PIE
SQUARED

to Michele
xo Cathy Barrow

PIE SQUARED

Irresistibly Easy Sweet & Savory

SLAB PIES

CATHY BARROW

Photographs by Christopher Hirsheimer

GRAND CENTRAL
Life&Style
NEW YORK · BOSTON

Grand Central Life & Style
Hachette Book Group
1290 Avenue of the Americas, New York, NY 10104
grandcentrallifeandstyle.com
twitter.com/grandcentralpub

First Edition: October 2018

Grand Central Life & Style is an imprint of Grand Central Publishing. The Grand Central Life & Style name and logo are trademarks of Hachette Book Group, Inc.

The publisher is not responsible for websites (or their content) that are not owned by the publisher.

The Hachette Speakers Bureau provides a wide range of authors for speaking events. To find out more, go to www.hachettespeakersbureau.com or call (866) 376-6591.

Library of Congress Cataloging-in-Publication Data
Names: Barrow, Cathy, author.
Title: Pie squared : irresistibly easy sweet and savory slab pies / Cathy Barrow.
Description: New York : Grand Central Life & Style, [2018] | Includes bibliographical references and index.
Identifiers: LCCN 2018003656| ISBN 978-1-5387-2914-4 (hardcover) | ISBN 978-1-5387-2916-8 (ebook)
Subjects: LCSH: Desserts. | Pies. | Pastry. | LCGFT: Cookbooks.
Classification: LCC TX773 .B3683 2018 | DDC 641.86—dc23
LC record available at https://lccn.loc.gov/2018003656

ISBNs: 978-1-5387-2914-4 (hardcover); 978-1-5387-2916-8 (ebook)

The illustration on pages 304 and 305 is copyright © 2018 by Marilyn Pollack Naron

Printed in China

IM

10 9 8 7 6 5 4 3 2 1

For my mother,
JAN,
*who taught me
everything about pie*

CONTENTS

Chapter Three

SAVOR A PIE

91

Chapter Four

SWEETIE PIES

197

THE SUM
OF ALL PARTS

If you wish to make an apple pie from scratch,
you must first invent the universe.

—CARL SAGAN

I've toted my signature sour cherry pie everywhere. I've made this pie for summer parties and winter birthdays. It's been double-crusted, streusel-topped, or decorated with lattice or cutout stars. The filling is barely sweetened. The cherries are suspended in a glaze, clear and never gloppy. The bottom crust is crisp, not soggy. I won a blue ribbon with that cherry pie. I am that person who makes four, and more often six, pies for Thanksgiving. Until recently, every one of those pies has been unapologetically round. It never occurred to me to make a pie in any other shape.

In June 2016, while tossing around story ideas with Bonnie Benwick, my editor at the *Washington Post*, she said, "How about a slab pie?" A pie baked in a baking sheet. Even though I am an experienced pie maker, I feared slab pie. I wasn't sure I could successfully roll out even my own trusted pie dough into a rectangle large enough to drape over a baking sheet. As it turned out, it was easier than I thought, and in

many ways, more straightforward than a round pie. For a few weeks, I became obsessed with slab pies. In time, I wrote a story for the *Post* with a recipe that tucked fruit and almond paste between two all-butter crusts (similar to Absolutely Peachy Slab Pie, page 214).

The story made a splash. We heard from pie makers far and wide sharing their admiration for the sheer functionality of a slab pie. Certainly, I wasn't the first to make a slab pie. Years earlier, Martha Stewart rolled out a slab pie on her television show. They've appeared in magazines and on blogs, and Pinterest is packed with slab pie images. It could be argued that baking sheet quiches, a staple of '80s cocktail parties, were the precursor to savory slab pies.

It's no wonder slab pies are welcome at potlucks, church socials, and neighborhood parties. In so many ways, there is no better contribution to a gathering than a slab pie. Slab pies are economical, easily transportable, and easy to portion out to serve a crowd.

Without even realizing it, I began to abandon the glass and ceramic round pie pans stacked in a drawer. The first slab pies I made were baked in a half sheet pan, 18 by 13 inches. Soon I realized that, while it might be the perfect size for a huge crowd, I wanted a slab pie that better suited the family dinner table. A different rectangular baking sheet, a quarter sheet pan 9 by 13 inches and just an inch high, fit the bill. And from that day forward, all my pies had corners: pie-squared.

I began to create recipes, playing with sweet and savory options. Over four months, I made 193 slab pies. At the end of my experimentation, after more than 70 pounds of all-purpose flour and nearly 60 pounds of unsalted butter, I had tweaked and nudged, tested and retested, until the crusts and fillings in the recipes that follow became utterly dependable and positively delicious.

To make a slab pie is not as straightforward as just doubling any old pie recipe. It's a different pie altogether. Right off the bat, the ratio is different: It's twice as much crust but only half as much filling. Along the way, I learned to approach pie making differently. I tweaked the seasonings, tinkered with the dough recipe, and learned to rely on a pattern of frequent chilling during the pie-making process.

Fruit pies were clear cut—add more fruit. Other sweet pies worked the same way, with more pudding, nuts, chocolate, or chiffon. The sweet pie recipes just needed a mathematical nudge.

Savory pies were different. Too much salt was catastrophic and too little was a crying shame. Seasonings had to be assertive. The fillings had to cook for just the right amount of time. And I wanted these mealtime pies packed with vegetables that were crisp and flavorful, not mushy and indistinguishable.

I set out to rework old favorites into Ham and Gruyère Slab Pie (page 176) and Chicken Pot Slab Pie (page 155) and soon moved on to other flavors I love at dinner, wondering how they might work when slipped between two layers of flaky crust. And while I considered sweet slab pies the ideal option for larger gatherings, savory pies were dinner and then the next day's lunch (Beefy Empanada Slab Pie, page 162). Or savory slab pies were the phoenix rising out of a stingy collection of leftovers (Cowboy Beef Stew Slab Pie, page 165, and "The Reuben" Slab Pie, page 159). We learned to love pie for lunch, as though we were eating in a proper London pub.

Along with savory pies came savory crusts: cheddar-flecked, studded with caramelized onion, decorated with seeds, or with cheese scattered over the top. And then came the combinations. That's the thing about pie. It's very adaptable.

Each recipe offers suggestions for Swaps for alternate crusts, filling ingredients, and toppings. Consider the Southern-Style Tomato Slab Pie (page 115), where an alternative to the Cheddar Cheese Crust (page 39) is an All-Butter Crust (page 30). Or the Loaded Baked Potato Slab Pie (page 101), where a Pretzel Crust (page 62), pressed in, can substitute for the Caramelized Onion Crust (page 42), which is rolled out. The Banana Pudding Slab Pie (page 281) is luscious and traditional in a Vanilla Wafer Crust (page 66), but a Chocolate Wafer Crust (page 66) with

a swipe of caramel raises this pie to a whole new level of indulgence.

A beautifully turned out pie is challenging without the right dough—one that is pliable, reliable, and, of course, delicious. My pie crust recipes are sized to fit the pan precisely, with a tidy crimp around the edges. The crust is flaky and crispy, sturdy yet tender, easy to manage, lattice, slice, and crimp. My favorite All-Butter Crust (page 30) swings from sweet to savory without skipping a beat and takes on flavorings generously. I hope it will become your favorite crust, too.

I am aware that there are *doughphobics* that walk among us. People for whom a terrible experience has so shaken them that they swear never again to make a pie. Slab pies may be a way back to pie. Keep in mind, pie making is a skill, not a talent. A person can learn a skill and perfect it with practice. I hope the Tools and Techniques section (page 1) will help you find your own personal rhythm in pie crust, the steady motion of the pin, the easy crimping, the insouciant slashing, all greeted with comfort and ease.

Nevertheless, I realize that some of you are not jumping on the rolled-out pie dough bandwagon no matter what I say. I've got you covered. Press-in crusts (pages 55 to 68) will fit both sweet and savory recipes. Whether speculoos or Ritz, amaretti or saltines, crumb crusts stand in with no rolling pin involved. An Olive Oil Crust (page 56) is flaky and complements most savory fillings, and the Shortbread Crust (page 59) works magic with the sweet pie fillings.

While 4 cups of filling makes for a perfectly plump 9-inch round pie, a slab pie demands a generous 5 or 6 cups to assure a sufficiency of satisfying filling. Slab pies are 2 to 3 inches deep at the most, with squared edges and corners. They're not like a round pie, where the filling might be twice as deep and the bottom crust is very slightly sloped at the edges. Some filling recipes tended to dry out when *slabified*. It took plenty of trial and error to find the sweet spot for thickeners where the filling has body, isn't watery, and is never pasty or gummy. Seasoning is vital. Without salt, the filling can be lost in a sea of crust.

Many of these pies sport a top crust which makes for a much sturdier slice, particularly if you're serving on paper plates. Lattice or cutout lids are icing on the pie, especially when the filling is extra juicy, as with cherries and blackberries. Turn to lattice or cutouts when a peek into the pie is part of the fun, as in the Just-Like-Artichoke-Dip Slab Pie (page 95). I've shown you some of my favorite lattices and coverings in the pages of this book, and how to do them on pages 26 to 29. Go ahead. Get fancy.

Slab pies are easier to portion, unlike extracting equal pieces from a round pie where the filling tumbles out and the top crust goes askew. And guests who want "just a sliver" create a whole other situation. Not so with a slab pie where pieces are square or rectangular and easily slivered or slabbed, portioning to meet the appetite. When your partner, roommate, kids, or neighbors show up at the table with a friend, I've given you a template for How to Slice a Slab Pie (page 304) to see just how easily these pies accommodate a crowd.

Change up your pie game with slab pies. Soggy Bottoms begone. Runny fillings won't do. Tough, pale crusts are history. I've honed a few techniques along the way and they appear as tips throughout the book: tricks that make slab pies roll off your pin, bake up deliciously, and lift right out of the pan.

You might wonder what a cookbook author does when baking so many pies. So did I. Coinciding with my deep dive into slab pie, we moved to a condominium in a building with more than forty other units. In the first weeks, I was turning out three or four pies a day and soon began to send all-building emails with subject lines like *Coconut Cream Pie on the way to the mailroom. Bring a plate.* If you are planning a move, consider slab pie. It's the ultimate in icebreakers; slab pies are community builders.

Make a pie, make a friend.

Chapter One

THE ELEMENTS OF PIE

IN MY PIE MAKING LIFE, THERE have been times I've put together pie in a kitchen equipped with nothing more than a paring knife and a pie pan (back in the day when I believed pies had to be round).

EQUIPMENT

It is possible to make slab pie with no special equipment except a slab pie pan. This 9- by 13-inch baking sheet, no more than 1 inch high, is called a *quarter sheet pan* in restaurant parlance. I may call it a slab pie pan, but it is sure to become one of the most useful pans in your kitchen. I have four. I use them for roasting vegetables or even a whole chicken, making scones, reheating leftovers, and toasting nuts. Some larger countertop "toaster" ovens fit a slab pie pan and you know what that means? Pie in the summer without turning on the big oven.

I do not line the pan in parchment or with a silicone baking mat. I never spray with cooking spray, coat with butter, dust with flour, or do anything else to prepare the pan. Baking the pie directly in the metal pan makes for the best, brownest, crispiest, flakiest crust.

Please do not let this list of equipment dissuade you from making a slab pie. Many of the following recipes require nothing more than the slab pie pan.

NEED TO HAVE
9- by 13-inch baking sheet (slab pie pan)

GOOD TO HAVE
Rolling pin
Ruler and painter's, or masking tape
Bench scraper
Pastry brushes

NICE TO HAVE
Full-size food processor, not a mini-prep
Baking Steel (also called a baking plate)
or baking stone (pizza stone)
Scale
Parchment paper or silicone baking mats

FUN TO HAVE
Fluted pastry wheel
Pizza wheel
Cookie cutters and other decorating tools
Docking tool

OVENS, STEELS, AND STONES
The worst offense of all the pie offenses has to be Soggy Bottom. I had been testing a variety of ways to ensure a crisp-bottomed slab pie, but none was perfect. Then one day, after heating the oven to 425°F, I realized my Baking Steel was still in there. Too hot, too heavy, and too difficult to remove at that moment, I shrugged and slid the slab pie pan on top of the steel. And that was that: The pie that emerged had a bottom crust that was crisp and browned and so darn perfect, I never looked back. That pie lifted right out of the pan in one piece. I placed it on a wooden serving board, cut squares, and served it. The bottom was deeply browned, crisp, and flaky. Yes, the bottom of the pie was perfectly, delightfully, deliciously flaky. That day, I hadn't

MACGYVERING A SLAB PIE PAN

If you don't have a 9- by 13-inch baking sheet, you can jury-rig a larger 18- by 13-inch pan, called a *half sheet* in the professional kitchen. Cut a piece of foil approximately 16 by 20 inches. Fold the foil accordion-style until it is 16 by 2 inches. Place this foil as if building a wall, making another edge, essentially forming a 9- by 13- inch space for the slab pie. Place the foil on edge, across the baking sheet, and fold the ends back so the folded piece fits snugly across the 13-inch centerpoint. Use painter's tape or masking tape to secure the foil to the pan's sides, then fit the bottom crust into half the pan. Form and bake the pie as instructed in the recipe. Remove the foil only after the pie has completely cooled or when serving, whichever comes first.

set out to combat Soggy Bottom, but I learned that baking the pie on top of a very hot surface did the trick.

While the Baking Steel (a 15-pound behemoth) does a great job as an oven heat booster, if you have a pizza stone it will provide the same result—a crisp-bottomed slab pie, one that slides right out of the pan. Simply heat the steel or stone while preheating the oven. If you don't have a stone or steel, invert a baking sheet and let it get hot in the preheating oven. Then, when the oven is at temperature, place the pie on top of the steel, pizza stone, or upside-down baking sheet. No more Soggy Bottom.

The best pies bubble over enthusiastically, so prepare ahead for easy cleanup. Place a piece of parchment paper on top of the stone, steel, or baking sheet, right under the pie pan. The paper will catch the drips and it's possible to dodge oven cleaning for one more week.

As for oven rack placement: Some people bake pie in the lower third of the oven, others put pie in the upper third. I like a slab pie to be right smack dab in the center of the oven so it's cooked all the way around. I almost always use the convection setting if it's available, because the breeze floating through the oven increases the flaky and crispy factors. When baking on a convection setting, I do not reduce or otherwise change the temperature.

CRUST + FILLING × OVEN = PIE

Pie is egalitarian, democratic, and fundamental, created from the most common ingredients.

FLAKIEST CRUSTS

The best crusts begin with the triumvirate, the trinity of pie crust: flour, fat, and cold liquid. But note that it's not always the most expensive or rarest elements that blend to make flaky, flavorful, tender pie crust.

Flour

Not all flour is the same. Winter wheat and summer wheat have different protein contents, making them perform differently. Consistency has me returning over and over to King Arthur Flour, a Vermont-based, employee-owned company. Those on the West Coast may not find King Arthur flours in the grocery store (although they may be ordered online); Gold Medal is an excellent substitute.

Butter

There's a time and place for European butter. Pie crust is not one of them. The higher butterfat and lower water content of fancy European butters cause them to soften too quickly, so the "cutting in" process is more challenging than with American-style butter. The recipes in this book were developed using ice cold, briefly frozen, unsalted, American-made butter.

Cold Water and Other Liquids

Any added liquids must be ice cold or the fats will melt as the dough is formed. If the fats melt at this point, the dough emulsifies, and the result is a tough, dense crust that fights back when it is rolled out.

Salt

The recipes in this book use Diamond Crystal **kosher salt**. If using Morton's kosher salt, cut back just a little as it's heavier by weight.

FABULOUS FILLINGS

There are more than sixty fillings in these pages, ranging from creamy custards to hearty stews. Each one is well spiced and assertively flavored because I've learned that once fillings are surrounded by crust, the flavor can be dulled. Taste and adjust salt and pepper. Squeeze a little more lemon juice in with the peaches. Use spices and herbs to make the fillings bold. Taste your way to a delicious pie by sampling the filling before it is encased in crust.

Never put a warm filling into a raw crust. That's a recipe for tough crust. Chill the filling first. Savory fillings often benefit from being made a day in advance so the flavors blend, meld, and develop.

TRUSTY THICKENERS—NOT GLOPPY. NOT RUNNY. JUST RIGHT.

There is no greater pie disappointment than Soggy Bottom, but runny fillings aren't welcome, either. I've got the fix for Soggy Bottom (see Ovens, Steels, and Stones, page 4). Runny fillings? It's all about the thickener.

Cornstarch thickens to a clear, not opaque, gel. I like it in fruit pies or with pudding fillings as there is no taste associated (as with flour). Once cornstarch is added, the filling must come to a boil to thicken. This happens as fruit pies bake.

Instant ClearJel is another form of cornstarch. It was developed for commercial use because it has a longer hold than standard cornstarch, allowing pies to sit for more days in a retail bakery setting. That's handy, I suppose (pies don't last that long around my house). I like using ClearJel with berry and cherry pies as they tend to be very juicy with a naturally runny gel. I never use ClearJel with custards or puddings—that's a recipe for glue. Instant ClearJel is found online at KingArthurFlour.com and other places. It keeps for years.

Tapioca pearls are often recommended for pie filling and I've had good luck with them, although they can be tricky to find in the grocery store. If you like using tapioca, substitute an equal amount wherever I use cornstarch or Instant ClearJel.

Flour makes gravy and that's why I choose to use it for many savory pie fillings. Browning the flour along with the fillings and before adding the liquid provides a much deeper, richer flavor: a *roux*. Cooking also overcomes any possibility of an unappealing raw flour taste.

Dried fruit thickens fruit pies; grind dried fruit with the recipe's sugar amount for a boost of sturdying **pectin** that gels the filling naturally. See So Very Apricot Slab Pie, page 211, for the method.

CHILLING

Pie loves cold. Pies take little active time, but a lot of inactive time, mostly to chill, relax, and get flaky. Chill the dough before rolling. When possible, refrigerate the dough between rolling and filling. Use cold filling, not hot. When possible, chill the assembled pie before baking. Not only does the secondary chill allow the fats to firm up again, to ensure some lift and flake, but it also helps the beautiful crimping and decorative work retain its shape.

ADJUSTING FOR ALTITUDE

Baking at high altitudes means evaporation occurs more quickly and pie crusts and fillings tend to dry out. To avoid a desiccated pie:

- Increase the oven temperature by 15°F at 3,000 feet; 20°F at 5,000 feet; and 25°F at 7,500 feet.

- Visual cues are always a better indication of doneness, but expect to decrease the baking time by around 5 minutes at 3,000 feet and 8 minutes at 7,500 feet.

- For all crusts, increase the flour by 1 tablespoon at 3,000 feet, and an additional 1 tablespoon for every 1,000 feet over 3,000. (Example: If baking at 6,000 feet, add 4 tablespoons flour to the crust recipe.)

- Decrease sugar in the filling by 1 tablespoon over 3,000 feet.

- Increase liquid in the filling by 2 tablespoons at 3,000 feet and 4 tablespoons at 7,500 feet.

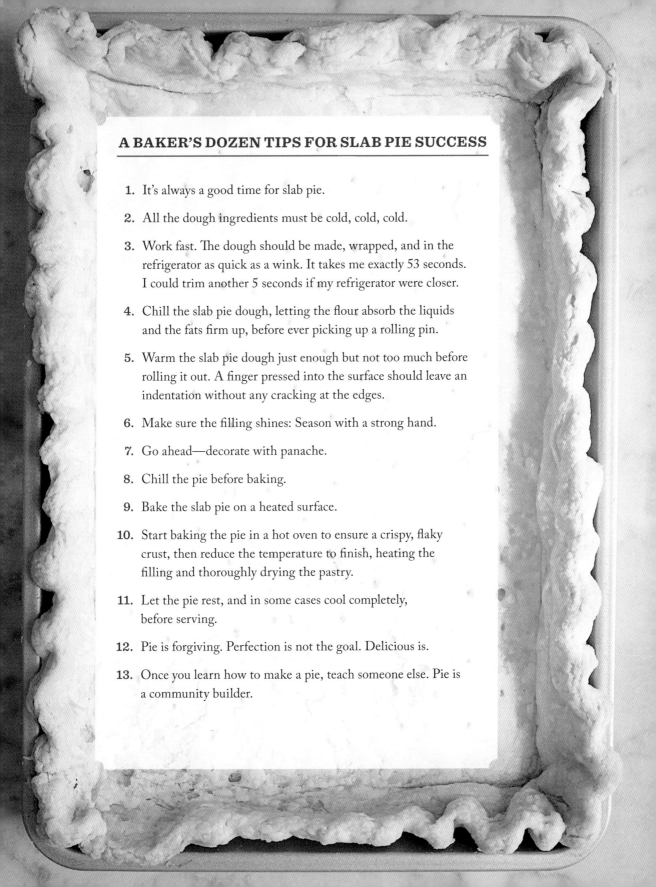

A BAKER'S DOZEN TIPS FOR SLAB PIE SUCCESS

1. It's always a good time for slab pie.

2. All the dough ingredients must be cold, cold, cold.

3. Work fast. The dough should be made, wrapped, and in the refrigerator as quick as a wink. It takes me exactly 53 seconds. I could trim another 5 seconds if my refrigerator were closer.

4. Chill the slab pie dough, letting the flour absorb the liquids and the fats firm up, before ever picking up a rolling pin.

5. Warm the slab pie dough just enough but not too much before rolling it out. A finger pressed into the surface should leave an indentation without any cracking at the edges.

6. Make sure the filling shines: Season with a strong hand.

7. Go ahead—decorate with panache.

8. Chill the pie before baking.

9. Bake the slab pie on a heated surface.

10. Start baking the pie in a hot oven to ensure a crispy, flaky crust, then reduce the temperature to finish, heating the filling and thoroughly drying the pastry.

11. Let the pie rest, and in some cases cool completely, before serving.

12. Pie is forgiving. Perfection is not the goal. Delicious is.

13. Once you learn how to make a pie, teach someone else. Pie is a community builder.

UPPING YOUR GAME—BIG SLABS

Once you become adept at rolling out rectangular crusts for slab pies, you may want to make a pie stretched across an entire baking sheet measuring 18 by 13. For potlucks, big parties, the office picnic, or the family reunion, a pie that serves thirty or more is a showstopper.

Making a double-size slab pie is not for the faint of heart: It takes serious muscles, a big flat surface, and plenty of determination to roll out a crust to 20 by 15 inches. Here are my workarounds.

- Make two separate batches of the slab pie crust recipe for a top and bottom crust and use one for the top crust and one for the bottom crust.

- For the bottom crust, cut the dough block in half and roll it out in two pieces. Patch them together in the bottom of the pan. No one will be the wiser.

- Plan for a lattice or cutout crust. Divide the dough block set aside for the top crust. Roll out each portion, fashioning strips, decorative cutouts, or any other method of topping the filling. Avoid attempting a full coverage crust, if possible.

- You've decided to attempt the full coverage top crust? Bless you and good luck. I've done it. The effort may have included some fiery language. Use masking tape to mark the 20- by 15-inch size on the counter. Work with everything—counter, pin, dough—as cold as possible.

- Make two slab pies instead.

HUMBLE PIE

Every pie is beautiful, so let's stop putting pressure on ourselves to put out an Instagram-worthy example. Don't let fear of rustic presentation get between you and pie.

Your first pie may not be gorgeous. Rather than focus on fancy decorating techniques, put your attention to speed and temperature. Work fast. Keep it cold. Roll out the dough with short, swift, confident strokes. Use a cold filling. Chill the pie before baking. Bake it on a hot surface. These steps will make a scrumptious slab pie, and isn't that the goal?

Chapter Two

THE POWER OF PIE CRUST

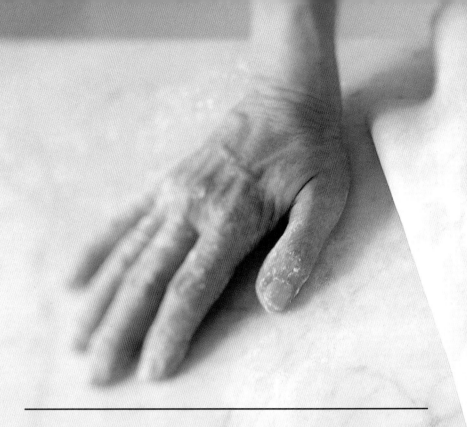

**ITHOUT CRUST, A PIE WOULD BE** a casserole, no more than a pan of filling, heated. Crust is pie's raison-d'être. From the beginning of my pie adventures, my mother's absolutely dependable pie dough recipe has paved the way to my success— paired with practice and persistence. Now, this recipe is in your hands, sized to fit a slab pie pan. It's easy to mix, easy to roll, easy to shape, and bakes up flaky, tender, and scrumptious. An indispensable, utterly reliable pie crust recipe delivers super powers.

In this chapter are other doughs made with butter or shortening, lard or cream cheese, cheddar, onion, chocolate, and rye. Or avoid a rolling pin altogether with press-in shortbread or olive oil crusts and crusts crushed from cookies and crackers. Grocery store phyllo, puff pastry, and even pie crusts all work with slab pies.

MIXING AND ROLLING OUT A SENSATIONAL SLAB PIE CRUST

Slab pies are for crust lovers. They're crowd pleasers, bronzed and golden, with scrumptious fillings burbling out of a flaky wrapping. There are more edges, more corners, and more opportunities for pie crust in a slab pie.

An ideal pie crust has flavor, loft, and crackly tenderness. A user-friendly pie dough rolls out without a fight and the crust emerges from the oven a pleasing color ranging from pale buttery tan to deeply bronzed and shiny. Your favorite pie crust will be all that, and will taste sensational.

When mixing the ingredients, speed and cold are important. No dawdling. Get the equipment and ingredients ready and go. Once the mixing begins, start to finish, the crust should be wrapped and in the refrigerator in about 3 minutes.

Cut in the cold fats so the flour coats each bit. "Cutting in" means combining the fat with the flour by blending flour and butter bits together until the bits are coated in flour. When cold liquid is added, the dampened flour becomes a shaggy mass, cohesive, with bits of butter here and there.

I know this directive can be confusing. Where, precisely, is the place where the dough has been worked enough but not too much? I like it to just barely form a ball in the food processor. I do the rest of the work of organizing the dough not with my warm hands, which are likely to melt the fats further, but by using a bench scraper as a tool. Here's how:

Form an X with two pieces of plastic wrap, one atop the other, and dust lightly with flour. Dump the dough onto the center point, scraping the food processor bowl clean. Fold the plastic wrap over the top and, with the bench scraper, push and prod the mass, aiming for a rectangular block that is 4 by 6 inches. Use a rolling pin to gently even the surface, right through the wrap, smoothing out any air bubbles or cracks in the dough. Flip the block over and use the rolling pin again to gently compact the block of dough. Make a few tidying moves to square up the edges. There will be pieces of the fat still visible and it will look like a block of dough, not a block of crumbly flour.

Refrigerate the dough for at least 4 hours. During this time, any bit of slight overworking will be forgiven, the flour will absorb the liquid, and the butter and other fats will firm up. The cold fats, when introduced into a hot oven, will steam and puff, giving the crust loft and flake.

WEIGHTY MATTERS

Success in baking is a direct result of precision. There are no two ways about it. Professional bakers know that weighing ingredients, instead of using cup (volume) measures, ensures precision and consistency, but home cooks have been resistant. Every recipe writer and cookbook author touts the kitchen scale, and I am yet another voice in the crowd vigorously nodding my head.

I'm going to let you in on a little secret: It's not only the consistent results that drive me to use the scale. Quite simply, using a kitchen scale means I wash fewer dishes. Weigh an ingredi-

Pulse to cut in the butter.

Process until the dough comes together.

ent right into the mixing bowl, hit zero, or *tare,* which resets the scale to zero, and weigh the next ingredient. Using a scale means cup measures become obsolete, and that fewer spatulas, spoons, and mixing bowls are used. Using a scale for the massively annoying task of measuring peanut butter, honey, and molasses means that instead of scraping these sticky substances first into and then out of a cup measure and into a mixing bowl, I can go instead from the jar directly into the bowl, weighing each sticky ingredient with ease.

But more than that, I have whisked, fluffed, spooned, and sifted flour to measure it by the cupful and weighed the results. Over ten tests, each time doing what I would swear was precisely the same set of actions, 1 cup of flour ranged from 110 to 135 grams (the most com-

monly attributed weight is 120 grams per cup). This means that for any given pie dough, it can vary from a little dry to a little wet. And while the resulting pie would be tasty, the crust might be tough or damp, and working with it may not be straightforward and easy. When rolling the dough out, it might stick, or it might crack.

Then I ran a few tests *weighing* the ingredients, making the same pie five times. Those tests produced the exact same crust every time.

To weigh ingredients for pie dough, set an empty bowl on the scale. If using the food processor or stand mixer, place the work bowl right on the scale, and there's no bowl to wash. Press Zero to take away the weight of the bowl (to *tare*). Add the flour, just enough to reach the desired weight. Tare again, clearing the scale back to zero, then weigh in the butter. Continue

Form a block.

Chill.

with all the ingredients, setting the scale to zero between each addition. Glance over at the sink. No bowls. No cup measures. No mess. I don't know about you, but I'm all about fewer dishes to wash.

Just do it. Get a scale (see Resources, page 309). Put it on the counter, or keep it inside a convenient drawer and make taking it out part of the preparations for baking. Soon it will be second nature and you'll join the rest of the voices complaining about recipes that don't include weights.

MIXING THE DOUGH

There are three ways to mix pie dough: Using a food processor, by hand, and (only in a pinch) with a stand mixer. My hands-down favorite is the food processor. In fact, pie crust may be the primary reason I own a food processor. Noth-

ing "cuts in" butter better. It also makes quick work of grating vegetables, mixing up scone and biscuit dough, and slicing mushrooms for gravy. But I digress.

The recipes in this book are written for the food processor. But you can use either of the other two methods with confidence. The dough that emerges is the same whether made in a machine or with your hands. But the food processor is as fast as a roadrunner and absolutely consistent and that's why I like it. Less than 2 minutes to dough, wrapped and ready for the refrigerator.

Mixing Pie Dough with a Food Processor

The food processor method is the default method in my recipes and explained in depth in each one. Be sure to use a processor with a 7-cup capacity or larger, not a mini processor. Place

THE POWER OF PIE CRUST

Weigh the flour and butter.

the processor work bowl on the scale. Weigh the flour into the work bowl as explained above, then weigh in the cold, cubed butter, and add the salt. Move the bowl to the food processor and use the Pulse function to cut the butter into the flour. Add the cold liquid all at once and process until the dough almost comes together in a rough ball. You'll hear the sounds change to *chunka chunka chunka* as the gathered clump hits the side of the bowl. All the flour will be dampened and the dough will be a shaggy clump. Scrape the processor clean and dump all the dough onto the flour-dusted plastic wrap and proceed.

Mixing Pie Dough by Hand

Mixing by hand is similar, but the rest period is even more important, allowing the flour to absorb all the moisture and avoid puffy pockets of unincorporated flour in the pie crust. I like to use a box grater to create flakes of frozen butter when making dough by hand because even though this method takes more time, the frozen butter doesn't lose structure and emulsify. Weigh the flour into a large bowl. Freeze the butter in sticks or blocks (not cubes) until solid. Using the largest holes on a box grater, shred the butter directly into the bowl containing the flour, intermittently fluffing the mixture so the butter doesn't clump. (If you don't have a box grater, cube the butter, chill, and use a pastry blender, two table knives, or simply pinch it between your fingers to cut it into the flour.) Using your hands, quickly combine the ingredients until the ribbons of butter are lightly coated in flour. Work thoroughly and quickly. Pour in the cold liquid and use your hands to gather the ingredients. Rather than squeeze the dough, instead toss and fold, lightly pressing it into a sort of cohesive mass. It will take time for the flour to absorb the

liquid, some of which happens while it rests, but work the mixture until all the flour is dampened and the dough is a shaggy clump. Scrape all the dough onto the flour-dusted plastic wrap and proceed.

Mixing Pie Dough with a Stand Mixer

This is a last resort dough-making option. It's the most challenging method because it is very difficult to control how rapidly the butter is cut in. Place the bowl of the stand mixer on the scale and weigh in the flour. Weigh in the very cold, not frozen, cubed butter. The butter should give under your fingertips, but should not smush. Add the salt. Set the bowl on the mixer and use the paddle attachment on the lowest speed to gradually cut in the butter. This should take about 20 seconds. Pour in the cold liquid and combine on the lowest speed for less than 1 minute. Dump the dough, which will be very loose and barely contained, onto the prepared, flour-dusted plastic wrap and proceed.

FORMING THE DOUGH BLOCK

Place two pieces of plastic wrap, each about 14 inches long, on the counter and crisscross them to form an X. Lightly dust with flour. Dump the dough on the centerpoint of the X, loose and rough, and dust the top with a little more flour. Fold the wrap over the dough and use the wrap and a bench scraper, not your warm hands, to press it into a 6- by 4-inch block (3 by 4 inches if making a single-crusted pie). The block should be firm, compact, and without cracks and fissures. The more precise this block is before chilling, the more straightforward it will be to roll out the dough to size, so be thoughtful and patient. At the same time, work quickly, so the butter doesn't melt.

THE POWER OF PIE CRUST

ROLLING OUT THE DOUGH

I want to assure you that rolling out pie dough is a skill that can be learned. No one is born with a rolling pin in their hand. With practice, making a pie and rolling out dough becomes a heavenly experience. A cold surface and a pin that fits will help you find your rolling mojo.

Counter, Board, or Cloth

Ideally, after forming the dough into a block in plastic wrap and a good long rest in the refrigerator, pie dough would be rolled out on a **cold stone counter.** I am fortunate. I have stone counters in my kitchen, but during the summer months or when the oven has been on for a while, they are not cold enough. I remedy the situation by placing a sealed bag of ice on the counter for 10 minutes, then remove, dry the counter, and roll out the dough. That right there is the perfect situation.

We all know perfect situations are rare. So, if you have a small kitchen and no good counter real estate, try to establish enough space on another table or surface in your home or with **an (extra-large) piece of smooth marble, stone, ceramic, or a wooden board** used only for this purpose. Remnants or odd pieces can be found at stone yards and countertop companies.

Any smooth surface works for rolling out pie dough, but the flour does get everywhere. Depending on how you feel about crevices filled with flour, you may want to use a **pastry cloth.** It will come with a matching cloth for a rolling pin, which is useful if your pin is scarred, dented, or uneven. Both should be linen and will arrive stiff as can be. Wash them to soften them up and use the heel of your hand to rub flour deep into the fibers. Pastry cloths only get better with time, when they are soft as a whisper

and thoroughly imbued with flour. Some people never wash their pastry cloth, but simply pack them away in a ziptop bag in the freezer, to be extracted when it's time to roll out a crust.

Find what works for you and perfect your technique with the tools that fit you, your kitchen, and your *pie-bility.*

The Rolling Pin

Finding the right rolling pin is a worthy pursuit. Go to a good kitchen shop or visit a baking friend who has a thing for rolling pins. Lift the pin, feel its heft, roll it forward, roll it toward you, see if you can press left or right comfortably, guiding the pin (or the dough, eventually) one way or the other. You'll find one that fits your hands, one that fills you with pie superpowers.

When testing out a rolling pin, engage your entire body: shoulders, wrists, hands. Tapered or straight? Handles or no handles? Heavy or light? Wooden or silicone? Marble or metal? I have a few to choose from, the tapered one for cookie dough and a heavy wooden cylinder I use to roll out yeast breads. For slab pies, when I need a wide swath of pie crust, I rely on a weighted silicone pin with handles. The handles keep my fingers out of the way and the weight helps stretch the dough efficiently, making quick work on the way to a thin, even swath that falls into the corners of the pan, holds a crimp, and stands up to decorating.

To roll out your pie dough, first prepare the rolling surface using blue painter's or masking tape to form a guide 11 inches wide by 15 inches high. Remove the dough from the refrigerator and let it warm slightly, no more than 10 minutes. Once a finger pressed into the surface makes an indentation without cracking, the dough is ready to roll. Do not let it get warmer

Divide the dough block.

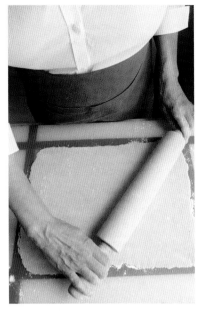

Roll to size.

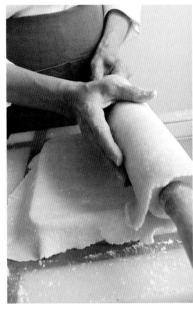

Drape over the pan.

Gently press into the pan.

Trim the overhang.

Chill.

or softer than this, and if it does, return it to the refrigerator for an hour before starting again. Rolling out dough that is too warm will smear the butter and other fats resulting in no flake, a tough crust, and a sad pie maker. Rolling out dough that is too cold? Crumbling edges, cracks and tears, and more frustration. Give the dough time to come to temperature. Use the time to gather ingredients for the filling, to heat the oven, get out the glaze or egg wash. As important as chilling the dough, bringing it to the correct temperature before rolling it out is equally important.

Liberally dust the countertop with flour. For a double-crusted pie, use a sharp knife or a bench scraper to divide the block of dough in two pieces, one slightly larger than the other. The larger piece will be used for the bottom crust. Keep the smaller piece covered while working with the other. If you doubt your ability to roll out the bottom crust within about 5 minutes, place the smaller piece in the refrigerator, then warm it slightly, again, before rolling it out. If making a pie with only one bottom crust, work with the entire block of dough.

Place the dough on the floured surface and smack the surface of the dough three times with the rolling pin, flip the dough and repeat on the other side. Smacking the dough is better at this point than rolling because it doesn't smear the fats, just compresses them. If the dough cracks when smacked, step back and allow additional time to warm, 2 or 3 minutes, then smack the dough again.

Begin to roll the dough from the center upward and downward using firm, sure strokes, then vaguely to one side or the other, diagonally, guiding the shape. Sliding a bench scraper under any spots that stick, lift the dough and turn it a quarter turn and roll again. Check the size against the taped guide periodically. Dust with additional flour whenever the dough begins to stick to the pin or the counter. Do not press down with all your might and do not roll back and forth; instead, pick the pin up and roll up and pick the pin up and roll down, each time deftly pushing the dough until it is consistently thick and large enough to fit in the pan. Turn it 90 degrees to stretch and form the block to fit the taped size, moving it all the time to keep it from sticking. Try to avoid rolling over and flattening the edges of the dough.

If the dough bounces back and fights with you, don't fight back. Wait it out, just a couple of minutes, until the dough relaxes. Continually and lightly dust the pin, the dough, and the counter with flour, moving the dough around, using the bench scraper to lift the dough and roll it from another angle. Be quick and agile. Any cracks can be repaired, so don't worry. Don't obsess. Remember the pan is 9 by 13 inches and use the tape to guide you.

When the dough is rolled to size, either loosely roll it up around the rolling pin and swiftly lift and lower it into the slab pie pan; or, alternatively, lightly fold it in half and in half again, placing the center point in the center of the slab pie pan, then unfold. Fit the dough into the corners and up the sides to drape over the rim, pressing gently with the side of your hand, not your fingertips (which would be more likely to rip it).

Place the pan in the refrigerator while rolling out the other, slightly smaller, half of the dough, about 10 by 14 inches, for the top crust. Place the top crust on a lightly floured sheet of parchment and refrigerate until ready to fill and bake the pie.

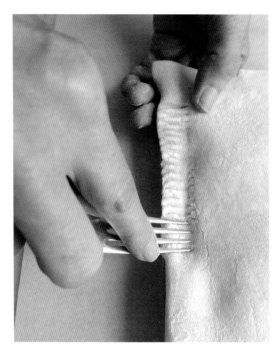

The Fork Pleat

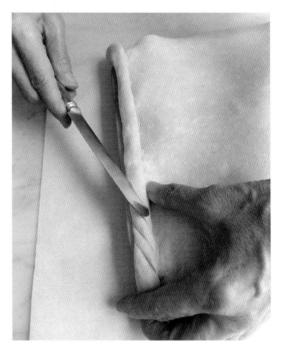

The Roll

Your dough is likely to tear. It might not be exactly to size, there may be more draping over the edge here, and nothing at all over there. Do not worry. Use kitchen shears to trim pieces from the excess to make up for the areas lacking crust. Simply press, tuck, patch, and poke until the crust is covering the bottom and draping over the top edge. Whatever happens on the way to pie stays between you and me.

In a pinch, a wine bottle, a broom handle, or any cylindrical object will stand in for a rolling pin, making pie possible in any situation.

THE FINISHING TOUCHES

You've filled the bottom crust and draped the top crust over the filling. Crimping the dough contains the filling, and slashing the surface releases steam, all of which encourages a juicy pie with a flaky lid. Make it as simple or as fancy as you please.

CRIMP AND SLASH

Think of "crimp and slash" as the final two steps in the pie-making dance.

Crimping seals together the top and bottom crusts so the filling stays put. Begin by trimming the dough evenly all around the pan. I like to use kitchen scissors. Use simple tools to make a decorative edge. I once saw a pie crimped using the head of an antique door key. The goal is to pinch

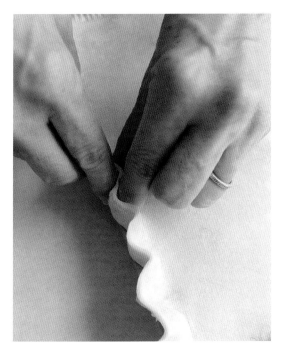

The Three-Finger Crimp

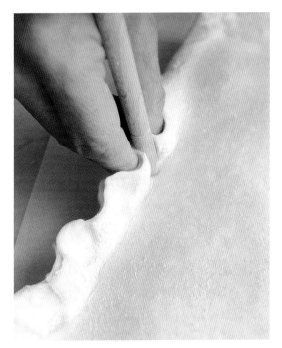

The Wooden Handle Ripple

the two crusts together. How you get there is up to your imagination. Here are some ideas.

The Fork Pleat

Start out simply, with the entry-level Fork Pleat. With a table fork, press the tines into the edge of the two crusts, squashing them together to seal, all along the edge of the pan.

The Roll

For a rolled crimp, form an even, plump, rounded ridge all around the pie by tucking the trimmed bottom crust over the top crust and rolling toward the center, gently and evenly, all around the pie. Decorate the edge with the blunt edge of a table knife, making gentle indentations along the edge, or the rim of a teaspoon to make a scalloped design.

The Three-Finger Crimp

For a classic finger crimp, place the thumb and index finger of one hand on the outside of the dough edge and push the index finger of the other hand between those two fingers to form a consistent pleat around the entire edge.

The Wooden Handle Ripple

I learned this tidy way of crimping from the great baker Sarabeth Levine. Just like the Three-Finger Crimp, the Wooden Handle Ripple forms a ruffled edge. For some people, using a tool makes crimping easier. Hold the rounded handle of a wooden spoon or similar tool in one hand and pinch the dough with the thumb and forefinger of the other for even and consistent, round, plump, professional-looking ripples.

Slashing opens the top crust and allows the filling to bubble up as the steam releases from inside the pie. Slashing keeps the top crust from splitting with joy as the filling cooks. Slashing can be simply functional, a few random knife slashes across the surface, or an artistic expression, using cutouts (see page 28) or even writing the type of pie in pretty script. Use a sharp knife and work quickly, slicing all the way through the top crust. A pie that is chilled will be easier to slash.

You will, at least once, put a pie in the oven and realize you have forgotten to slash it. It's never too late. Open the oven and slash that pie or risk a spillover. Slashing does not stop a pie from burbling enthusiastically from the slashes, so always place a piece of parchment under the pie, atop the Baking Steel. Pies can be messy.

LATTICES, CUTOUTS, STAMPS, AND SHAPES

A double-crusted pie with a straightforward slash will always have a place on the table. On the other hand, I'll admit to loving the collective "ahhhh" when a pie with a decorative lattice top is revealed. Lattice crusts look so fancy and pretty and difficult. They aren't. If you can roll out a top crust, you can make lattice strips or cutouts.

Lattice crusts with their crisscrossed strips of dough work especially well for pies with juicy fillings, because more filling is exposed to the heat of the oven so any sauciness reduces, gets thick and jammy, deeply delicious, and not runny at all.

To make a lattice, roll the dough out to 10 by 14 inches, as if for a top crust. Use a sharp paring knife, pizza cutter, or fluted pastry wheel (or all of the above) to cut long strips of dough either parallel with the edges or on the diagonal, so they are as long as possible. For precision, use the edge of a pan or a ruler for guidance forming straight lines. The strips may be of varied widths or precisely consistent. I tend to make a varied width lattice because precision is so elusive. Whatever size and shape the lattice, it will look beautiful when the pie emerges from the oven, glossy and crispy.

Lazy Lattice

Start with the **Lazy Lattice;** there's no weaving involved. Begin by placing strips of dough from edge to edge in one direction, either width-wise, length-wise, or diagonally. I like to begin the "long way" to make sure I have enough long strips to fit. Once the strips are placed in one direction, starting at one edge of the pan, place the strips at a right angle to the first row, creating a tic-tac-toe top.

Basket Weave Lattice

To basket weave the strips, which is a little more work but looks very pretty, place the strips across the pie in one direction, leaving some breathing room between. Lift and fold back every other strip and place a dough strip across the center of the pan, over and under the existing ones. Replace the dough strips, lifting and folding the other strips back. Place another perpendicular strip and basket weave. Continue in this fashion, working from the center in both directions until the pie is covered. It can be helpful to build this not-lazy version of a lattice on a piece of parchment paper first and use the paper to transfer the entire woven lattice as a fait accompli to the surface of the pie.

Lazy Lattice

Basket Weave Lattive

Brawny Lattice

Fancy Lattice

THE POWER OF PIE CRUST

Brawny, Skinny, or Irregular Lattice

Make wide strips and lattice them close together for a nearly seamless top crust, or make thin dough strips and run them in one direction only, like the stripes on a zebra. Hand cut the strips for wavy, unconventional, modern art–inspired, irregular lattice. Use a fluted pastry wheel to make them ruffled.

Using scissors, trim the strips and bottom crust to a half inch beyond the edge of the pan. Use any trimmed pieces to patch skimpy areas. Crimp the lattice and bottom crust together.

If a super-fancy lid is your goal, it's helpful to have an additional half-recipe (for a single crust) of pie dough. With plenty of dough at hand, try braiding strips to vary among the lattice strips. Use the extra to make a special edge, overlapping leaves, hearts, or alphabet cutouts spelling "Happy Birthday."

Cutouts

My pie dough loves to be a cutout, so long as it's kept cold. Stamp out enough forms to cover the pie, and chill before placing on the surface of the filled pie.

Stamps

If the pie has a top crust, roll it out, chill it hard, and rather than slashing the surface, use cookie cutters, a small glass, or a sharp knife to stamp out shapes before draping the crust over the filling. They'll allow the filling to breathe and evaporate and look festive in the meantime.

Shapes

Sculpt a decoration that tells the crowd what's in the pie. Top a chicken pot pie with a cutout chicken. Grape clusters on a grape pie. Use your imagination and have fun.

SHINY OBJECTS— WASHES AND SPRINKLES

When the crimped, slashed, decorated pie is just about to slide into the oven, a wash is the crowning touch to ensure a glossy, shiny, burnished crust. It only takes a moment to pick up a pastry brush and paint the top crust; just make sure to leave the edges bare. (Painting the crust edges can make them tough and difficult to cut through.) Out of eggs? No cream in the refrigerator? Use cool water or bake a naked pie. It will not change the flavor or the flake in the crust.

Here are some of my favorite washes from Low-Shine to High-Gloss.

Beat the ingredients together until well mixed before brushing the pie dough.

Low-Shine Wash: 1 egg white *or* 1 tablespoon whole milk *or* 1 tablespoon cool water
Cream Wash: 2 to 3 tablespoons heavy cream
Sweet or Salty Egg Wash: 1 egg yolk; 1 tablespoon cool water; 1 tablespoon granulated sugar *or* ½ teaspoon kosher salt
High-Gloss Egg Wash: 1 egg yolk; 1 tablespoon cool water

For a textural finish, start with any wash and scatter on 2 or 3 tablespoons of sparkling or raw sugar, sprinkles, grated hard cheese, toasted bread crumbs, or a scant half teaspoon of flaky salt like Maldon or *fleur de sel.*

BLIND BAKING

Because single-crusted pies, once filled, often bake for less than the time needed to fully, deeply bake the dough, the crust can end up damp or soggy or even a bit raw. Therefore, some recipes call for blind baking the bottom crust—pre-baking the crust, before filling the pie.

Pie dough is lofty and flaky and that's a good thing until it is baked without a filling, because the crust will rise up and blister in the oven. Before blind baking, dock, or pierce the crust with a fork or a docking tool, to tamp down that tendency, then crimp the edge of the crust decoratively and refrigerate for at least 20 minutes.

Heat the oven to 400°F, placing a baking stone, Baking Steel, or inverted baking sheet on the center rack. Line the unbaked crust with parchment paper or foil with plenty of overhang for easy lifting. Fill with uncooked beans, raw rice, pennies, or pie weights right up to the rim. This will keep the sides of the crust from collapsing while baking.

Slide the pan into the oven, on top of the steel, stone, or baking sheet and bake for 25 minutes if the pie will be filled and baked again. Bake for 40 minutes if the crust will be filled and chilled, with no additional baking.

Carefully remove the paper or foil from the crust, taking with it the beans, rice, or pie weights, and return the pan to the oven to bake another 7 to 10 minutes, until dry to the touch. Cool on a rack before continuing with the recipe.

THE POWER OF PIE CRUST

ALL-BUTTER CRUST

For a Double- or a Single-Crust Slab Pie

This is my hands-down favorite crust. It is easy to handle, freezes beautifully, crimps like a dream. The edges and top crusts lift up all flaky and appealing and the bottom crust browns into a sturdy, buttery base. Learning to make one great crust is an indispensable life skill. Memorize the ingredient list and you'll be ready if you stumble across a berry patch or have a bit of leftover stew, as this crust shape shifts from sweet to savory easily, the butter is flavor-forward, and the flake and crisp finish extra special. (See page 19 to make the dough by hand or in a stand mixer.)

FOR A DOUBLE CRUST

2½ cups plus
2 tablespoons (325 g)
all-purpose flour

16 tablespoons (225 g)
unsalted butter, cubed and
frozen for 20 minutes

¼ teaspoon kosher salt

½ cup (120 ml) ice water

FOR A SINGLE CRUST

1⅓ cups (160 g)
all-purpose flour

8 tablespoons (113 g)
unsalted butter, cubed and
frozen for 20 minutes

⅛ teaspoon kosher salt

¼ cup (60 ml) ice water

Place the work bowl of the food processor on the scale, set the scale to zero, and weigh the flour into the bowl. Weigh in the butter, and add the salt. Move the bowl to the food processor base, insert the metal blade, cover, and use the Pulse function to cut the flour and butter into flour-covered, pea-sized pieces, about 15 quick pulses. Add the ice water all at once and process until the dough almost comes together in a ball. All the flour will be dampened and the dough will clump.

Spend time on this next step because the more compact and precise the dough, the easier it is to roll to the correct size and thickness to fit the slab pie pan. Form an X with two long pieces of overlapping plastic wrap and lightly flour the surface. Dump the dough onto the center of the plastic wrap, scraping the processor bowl clean. Wrap the sloppy gathering of dough in plastic and, at the same time, use a bench scraper (not your warm hands that might melt the butter clumps) to form the squared sides of a block about 6 by 4 inches (or 3 by 4 inches if making a single crust). Once wrapped, use a rolling pin to gently press across the surface of the block. Flip it over and do the same on the other side. Now let it rest: Refrigerate the dough for at least 4 hours or preferably overnight.

(Continued)

RECIPES THAT USE AN ALL-BUTTER CRUST

These pies call for an All-Butter Crust, but feel free to mix and match. Each recipe offers Swaps with suggestions for alternate crusts, fillings, and toppings.

BUTTER AND SHORTENING CRUST

For a Double- or a Single-Crust Slab Pie

Shortening is the vegetarian version of lard and a pie maker's friend for flaky yet sturdy, tender yet sandy, bronzed yet crisp pie crust. As opposed to the All-Butter Crust, which is meltingly delicious but quicker to dampen and get soggy, a pie crust with some shortening in it has a longer shelf life. But I still like to include at least half butter for the flavor alone. Half and half results in a crisp, layered edge; the boost of vodka in the cold liquids is a shot in the arm for the flake. This is a sturdy crust, easy to roll and patch, happy to be a lattice, utterly crimpable. (See page 19 to make the dough by hand or in a stand mixer.)

FOR A DOUBLE CRUST

2½ cups plus
2 tablespoons (325 g)
all-purpose flour

8 tablespoons (113 g)
unsalted butter, cubed
and frozen for 20 minutes

8 tablespoons (113 g)
Spectrum or other
vegetable shortening,
cubed and frozen for
20 minutes

¼ teaspoon kosher salt

½ cup (120 ml) ice water

3 teaspoons
vodka, optional

(Continued)

Place the work bowl of the food processor on the scale, set the scale to zero, and weigh the flour into the bowl. Weigh in the butter, then the shortening; add the salt. Move the bowl to the food processor base, insert the metal blade, cover, and use the Pulse function to cut the flour, butter, and shortening into flour-covered, pea-sized pieces, about 15 quick pulses. Add the ice water and vodka (if using) all at once; process until the dough almost comes together in a ball. All the flour will be dampened and the dough will clump.

Spend time on this next step because the more compact and precise the dough, the easier it is to roll to the correct size and thickness to fit the slab pie pan. Form an X with two long pieces of overlapping plastic wrap and lightly flour the surface. Dump the dough onto the center of the plastic wrap, scraping the processor bowl clean. Wrap the sloppy gathering of dough in plastic and, at the same time, use a bench scraper (not your warm hands) to form the squared sides of a block, about 6 by 4 inches (or 3 by 4 inches if making a single crust). Once wrapped, use a rolling pin to gently press across the surface of the block. Flip it over and do the same on the other side. Now let it rest: Refrigerate the dough for at least 4 hours or preferably overnight.

(Continued)

FOR A SINGLE CRUST

1⅓ cups (160 g)
all-purpose flour

4 tablespoons (56 g)
unsalted butter, cubed and
frozen for 20 minutes

4 tablespoons (56 g)
Spectrum or other
vegetable shortening,
cubed and frozen for
20 minutes

⅛ teaspoon kosher salt

¼ cup (60 ml) ice water

1½ teaspoons vodka,
optional

RECIPES THAT USE A BUTTER
AND SHORTENING CRUST

These pies call for a Butter and Shortening Crust, but feel free to mix and match. Each recipe offers Swaps with suggestions for alternate crusts, fillings, and toppings.

After-Thanksgiving Turkey Slab Pie (page 157)
Merry Mince-ish Slab Pie (page 257)
Mostly Rhubarb and Just a Little Strawberry Slab Pie (page 205)

WHY VODKA?

Vodka in the crust tightens the crumb, increases the flake, and, when paired with shortening, is the best guarantee against a tough crust. If vodka isn't in your house, skip it. There is no need to increase the water if the vodka is omitted.

CREAM CHEESE CRUST

For a Double- or a Single-Crust Slab Pie

This tender, slightly tangy crust snuggles up to both sweet and savory fillings. It's sturdy enough to cut shapes, loves a good crimp, stands tall on the sides, and shines under an egg wash. Use full-fat cream cheese in a block, not whipped. (See page 19 to make the dough by hand or in a stand mixer.)

FOR A DOUBLE CRUST

2½ cups plus
2 tablespoons (325 g)
all-purpose flour

8 tablespoons (113 g)
unsalted butter, cubed and
frozen for 20 minutes

8 tablespoons (113 g)
cream cheese, cubed and
refrigerated for 20 minutes

¼ teaspoon kosher salt

½ cup (120 ml) ice water

FOR A SINGLE CRUST

1⅓ cups (160 g)
all-purpose flour

4 tablespoons (56 g)
unsalted butter, cubed and
frozen for 20 minutes

4 tablespoons (56 g)
cream cheese, cubed
and refrigerated for
20 minutes

⅛ teaspoon kosher salt

¼ cup (60 ml) ice water

Place the work bowl of the food processor on the scale, set the scale to zero, and weigh the flour into the bowl. Weigh in the butter, then the cream cheese; add the salt. Move the bowl to the food processor base, insert the metal blade, cover, and use the Pulse function to cut the flour, butter, and cream cheese into flour-covered, pea-sized pieces, about 15 quick pulses. Add the ice water all at once and process until the dough almost comes together in a ball. All the flour will be dampened and the dough will clump.

Spend time on this next step because the more compact and precise the dough, the easier it is to roll to the correct size and thickness to fit the slab pie pan. Form an X with two long pieces of overlapping plastic wrap and lightly flour the surface. Dump the dough onto the center of the plastic wrap, scraping the processor bowl clean. Wrap the sloppy gathering of dough in plastic and, at the same time, use a bench scraper (not your warm hands) to form the squared sides of a block, about 6 by 4 inches (or 3 by 4 inches if making a single crust). Once wrapped, use a rolling pin to gently press across the surface of the block. Flip it over and do the same on the other side. Now let it rest: Refrigerate the dough for at least 4 hours or preferably overnight.

(Continued)

THE POWER OF PIE CRUST

RECIPES THAT USE A CREAM CHEESE CRUST

These pies call for a Cream Cheese Crust, but feel free to mix and match. Each recipe offers Swaps with suggestions for alternate crusts, fillings, and toppings.

Beefy Empanada Slab Pie (page 162)
Frosted Strawberry Slab Pie (page 207)
Just-Like-Artichoke-Dip Slab Pie (page 95)
Spinach, Gorgonzola, and Walnut Slab Pie (page 109)
Raspberry Rugelach Slab Pie (page 250)
Sugar-Free Fig Slab Pie (page 255)
Walnut "Baklava" Slab Pie (page 264)

CHEDDAR CHEESE CRUST

For a Double- or a Single-Crust Slab Pie

A cheddar cheese crust is decadent. I like to use orange cheese so the nuggets melting into the flaky layers are obvious and seductive. Take your time to both grate and chop the cheese. Shreds and pieces that are too small will disappear into the crust; too large and the crust is lumpy. (Please do not use pre-shredded cheese, which is often coated in cornstarch.) Because of the cheese, the crust may brown more quickly, so tent the top of the pie with aluminum foil if the filling needs more time to warm through. Wrap this crust around thick slices of beefsteak tomatoes so the heat of the oven can turn those red slabs warm and juicy, a combination that is positively breathtaking. (See page 19 to make the dough by hand or in a stand mixer.)

FOR A DOUBLE CRUST

4 ounces (113 g) extra sharp cheddar cheese, preferably orange, cold

2½ cups plus 2 tablespoons (325 g) all-purpose flour

16 tablespoons (225 g) unsalted butter, cubed and frozen for 20 minutes

¼ teaspoon kosher salt

½ cup (120 ml) ice water

FOR A SINGLE CRUST

2 ounces (56 g) extra sharp cheddar cheese, preferably orange, cold

1⅓ cups (160 g) all-purpose flour

8 tablespoons (113 g) unsalted butter, cubed and frozen for 20 minutes

⅛ teaspoon kosher salt

¼ cup (60 ml) ice water

If making a double crust, prepare the cheese by grating some of it on the large holes of a box grater and chopping some of it into pea-sized pieces. It should be an irregular pile of cheese nuggets, with some pieces larger than others, totaling about 1 packed cup. If making a single crust, roughly chop the cheese into pea-sized pieces, about ½ cup packed.

Place the work bowl of the food processor on the scale, set the scale to zero, and weigh the flour into the bowl. Weigh in the butter, then add the salt. Move the bowl to the food processor base, cover, and use the Pulse function to cut the flour and butter into flour-covered, pea-sized pieces, about 15 quick pulses. Remove the cover of the processor and scatter the cheese over the dough. Cover and add the water all at once. Process until the dough barely comes together in a ball. All the flour will be dampened and the dough will clump.

Spend time on this next step because the more compact and precise the dough, the easier it is to roll to the correct size and thickness to fit the slab pie pan. Form an X with two long pieces of plastic wrap and lightly dust the surface with flour. Dump the dough onto the center of the overlapping plastic wrap, scraping the processor bowl clean. Wrap the sloppy gathering of dough in plastic and, at the same time, use a bench scraper (not your warm hands) to form the squared sides of a block, about 6 by 4 inches (or 3 by 4 inches if making a single crust).

(Continued)

It should be studded with pieces of cheese. Once wrapped, use a rolling pin to gently press across the surface of the block. Flip it over and do the same on the other side. Now let it rest: Refrigerate the dough for at least 4 hours or preferably overnight.

RECIPES THAT USE
A CHEDDAR CHEESE CRUST

These pies call for a Cheddar Cheese Crust, but feel free to mix and match. Each recipe offers Swaps with suggestions for alternate crusts, fillings, and toppings.

Not-So-Old-Fashioned Apple Slab Pie (page 236)
Southern-Style Tomato Slab Pie (page 115)

CARAMELIZED ONION CRUST

For a Double- or a Single-Crust Slab Pie

While baking, this crust smells like onion soup mix. In a good way. It is the perfect envelope for a filling that might benefit from some zip. Plan plenty of time for the two rounds of chilling: One for the butter and a second for the crust. Chop the onions very finely so they disperse throughout the butter and the dough. Flour the board and rolling pin generously before beginning to roll it out; this is a sticky dough and it warms quickly. (See page 19 to make the dough by hand or in a stand mixer.)

FOR A DOUBLE CRUST

2½ cups plus
2 tablespoons (325 g)
all-purpose flour

16 tablespoons (225 g)
Onion Butter (recipe
follows)

½ teaspoon kosher salt

½ cup (120 ml) ice water

FOR A SINGLE CRUST

1⅓ cups (160 g)
all-purpose flour

8 tablespoons (113 g)
Onion Butter
(recipe follows)

¼ teaspoon kosher salt

¼ cup (60 ml) ice water

Place the work bowl of the food processor on the scale, set the scale to zero, and weigh the flour into the bowl. Weigh in the onion butter; add a pinch of salt. Move the bowl to the food processor base, insert the metal blade, cover, and use the Pulse function to cut the flour and butter into flour-covered, pea-sized pieces, about 15 quick pulses. Add the ice water all at once and process until the dough almost comes together in a ball. All the flour will be dampened and the dough will clump.

Spend time on this next step because the more compact and precise the dough, the easier it is to roll to the correct size and thickness to fit the slab pie pan. Form an X with two long pieces of plastic wrap and lightly dust the surface with flour. Dump the dough onto the center of the overlapping plastic wrap, scraping the processor bowl clean. Wrap the sloppy gathering of dough in plastic and, at the same time, use a bench scraper (not your warm hands) to form the squared sides of a block, about 6 by 4 inches (or 3 by 4 inches if making a single crust). It should be studded with tiny pieces of onion. Once wrapped, use a rolling pin to gently press across the surface of the block. Flip it over and do the same on the other side. Now let it rest: Refrigerate the dough for at least 4 hours or preferably overnight.

(Continued)

RECIPES THAT USE A CARAMELIZED ONION CRUST

These pies call for a Caramelized Onion Crust, but feel free to mix and match. Each recipe offers Swaps with suggestions for alternate crusts, fillings, and toppings.

Loaded Baked Potato Slab Pie (page 101)
Christine's Smoky Fish Slab Pie (page 137)
Curried Chicken Slab Pie (page 151)
Lamb Vindaloo Slab Pie (page 173)

ONION BUTTER

Makes 16 tablespoons

16 tablespoons (225 g) unsalted butter, at room temperature

1 medium onion (142 g), diced small (about 1 cup)

Cube the butter into ½-inch pieces and place them in a large mixing bowl. Take out a good-sized knob of butter from the bowl, about 2 tablespoons, and heat until bubbling in a small skillet over low heat. Add the onions to the melted butter, stir well, and cook over low heat for 20 to 25 minutes, stirring lazily from time to time. The onions should be soft, browned, and smelling nice and sweet. Let cool for a few minutes.

Scrape the onions, any melted butter, and all the delicious brown bits into the bowl with the butter cubes. Knead the onions into the butter with your fingers or a rubber spatula. Wrap the butter in plastic wrap, then form it into a block. Refrigerate until very cold, at least 2 hours. Cube the onion butter and chill until ready to make the crust.

LARD OR LEAF LARD CRUST

For a Double- or a Single-Crust Slab Pie

Before turning away from a recipe that includes the word *lard,* let me introduce you to this wonderful addition to pie crust. Lard has less saturated fat than butter, so stop fretting. I'm not going to pretend it's a health food, but in the world of pies, lard is a welcome addition. A lard-based crust keeps longer and will not become soggy.

Lard is a beautiful thing. The larger fat crystals mean the lift it gives a pie crust is unbeatable. It adds flake, structure, and an unctuousness that's unmistakable. Smell the lard before using it. If there's a whiff of bacon, it may make a better crust for a savory pie.

Leaf lard, harder to find but so worth it, is my personal preference. Leaf lard is the clean fat surrounding a pig's kidney. Because it has no blood lines that run through it, leaf lard's color is pure white and there is hardly any flavor, only benefits.

While it is a straightforward task to render lard using a slow cooker, ready-to-use is a lot easier. These days, it's available online, at better butcher shops, and some farmers' markets.

Lard-based dough softens quickly—those larger fat crystals won't hold the chill in the same way as butter—so work quickly on a cold surface and chill—and rechill—the crust at every stage. Make sure fillings are completely cold before putting them in the pie, not even slightly warm, or the crust may end up soggy and tough. Once baked, this is a gloriously flaky crust, a little sandy, with a clean flavor. (See page 19 to make the dough by hand or in a stand mixer.)

FOR A DOUBLE CRUST

2½ cups plus
2 tablespoons (325 g)
all-purpose flour

12 tablespoons (170 g)
rendered lard or leaf lard,
cubed and frozen for
20 minutes

4 tablespoons (56 g)
unsalted butter, cubed and
frozen for 20 minutes

¼ teaspoon kosher salt

½ cup (120 ml) ice water

(Continued)

Place the work bowl of the food processor on the scale, set the scale to zero, and weigh the flour into the bowl. Weigh in the lard and then the butter; add the salt. Move the bowl to the food processor base, insert the metal blade, cover, and use the Pulse function to cut the flour and fats into flour-covered, pea-sized pieces, about 15 quick pulses. Add the ice water all at once and process until the dough almost comes together in a ball. All the flour will be dampened and the dough will be wet pearls and clumps.

(Continued)

THE POWER OF PIE CRUST

FOR A SINGLE CRUST

1⅓ cups (160 g)
all-purpose flour

6 tablespoons (85 g)
rendered lard or leaf lard,
cubed and frozen for
20 minutes

2 tablespoons (28 g)
unsalted butter, cubed and
frozen for 20 minutes

⅛ teaspoon kosher salt

¼ cup (60 ml) ice water

Spend time on this next step because the more compact and precise the dough, the easier it is to roll to the correct size and thickness to fit the slab pie pan. Form an X with two long pieces of overlapping plastic wrap and lightly flour the surface. Dump the dough onto the center of the plastic wrap, scraping the processor bowl clean. Wrap the sloppy gathering of dough in plastic and, at the same time, use a bench scraper (not your warm hands) to form the squared sides of a block, about 6 by 4 inches (or 3 by 4 inches if making a single crust). Once wrapped, use a rolling pin to gently press across the surface of the block. Flip it over and do the same on the other side. Now let it rest: Refrigerate the dough for at least 4 hours or preferably overnight.

RECIPES THAT USE A LARD CRUST

These pies call for a Lard Crust, but feel free to mix and match. Each recipe offers Swaps with suggestions for alternate crusts, fillings, and toppings.

Asparagus, Fontina, and Pancetta Slab Pie (page 111)
Cowboy Beef Stew Slab Pie (page 165)

RYE CRUST

For a Double- or a Single-Crust Slab Pie

The addition of rye flour makes a tangy crust with a more pronounced grain flavor than one made entirely from all-purpose flour. I developed this crust initially for "The Reuben" Slab Pie (page 159), but once I tried it with the sweet berries of summer (page 227), I was sold on its adaptability, from savory to sweet. If you're looking for a crust with a little character, give this one a try. Whole grains can make for a dense crust, so I add vodka to pump up the flakiness and shortening to help with the lift. (See page 19 to make the dough by hand or in a stand mixer.)

ROLLING PIN CRUSTS

FOR A DOUBLE CRUST

1¾ cups plus 1 tablespoon (225 g) all-purpose flour

1 cup (100 g) rye flour

8 tablespoons (113 g) unsalted butter, cubed and frozen for 20 minutes

8 tablespoons (113 g) Spectrum or other vegetable shortening, cubed and frozen for 20 minutes

½ teaspoon kosher salt

½ cup (120 ml) ice water

3 teaspoons ice cold vodka, optional

FOR A SINGLE CRUST

1 cup (120 g) all-purpose flour

⅜ cup (40 g) rye flour

4 tablespoons (56 g) unsalted butter, cubed and frozen for 20 minutes

(Continued)

Place the work bowl of the food processor on the scale, set the scale to zero, and weigh the all-purpose flour into the bowl. Weigh in the rye flour, then the butter and the shortening; add the salt. Move the bowl to the food processor base, nestle the sharp metal blade into the work bowl, cover, and use the Pulse function to cut the flour and fats into flour-covered, pea-sized pieces, about 15 quick pulses. Add the ice water and vodka all at once and process until the dough almost comes together in a ball. All the flour will be dampened and the dough will be craggy and clumpy.

Spend time on this next step because the more compact and precise the dough, the easier it is to roll to the correct size and thickness to fit the slab pie pan. Form an X with two long pieces of overlapping plastic wrap and lightly flour the surface. Dump the dough onto the center of the plastic wrap, scraping the processor bowl clean. Wrap the sloppy gathering of dough in plastic and, at the same time, use a bench scraper (not your warm hands) to form the squared sides of a block, about 6 by 4 inches (or 3 by 4 inches if making a single crust). Once wrapped, use a rolling pin to gently press across the surface of the block. Flip it over and do the same on the other side. Now let it rest: Refrigerate the dough for at least 4 hours or preferably overnight.

(Continued)

4 tablespoons (56 g)
Spectrum or other
vegetable shortening,
cubed and frozen for
20 minutes

¼ teaspoon kosher salt

¼ cup (60 ml) ice water

1½ teaspoons ice cold
vodka, optional

RECIPES THAT USE A RYE CRUST

These pies call for a Rye Crust, but feel free to mix and match. Each recipe offers Swaps with suggestions for alternate crusts, fillings, and toppings.

Cheesy Cauliflower Rarebit Slab Pie (page 127)
"The Reuben" Slab Pie (page 159)
Blackberry, Sweet Corn, and Basil Slab Pie (page 227)

CHOCOLATE CRUST

For a Double- or a Single-Crust Slab Pie

My friend Jennifer claimed that while she was adept at yoga handstands, rolling this dough took all her might and more. I'm going to be straight with you: The dough is tricky. It takes strength to roll it out, especially if it's too cold; but if it gets too warm, it's a smeary mess. But give it a shot. It's a delicious and surprising crust, not too sweet, but flaky and crisp. Do not flour the counter when rolling the crust—it will only make the dough tough and hard to work. Instead, use powdered sugar and use it generously. You will not make the crust too sweet. (See page 19 to make the dough by hand or in a stand mixer.)

FOR A DOUBLE CRUST

2½ cups plus
2 tablespoons (325 g)
all-purpose flour

⅓ cup (35 g) natural (not Dutched) cocoa powder

⅓ cup (67 g)
granulated sugar

16 tablespoons (225 g) unsalted butter, cubed and frozen for 20 minutes

¼ teaspoon kosher salt

⅔ cup coffee (160 ml),
ice cold

FOR A SINGLE CRUST

1⅓ cups (160 g)
all-purpose flour

Scant 3 tablespoons (18 g) natural (not Dutched) cocoa powder

Scant 3 tablespoons (40 g) granulated sugar

(Continued)

Place the work bowl of the food processor on the scale, set the scale to zero, and weigh the flour into the bowl. Weigh in the cocoa, then the granulated sugar and the butter; add the salt. Move the bowl to the food processor base, insert the metal blade, cover, and use the Pulse function to cut the dry ingredients and butter into flour-covered, pea-sized pieces, about 15 quick pulses. Add the coffee all at once and process until the dough almost comes together in a ball. All the flour will be dampened and the dough will clump.

Spend time on this next step because the more compact and precise the dough, the easier it is to roll to the correct size and thickness to fit the slab pie pan. Form an X with two long pieces of overlapping plastic wrap and lightly dust the surface with powdered sugar. Dump the dough onto the center of the plastic wrap, scraping the processor bowl clean. Generously dust the dough with powdered sugar. Wrap the sloppy gathering of dough in plastic and, at the same time, use a bench scraper (not your warm hands) to form the squared sides of a block, about 6 by 4 inches (or 3 by 4 inches if making a single crust). Once wrapped, use a rolling pin to gently press across the surface of the block. Flip it over and do the same on the other side. Now let it rest: Refrigerate the dough for at least 4 hours or preferably overnight.

(Continued)

THE POWER OF PIE CRUST

8 tablespoons (113 g)
unsalted butter, cubed and
frozen for 20 minutes

⅛ teaspoon kosher salt

¼ cup coffee (60 ml),
ice cold

Powdered sugar for
dusting and rolling
the dough

RECIPES THAT USE A CHOCOLATE CRUST

These pies call for a Chocolate Crust, but feel free to mix and match. Each recipe offers Swaps with suggestions for alternate crusts, fillings, and toppings.

Chocolate Pecan Slab Pie (page 261)
Double Chocolate Slab Pie (page 271)

NO COFFEE?

I love the undercurrent coffee adds to almost anything chocolate, from cookies to ice cream, so it made perfect sense to add it to the chocolate crust. If you're not a coffee drinker, or even if you are, cold coffee may not be easy to find in your house. Keep a jar of espresso powder on hand for any such situation. Depending on how prevalent you would like the coffee flavor to be, spoon anywhere from a teaspoon to a healthy tablespoon of espresso powder into ½ cup boiling water, stir, cool, and use in this recipe.

HOT WATER CRUST

For a Double-Crust Slab Pie

A hot water crust is the genius invention of some long ago British pastry chef. Those British know a thing or two about savory pies. They know how to put together a crust that stands up tall, never slumping, that stays delicious for a few days, never becoming gummy, and that keeps the meaty filling moist, never dry. Work quickly because once the dough cools, it's a beast to roll and form.

Hot water dough is counterintuitive to those of us who revere a keep-it-cold method and, I'll admit, when I made it the first time, I was certain it would be horrible. And yet, it was divine. It is a remarkably easy crust to crimp, stamp, and mold. Fancy leaves, turned roses, bunnies, and birds are all possible. Wait until you see the sturdy golden pie emerge from the oven. It's positively breathtaking. Unlike the other American-style pie crusts in this book, this very British Hot Water Crust must not be made by machine or one risks a tough and obstreperous pie.

This crust is the right choice for a picnic pie—any savory, meaty pie to be eaten cold or at room temperature. The classic British meat pie was made to last for a few days, so a thin layer of gelatin is added after baking to hold in the juices of the filling without letting the crust get soggy.

2¼ cups (265 g) all-purpose flour

½ cup (60 g) bread flour

1 teaspoon kosher salt

4 tablespoons (56 g) unsalted butter, cubed and cold but not frozen

6 tablespoons (85 g) rendered lard or leaf lard, cubed and cold but not frozen

½ cup (120 ml) boiling water

Place a large deep bowl on the scale, set the scale to zero, and weigh the all-purpose flour into the bowl. Weigh in the bread flour, then add the salt. With floured fingers, rub the butter and lard into the flours until the mixture is coarse and sandy. Pour the boiling water over the mixture and beat with a firm wooden spoon. As soon as the dough is smooth, tip it out onto a lightly floured countertop. Form a ball and if it is at all lumpy with flour, knead it further. Divide the dough into two pieces, one slightly larger than the other, and proceed with the recipe immediately. This dough must be worked while still warm.

RECIPES THAT USE A HOT WATER CRUST

Christmas in London Slab Pie (page 188)
English-Style Pork Slab Pie (page 185)

For the *doughphobic*, a press-in crust is a lifesaver. But that doesn't mean it's a lazy crust. There is still a technique, a method, which results in a great crust. Without some firm pressure, they're too crumbly. Too much butter and they're mushy and never dry out enough. Not enough butter and they're sandy and ineffective. Take the time to carefully prepare the crust and the pie will cut and serve satisfactorily.

Cookbook author, writer, and Food52 cofounder Amanda Hesser described the "sides first" crust method in her recipe for a press-in tart shell and I've adhered to this principle ever since I first saw it. Empty the dough into the pan and, taking walnut-sized pieces, press these smaller amounts of dough into the sides and corners of the pan first. Build the sides evenly thick, about ¼ inch, all the way around and square up the top surface. Use the side of your hand and your knuckles, not your fingertips, to make an even, firm edge. Use a metal cup measure or the flat bottom of a drinking glass to press the remaining dough evenly across the bottom of the pan. Steal from the sides to fill in the base only if needed. With a table knife, fork, or other tool, lightly press a design evenly spaced along the top edge. After all, it is the only part of the crust that will show. This method works best with the Shortbread Crust (page 59), the Olive Oil Crust (page 56), and the Cracker Crumb Crusts (page 61). Chill the crust for 20 minutes before baking; this will help it retain its shape, and avoid any slumping in the hot oven.

Alternatively, for Cookie Crumb Crusts (page 65) and the Hash Brown Crust (page

67), it's more effective to work from the base of the pan moving the crust to the sides. Dump the dough into a 9- by 13-inch slab pie pan. It's likely to be crumbly and not cohesive. Use a metal cup measure or the flat bottom of a glass to press the crumbs evenly on the bottom of the pan, working the sides last. Make the sides as thick as possible and press firmly so the crust keeps its shape in the oven. Decorate the top edge along all four sides with a table knife, fork, or other tool, making evenly spaced designs. Refrigerate the crust for 20 minutes before baking.

Remember: No one sees the bottom crust.

OLIVE OIL CRUST

For a Single-Crust Slab Pie

One bowl, one fork, one pan. It could not be simpler to make a delicious bottom crust for any savory pie. Use a high-quality, lightly flavored olive oil because green, bitter, sharp oil will pass those qualities on to the crust and permeate the pie. With a buttery, smooth olive oil, this crust is a revelation. Slightly sandy and not at all oily, the Olive Oil Crust is a great no-rolling-pin crust for almost any savory pie.

I prefer to press the dough out, but if making a double-crusted pie, you'll have to roll the top crust. Be aware: This dough can be tricky to roll. Grab your socks, as they say, and be confident. Make a double batch of the recipe, press half of the dough into a 9- by 13-inch baking sheet, and add the filling. Flour a piece of parchment paper, flour the remaining dough, flour the rolling pin often and confidently, and work fast to roll out the top crust on top of the parchment. Roll out the dough briskly from the center outward to the edges. Patch where needed. Brush away the excess flour and slide the crust from the parchment onto the filling. Fork crimp the edge; this is a crumbly dough and will act up with any other crimp. It's impossible for cutouts; don't even go there.

1⅔ cups (200 g) all-purpose flour

1½ teaspoons kosher salt

⅔ cup (156 ml) mild olive oil

2 tablespoons plus 2 teaspoons water

Heat the oven to 350°F; if you have one, place a baking stone, Baking Steel, or inverted baking sheet on the center rack to heat (see page 4).

Mix the flour and salt in a medium bowl using a table fork. With the same fork, whisk the olive oil and water right in the measuring cup.

Make a well in the center of the flour mixture and pour in the oil mixture. Using the fork, draw flour into the oil, turning the bowl at the same time. Once the dough starts to come together, switch to your hands to mix until the dough is smooth and comes together in a ball. You cannot overwork this dough; if it looks and feels cohesive, you're ready to go, about 5 minutes at the most.

Gather the ball of dough and plop it into a 9- by 13-inch baking sheet. Pinch off pieces of dough and begin building up the sides and corners. Make the edge about ¼ inch thick and as high as the sides of the pan. Use a measuring cup or the flat bottom of a drinking glass to spread the remaining dough along the bottom of the pan. Work deliberately: It can take a while to press the dough about ⅛ inch thick into a crust that goes across the entire pan. Be confident it will eventually do so. Patience.

(Continued)

This crust needs to bake for 40 minutes. If the recipe calls for the assembled pie to cook for 40 minutes or more, fill the unbaked shell. If the recipe calls for less time in the oven, blind bake the crust for 20 minutes (see Blind Baking, page 29).

Fill the unbaked crust and pop the pie into the oven, (on top of the steel, stone, or baking sheet if using) until the filling is bubbling and the crusty edges are browned, about 40 minutes.

VARIATIONS

Choose grapeseed, safflower, or corn oil for a more "unflavored" crust. Peanut oil tastes like, well, peanut oil. Walnut and hazelnut oils will burn, but you can add 2 tablespoons of nut oil to a neutral oil like grapeseed for a slightly flavored crust. Add 2 tablespoons of toasted sesame oil for a completely different take.

Spice this crust with abandon. Add any of the following to the flour and salt mixture:

1 teaspoon black pepper

1 teaspoon granulated onion

1 teaspoon chili powder

1½ teaspoons smoked paprika

1 teaspoon fennel seeds

1 tablespoon sesame seeds

RECIPES THAT USE AN OLIVE OIL CRUST

This crust works with any savory pie filling.

Carbonara Zoodle Slab Pie (page 179)

Moroccan-Style Shepherd's Slab Pie (page 168)

SHORTBREAD CRUST

For a Single-Crust Slab Pie

With a tender crumb like a cookie, this quick-to-make crust pairs with any fruit or custard filling, and there's no rolling pin involved. This is the crust I make when I discover a patch of blackberries behind a rented weekend cottage, as it requires no rolling pin and only 30 minutes of chilling before I can bake up something berry-full.

6 tablespoons (85 g) unsalted butter, at room temperature

⅓ cup (67 g) granulated sugar

1 egg yolk

1½ cups (180 g) all-purpose flour

¼ teaspoon kosher salt

Heat the oven to 350°F; if you have one, place a baking stone, Baking Steel, or inverted baking sheet on the center rack to heat (see page 4).

Using a stand mixer, hand mixer, or strong wooden spoon, beat the butter and sugar until smooth, lightened, and fluffy, about 5 minutes with the stand mixer. Add the egg yolk and beat until fully incorporated. Add the flour and salt and stir until a crumbly dough is formed.

Scrape the dough into a 9- by 13-inch baking sheet and, working with pieces no larger than a walnut, press the crust up the sides and well into the corners of the pan before worrying about the bottom. Then use a metal cup measure or a flat-bottomed glass to press out the remaining dough as uniformly as possible to about a ¼-inch thickness. Decorate the top edge using a table knife, a fork, or another tool, making slight indentations all the way around. Chill the crust for at least 20 minutes.

Slide the pan into the center of the oven (on top of the steel, stone, or baking sheet if using) and bake for 15 to 20 minutes, until pale golden brown on the edges. Cool the crust before filling.

(Continued)

VARIATIONS

This crust will take on flavor beautifully. Simply add any of the following enhancements:

½ teaspoon grated lemon or orange zest
½ teaspoon culinary lavender flowers
½ teaspoon fresh lemon thyme leaves
½ teaspoon fresh rosemary leaves, minced
1 teaspoon ground cinnamon
1 teaspoon cardamom seeds, crushed with the side of a knife
Seeds scraped from one vanilla bean
1 tablespoon poppy seeds
1 tablespoon sesame seeds

RECIPES THAT USE A SHORTBREAD CRUST

This crust works with any sweet pie filling.

Grande Mocha Cappuccino Slab Pie (page 297)
Leftover Cranberry Sauce Slab Pie (page 243)
Blueberry Streusel Slab Pie (page 224)

CRACKER CRUMB CRUSTS

For a Single-Crust Slab Pie

I grew up with graham cracker crumb crust pies, but making a crumb crust from another kind of cracker? It never occurred to me. Then I traveled to North Carolina and tasted Atlantic Beach Pie at Crook's Corner restaurant. That saltine crust slayed me. I've been playing with savory versions of crumb crust ever since and offer up four options below. Unlike cookie crumb crusts, which I like crushed to fine crumbs, I prefer shards of crackers here. Rather than use a blender or food processor, place the crackers in a ziptop bag and bash with a rolling pin until there are many different-sized small pieces but the crumbs are not powdered. Alternatively, use your hands to crush them. Cracker crumb crusts are always pre-baked and cooled before filling.

FOR A SALTINE CRUST

1½ sleeves (170 g)
saltine crackers
(about 60 crackers),
(about 2 cups crushed)

⅓ cup (67 g)
granulated sugar

10 tablespoons (140 g)
unsalted butter, cubed,
at room temperature

FOR A RITZ
CRACKER CRUST

60 Ritz crackers (225 g),
(about 2 cups crushed)

8 tablespoons (113 g)
unsalted butter, cubed,
at room temperature

(Continued)

Heat the oven to 350°F; if you have one, place a baking stone, Baking Steel, or inverted baking sheet on the center rack to heat (see page 4).

Place the crackers/pretzels/matzo in a ziptop bag and bash them with a rolling pin until they are in small pieces but not powdered, or use your hands to crush them.

Pour the crushed crackers into a medium bowl, add the remaining ingredients, and knead until a cohesive dough forms. This will take 8 to 10 minutes of hard work. Using your knuckles and the side of the hand, not your fingertips, press the dough into the sides and corners of a 9- by 13-inch baking sheet, forming a sturdy edge. Then use a metal cup measure or the flat bottom of a drinking glass to press the crust evenly across the bottom of the pan.

Slide the pan into the center of the oven (on top of the steel, stone, or baking sheet if using) and bake the crust for 20 to 25 minutes, until browned at the corners and edges. Cool on a rack.

(Continued)

THE POWER OF PIE CRUST

½ pound (225 g) fat
pretzels, knots, or rods,
(about 2 cups crushed)

8 tablespoons (113 g)
unsalted butter, cubed,
at room temperature

FOR A MATZO CRUST

8 or 9 sheets (225 g)
matzo, (about 2 cups
crushed)

¼ cup (50 g) granulated
sugar

1 teaspoon kosher salt

10 tablespoons (140 g)
unsalted butter, cubed,
at room temperature

RECIPES THAT USE A CRACKER CRUMB CRUST

Cracker crumb crusts suit most savory pies and certain sweet ones,
like lemon and coconut.

Sausage and Biscuit Slab Pie (Ritz crackers, page 193)

Niçoise-Style Tuna and Spring Greens Slab Pie (pretzels, page 121)

Fried Green Tomato Slab Pie (Ritz crackers, page 133)

Coconut Cream Slab Pie (saltines, page 290)

Dairy-Free and Passover-Perfect Coconut Cream Slab Pie
(matzo, page 294)

COOKIE CRUMB CRUSTS

For a Single-Crust Slab Pie

Crusts made with cookie crumbs are easy as pie. Crush cookies into crumbs and store them in the freezer (because cookie crumbs can turn rancid quickly). I prefer butter mixed in, but mild oils like grapeseed and safflower work as well. Each of the crust options below is no more than a giant cookie that is crushed and glued back together with butter. The goal is to create a sturdy frame. I use a metal cup measure or a flat-bottomed glass to press the wet crumbs firmly into the pan. In many cases, the pie crumbs won't quite reach up the sides of the pan. Don't worry. Aim to fashion a solid base that cuts and lifts easily. Always pre-bake cookie crumb crusts and let them cool before filling. And contemplate adding a swath of melted chocolate, caramel, or raspberry jam between the crust and the filling.

FOR A GRAHAM CRACKER CRUST

9 graham crackers (143 g), crushed to a powder (about 1¼ cups)

6 tablespoons (85 g) unsalted butter, melted

⅓ cup (67 g) granulated sugar

1 teaspoon kosher salt

FOR A GINGERSNAP CRUST

35 gingersnaps (8 ounces, 225 g), crushed to a fine powder (about 2 cups)

8 tablespoons (113 g) unsalted butter, melted

¼ teaspoon kosher salt

(Continued)

Heat the oven to 350°F; if you have one, place a baking stone, Baking Steel, or inverted baking sheet on the center rack to heat (see page 4).

Combine all the ingredients, kneading the mixture until it is cohesive and the crumbs are thoroughly buttered.

Dump the damp crumbs into a 9- by 13-inch baking sheet and press the mixture evenly along the bottom. Take your time pressing the crust in, using the side of your hand or a metal measuring cup to form a smooth base and a good edge until the crust feels firm to the touch.

Slide the pan into the oven (on top of the steel, stone, or baking sheet if using) and bake until the crust is lightly browned, about 20 minutes. The crust may emerge still damp, but as it cools it will firm up.

THE POWER OF PIE CRUST

FOR A VANILLA OR CHOCOLATE WAFER CRUST

1 (11-ounce) package standard size Nilla Wafers (311 g), about 80 cookies, or 1 (9-ounce) package Famous Chocolate Wafers (255 g), about 40 cookies, crushed to a fine powder (about 2 cups)

8 tablespoons (113 g) unsalted butter, melted

¼ teaspoon kosher salt

FOR A SPECULOOS CRUST

29 Biscoff (or other speculoos) cookies (225 g; from an 8.8-ounce package), crushed to a fine powder (about 2 cups)

8 tablespoons (113 g) unsalted butter, melted

¼ teaspoon kosher salt

FOR AN AMARETTI CRUST

29 amaretti cookies (225 g), crushed to a fine powder (about 2 cups)

8 tablespoons (113 g) unsalted butter, melted

¼ teaspoon kosher salt

RECIPES THAT USE A COOKIE CRUMB CRUST

Long before I learned to roll out a crust, I made pies with cookie crumbs. Cookies go with anything sweet, so of course, a cookie crust is just the ticket for custards, creams, and fruit pie crusts.

Banana Pudding Slab Pie (vanilla wafers, page 287)

Lemon Cream Slab Pie (speculoos, page 281)

Lemon Meringue Slab Pie (gingersnaps, page 284)

No-Campfire-Necessary S'Mores Slab Pie (graham crackers, page 275)

Peanut Butter Slab Pie (chocolate wafers, page 269)

Pumpkin Chiffon Slab Pie (amaretti cookies, page 247)

Sesame Sweet Potato Slab Pie (gingersnaps, page 130)

HASH BROWN CRUST

For a Single-Crust Slab Pie

The idea for a crust made from potatoes may not have begun with Mollie Katzen's *Moosewood Cookbook,* but that is where I learned to press potatoes into a pie pan and call it crust. It's a shoo-in for a breakfast pie, and swaps in to any savory pie recipe when gluten-free friends are visiting. No flour is used for binding; rely instead on the naturally occurring potato starch to hold the crust together.

2 tablespoons neutral oil like canola or grapeseed

1 medium (142 g) onion, peeled

1½ pounds (680 g) medium russet potatoes, scrubbed (not peeled), about 4

1 large egg plus 1 egg white, beaten

1 teaspoon kosher salt

½ teaspoon coarsely ground black pepper

Heat the oven to 425°F; if you have one, place a baking stone, Baking Steel, or inverted baking sheet in the center rack to heat (see page 4). Use a pastry brush to paint 1 tablespoon of the oil into the corners, up the sides, and across the bottom of a 9- by 13-inch baking sheet.

Grate the onion on the medium holes of a box grater or use a food processor's grating disk (my preference) and place in a medium mixing bowl. Grate the potatoes on the large shredding side of the box grater or with the food processor's grating disk. Taking a handful of shredded potatoes at a time, squeeze them over a small bowl to capture the liquid, then place the potato shreds in the bowl with the onions. Work quickly.

Let the potato liquid sit for about 5 minutes, until the starch and liquid separate. Pour off the liquid, keeping the starchy white paste at the bottom of the bowl. Add the potato starch to the grated onions and potatoes, then add the egg and egg white, salt, and pepper. Mix well. I use my hands.

Press the potato mixture firmly into the pan. Brush the surface of the potatoes with the remaining 1 tablespoon oil. Roast until toasty brown on the edges and across the surface, 40 to 45 minutes.

RECIPES THAT USE A HASH BROWN CRUST

Potatoes are a glorious base for so many delicious foods; try this crust with any savory filling. Meaty stews are especially complementary.

Eggs Florentine Slab Pie (page 190)
Poblano and Chorizo Slab Pie (page 144)

PRESS-IN CRUSTS

67

THE POWER OF PIE CRUST

CORNBREAD CRUST

For a Single-Crust Slab Pie

This corn-y crust is tender and cake-like. Look for high-quality cornmeal: I favor a coarse grind, but you may prefer a less textural cornbread, so feel free to use a fine grind instead. This crust is sturdy enough to rise and bake even with a filling spooned right on top of the batter. When it comes to cornbread recipes, I fall on the no-sugar side of the debate. If you prefer a sweeter cornbread, add 2 tablespoons of granulated sugar to the batter.

There's one important trick to this crust: I'm not kidding around when I tell you to remove ½ cup of the batter before pouring the rest into the buttered slab pie pan. If you don't, I guarantee that the batter will spill over the side (and onto the bottom of the oven). Instead, butter a ramekin, pour in that extra batter, and bake it with the pie (for 25 to 30 minutes). That little baby cornbread is all yours.

To serve the cornbread as a side dish and not a crust, place a 9- or 10-inch cast iron skillet in the oven while it preheats to 400°F. Cautiously butter the screamingly hot pan and spoon the batter in, smoothing the surface. Bake for 25 to 30 minutes, until golden brown and pulling away from the sides of the pan.

6 tablespoons (85 g) unsalted butter, melted

¾ cup (90 g) all-purpose flour

¾ cup (115 g) stone-ground cornmeal

1½ teaspoons baking powder

1 teaspoon baking soda

1 teaspoon kosher salt

1 cup (240 ml) buttermilk

2 large eggs, beaten

Heat oven to 400°F. Brush a 9- by 13-inch baking sheet with the 1 tablespoon melted butter, especially in the corners and up the sides; also butter a 4-ounce ramekin.

In a deep bowl, whisk the flour and cornmeal with the baking powder, baking soda, and salt. In another bowl, whisk together the 5 tablespoons butter, the buttermilk, and eggs. Add the egg mixture to the flour mixture and, using no more than a fork, quickly incorporate the ingredients. Lumps are okay. Scoop out ½ cup of the batter into the buttered ramekin. Pour the remaining batter into the slab pie pan.

Pour the filling right on top of the batter. Everything will work out in the oven, with the cornbread enveloping the filling. Bake the pie for 25 to 30 minutes until golden brown and pulling away from the sides of the pan.

RECIPES THAT USE A CORNBREAD CRUST

The sweet corn flavor complements hearty meaty fillings.

Favorite Turkey Chili Frito Slab Pie (page 141)
Nacho Slab Pie (page 97)

STORE-BOUGHT PIE CRUST

I know. I get it. It seems so much easier to buy pie crust than to make it. Perhaps you hesitate to make the dough, or you fear rolling it out and that is what has led you to the refrigerator or freezer case at your local grocery store. Whatever the reason, now that I've got you looking at this book, I'm going to make one more play for the real deal. Try my go-to pie crust (All-Butter Crust, page 30) or press in an Olive Oil Crust (page 56) or Shortbread Crust (page 59) instead of turning to the pre-made.

But if you're not there yet, and you plan to buy a crust this one time, here is what to consider when shopping for a pre-made crust. Check the ingredient list carefully. Look for butter or organic shortening and look away from those containing partially hydrogenated oil, an ingredient that leaves an odd coating in the mouth. Most grocery store crusts will come already pressed into a round pan, but for a slab pie, find the ones that come rolled up in a box, sometimes in the freezer section, sometimes in the refrigerated section.

Every store-bought crust I tested benefited from a scattering of salt and, if making a sweet pie, a sprinkling of sugar, too. Add these seasonings on top of the bottom crust before filling the pie. The salt is especially important.

Handling Tips

Defrost frozen pie dough overnight in the refrigerator. Once defrosted, remove one crust at a time from the refrigerator and allow it to warm slightly, at most only 5 to 10 minutes. Each crust will likely be individually packaged, often between two pieces of coated paper. Use

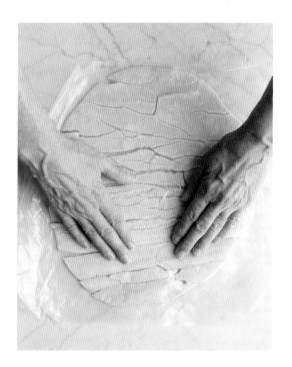
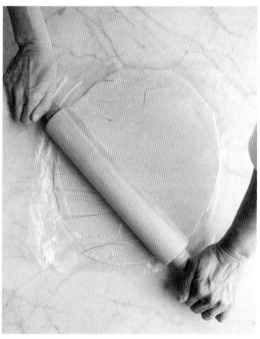

those papers to guide the dough while rolling it out and making the round shape more rectangular. If the dough is not packaged between coated paper, use two pieces of parchment paper lightly dusted with flour, as noted below, and roll the dough out.

Carefully unroll the pie dough onto a floured sheet of parchment. Dust the crust with flour and place a second sheet of parchment on top of the crust. The crust is likely to crack while unrolling it, but will crumble less horribly if it is at room temperature. Don't worry about the cracks, use a rolling pin to smooth out the crevices and guide the crust into a cohesive sheet. Using the rolling pin, gently press the crust into a rectangular-ish shape so it will fit the bottom of a 9- by 13-inch baking sheet and slightly rise up on the sides; aim for approximately 10 by 14 inches. If the dough is too soft, too warm, and smears when rolled, put it back in the refrigerator for at least 20 minutes before starting again. Peel off the top piece of parchment, invert the slab pie pan over the dough, and invert both pan and crust, using the bottom piece of parchment for leverage. Fit the crust in the pan, gently pressing it into the corners and up the sides as much as possible, and refrigerate. A round 9-inch pie crust will never thoroughly fill a squared pan, but it will make a good effort. Repeat rolling out the other crust and refrigerate it between the parchment sheets until ready to fill the pie.

To make a lattice topper or a cutout topper, follow the instructions on page 26.

Follow the pie recipe as written to make the filling. Fill the bottom crust and scatter salt across the surface. Peel back the top parchment paper and invert and drape the top crust over the filling. Use your fingers to pinch the two crusts together (see Crimp and Slash, page 24).

Grocery store crusts need less time to bake than homemade crusts. If using a grocery store crust, reduce the overall baking time to no more than a total of 45 to 50 minutes, and reduce the baking temperature by 25°F. Tent the pie with foil if it browns too quickly. Using visual cues (bubbling filling, browning crust) to determine when the pie is done is always the best bet.

PHYLLO

Phyllo is a simple dough of flour and water rolled into very thin sheets that are then brushed with butter and layered to make a papery, rich pastry. Because there are no eggs or fats in the dough, phyllo needs plenty of butter or another fat to form crispy, flaky, ethereal layers. If you've never phyllo'd before, try it once and the secret to phyllo will be revealed: You can't make a mistake. Seriously. This stuff is foolproof. Rips and tears? Patch them with another piece of phyllo, add butter to glue it together, and soldier on. It's delicious every single time. That said, there are some tricks to help you keep your cool when working with this dough.

Phyllo sheets are available in two sizes, but the smaller, 9- by 14-inch sheets, are best suited for the slab pie pan. If you can only find the 14- by 18-inch sheets, use kitchen scissors or a long sharp knife to cut them in half along the 18-inch edge. Phyllo demands we plan ahead: The resulting pastry is well worth it. Defrost a 16-ounce package of phyllo dough in the refrigerator for one full day (24 hours). There is no way to speed up this process. Do not leave the dough out on the counter to defrost; it will become gummy and difficult to work with.

Make the layers as quickly as possible, keeping the phyllo covered with a sheet of plastic

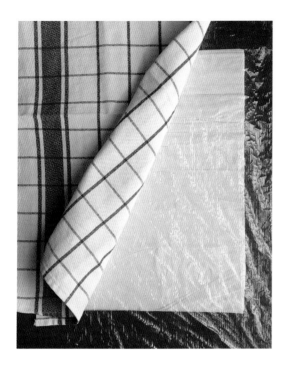

wrap and a slightly damp cotton kitchen towel on top of the plastic wrap while buttering.

Butter is the most common fat used to lubricate phyllo, but duck fat, lard, bacon fat, and olive oil all work beautifully. There is no denying the benefit of butter for the flavor and the way it browns and burnishes the crust, but bacon fat is gosh darn amazing, too.

When buttering between the layers, use a gentle touch with a soft pastry brush. I like a natural bristle brush, 1 or 2 inches wide. Use a dabbing motion, do not brush or the sheets will tear, and be generous. On a buttered 9- by 13-inch baking sheet, place a phyllo sheet, allowing some drape over the edges. Butter this first sheet well. Now, pick up two more sheets, placing them on top of the buttered one. Butter the top sheet and repeat two more times, until there are seven sheets on the bottom of the pan.

Fill the pie with cooled filling and repeat the process with the phyllo, first draping a single layer of phyllo, buttering and adding six more sheets in three additions with butter dabbed between each pair of phyllo sheets. The phyllo will rip and tear; simply patch and keep going. No one will see these repairs once the pie is baked! Generously brush the top layer with every bit of the butter. Trim the edges, fold the bottom layers over the top layers, rolling toward the center to make a chubby edge.

If there is time, I like to chill the pie for an hour or more at this juncture. Cold, it's much easier to make the required shallow cuts through the top layers of phyllo. Portion the pie with these surface cuts sliced all the way through the top layers of phyllo, but not all the way through the pie's bottom layer. These cuts are traditionally made in a diamond pattern (think baklava), but use whatever pattern portions the pie correctly for your crowd (see How to Slice a Slab Pie, page 304). These cuts are a must-do. It's impossible to slice into phyllo after it's cooked to crackly perfection without shattering it. Hidden benefit? With even more crispy corners, every piece is an edge piece. Phyllo pies cook at around 400°F until golden brown with a bubbly filling, about an hour.

Recipe That Uses a Phyllo Crust
Get creative and use phyllo to wrap up any sweet or savory pie.

Sumac-Scented Eggplant Slab Pie (page 124)

PUFF PASTRY
If you have enjoyed a *palmier* or cheese straw, you know—and likely love—puff pastry. What's not to love? Puff pastry is made with butter, lots and lots of butter, and that is what makes it so darn delicious. Puff pastry, straight from the grocery store, without the need to beat butter, fold it, turn it, and otherwise manipulate your way to fancy pastry, is one of the great pleasures of modern life. Most puff is found in the freezer section, somewhere around the frozen bread, pie crusts, and rolls. There is no way to speed the defrosting process, so move the box from the freezer to the refrigerator the night before. And note that puff pastry, once defrosted, keeps only two or three days.

Commercial puff pastry is often made with non-buttery fats like palm, cottonseed, and other partially hydrogenated oils. I prefer puff that is all butter, like Dufour, but it can be expensive and is often difficult to find. Simply Enjoy brand is found in some parts of the country; it's a private label brand and has a higher percentage of butter in the blend. It bakes beautifully. Trader

Joe's brand puff pastry is well made and delicious, and more likely to be in the freezer case during the holidays. Pepperidge Farm is widely available, easy to use, and has some buttery flavor. It's dependable. Wewalka brand is found in the refrigerated section (no defrosting) but has no butter at all in the mix.

Keeping puff pastry chilled is essential. Puff is made by folding buttery dough over and over making layers and layers of paper-thin dough with swipes of cold butter in between. These buttery bits release steam in the oven and each layer lifts up tall and airy and flaky and buttery. There's nothing quite like it.

I have different expectations for a slab pie made from puff pastry. These pies will serve fewer people than a classic crusty slab pie, because the puff isn't as sturdy as a traditional pie crust; once baked it doesn't easily portion into little bites without deflating the layers. Think of the puff as a platform for delicious, rich toppings, best for a small gathering.

Start with the obvious: Grocery store puff pastry will not immediately fit the slab pie pan. So you'll need to use a rolling pin to stretch the dough, but do so gently and cautiously. Too much pressing and the layers are smashed, the lift is altered, and the puff is dull, mushy, and disappointing.

Work with the defrosted, but still cold, pastry on a lightly floured surface. Unfold the pastry and use a rolling pin to gently roll it out, working to smooth the folds from the box and making the dough slightly longer than it is wide, about 10 by 12 inches. Use a sharp knife or pastry wheel to cut ½- to 1-inch strips from each edge. Tuck the remaining pastry into the bottom of a 9- by 13-inch baking sheet and use the trimmed strips to stack a raised edge all around the crust.

At this point cover the pan and chill the pastry again for at least 30 minutes. This resting period is critical to chill the buttery bits again, avoiding tough pastry and encouraging lift.

When using puff pastry for slab pies, do not weigh down the pastry with too much filling. You will need to use less filling than you think,

so the pastry will still be lofty and bronzed. Plan ahead for eight or twelve pieces, lightly scoring the surface of the pastry into portions before topping with the filling.

Consider using more puff pastry as a topper, cutting out shapes that cover each serving. I like randomly shaped triangles or different sizes of circles, but stars and hearts are adorable! Use these toppers on Chicken Pot Slab Pie (page 155), any berry pie, or an appetizer pie like Asparagus, Fontina, and Pancetta Slab Pie (page 111).

Bake puff pastry slab pies or toppers in a hot oven, anywhere from 400°F to 450°F, depending on package instructions, until deeply golden brown, 25 to 30 minutes.

Recipes That Use a Puff Pastry Crust

Keep puff pastry in the freezer for hosting emergencies. Improvise assuredly: Fruit fillings, in small quantities, sitting on a spoonful of mascarpone or ricotta atop puff pastry. Or go savory with a dollop of a rich, meaty filling instead.

Zucchini, Feta, and Kalamata Olive Slab Pie (page 117)
Pear and Frangipane Slab Pie (page 241)
Good Morning Cheese Danish Slab Pie (page 299)

WHIPPED AND MASHED TOPPINGS

When a pie has no top crust, or even when it does, whipped cream wants to cozy up to a piece of pie. It's the next best thing to ice cream. Here are some whipped toppings to pretty up your next pie, including meringues and, not wanting to ignore savory pies, a cloud of whipped, light-as-air potatoes, too.

These whipped toppers should be sturdy so they do not weep or droop—aim for very stiff peaks. A piping bag and star decorating tip will make any of these toppings look fancy. Or use the back of a spoon and a light touch for whimsical peaks and valleys.

WHIPPED CREAM

Makes 4 cups

2 cups (480 ml)
heavy cream

½ cup (100 g)
granulated sugar, optional

½ teaspoon vanilla extract

Beat the cream at high speed with an electric mixer until foamy. Add the sugar, if using, 1 tablespoon at a time. Whip on high until stiff peaks form and the beater leaves a trail in the cream. Spread or pipe the whipped cream over the pie.

WHIPPED COCONUT CREAM

Makes 3 cups

1 can (350 ml) coconut cream, chilled in the can in the refrigerator for several hours

¼ cup (59 g) powdered sugar

½ teaspoon vanilla extract

Beat the coconut cream at high speed with an electric mixer until foamy. Add the sugar 1 tablespoon at a time, beating until stiff peaks form. Beat in the vanilla. Chill for 1 hour before spreading or piping the whipped topping over the pie.

MERINGUE

Makes 4 cups

3 egg whites (90 g),
at room temperature

¼ teaspoon cream of tartar

½ cup (100 g)
granulated sugar

¼ teaspoon vanilla extract

Heat the oven to broil with a rack in the upper third of the oven.

In a stand mixer, beat the egg whites on medium until foamy. Add the cream of tartar (which helps to stabilize the lift). Continue beating, increasing the speed to high while adding the sugar 1 tablespoon at a time. When half the sugar has been added, add the vanilla extract. Continue adding the sugar 1 tablespoon at a time; when the egg whites are shiny and form tall, stiff peaks when the beater is lifted, check to see if the sugar is dissolved by rubbing a little meringue between two fingers. There should be no grit. If it's still gritty, continue beating and test again after another minute.

To use, plop the meringue here and there over a pie filling and gently disperse it across the surface with the back side of a large spoon, making fluffy peaks and ensuring the meringue securely touches the entire edge of the crust. Or spoon the meringue into a pastry bag and pipe a pretty design across the surface. Slide the pie into the oven and broil the meringue until it is browning here and there and smells like toasted marshmallows, 3 or 4 minutes. Cool slightly and serve soon.

POTATO MASH

Makes 4 cups

2½ pounds (1.14 kg)
russet potatoes, peeled
and cut into chunks

Kosher salt

3 tablespoons (42 g)
unsalted butter, cubed

½ teaspoon coarsely
ground black pepper

¼ cup (60 ml) whole milk,
warmed)

In a medium saucepan over high heat, cover the potatoes with cool water and a big pinch of salt. Cover and boil until the potatoes are fork-tender and soft, 12 to 15 minutes. Drain all the water from the pan, remove from the heat, and cover, leaving the potatoes to steam for 5 minutes.

Mash the potatoes with a stand mixer fitted with the whisk attachment, a hand mixer, or a good old handheld masher, adding the butter, 1 teaspoon salt, and the pepper. Pour in the milk slowly, whipping all the time, until the potatoes are smooth and velvety and not too stiff.

To use, spoon your savory filling into a crust and spread it out from edge to edge. Dollop the potatoes across the filling here and there. Gently spread the potatoes from edge to edge leaving none of the filling exposed. Slide the pie into the oven to bake for the time noted in the recipe.

If you prefer to use a pastry bag and a decorating tip, and if the potatoes are too stiff, loosen them with no more than one additional tablespoon of milk.

THE POWER OF PIE CRUST

GLAZES, SQUIGGLES, AND DRIZZLES

GLAZES

FOR A VANILLA GLAZE

1 cup (113 g) powdered sugar

3 to 6 tablespoons cold milk

1 teaspoon vanilla extract

FOR A LEMON GLAZE

1 cup (113 g) powdered sugar

3 to 6 tablespoons cold milk

½ teaspoon grated lemon zest

1 tablespoon fresh lemon juice

FOR AN ORANGE GLAZE

1 cup (113 g) powdered sugar

3 to 6 tablespoons cold milk

½ teaspoon grated orange zest

1 tablespoon fresh orange juice

FOR A COFFEE GLAZE

1 cup (113 g) powdered sugar

3 to 6 tablespoons cold milk

1 teaspoon espresso powder dissolved in 1 tablespoon cool water

Makes 1¼ cups

Whisk the powdered sugar and 3 tablespoons milk together until smooth. Add the flavoring. Continue to whisk until velvety smooth, adding more liquid as needed to reach the desired consistency.

Flood the entire surface of your pie with the glaze using an offset spatula. Or squiggle on with a pastry bag. Or drizzle on with a fork. Once the pie has been decorated, chill to set the glaze.

THE POWER OF PIE CRUST

POURABLE CHOCOLATE

Makes ⅔ cup

4 ounces (113 g) semisweet or bittersweet chocolate, chopped

Up to 2 tablespoons heavy cream

A drop or 2 of light corn syrup, optional

Add half the chocolate to a heatproof bowl set over barely simmering water, stirring from time to time. (See How to Melt Chocolate, page 263, and How to Make a Double Boiler, below). When smooth and thoroughly melted, remove from the heat and whisk in the remaining chocolate until melted. Thin to the desired consistency with the cream, continuing to whisk until the glaze is smooth. Whisk in the corn syrup, which will make the chocolate shiny. After decorating, chill the pie to firm up the chocolate.

HOW TO MAKE A DOUBLE BOILER

I am no fan of single-use kitchen equipment, so I do not own an actual double boiler. Double boilers are nothing more than one pan that sits inside another, with simmering water in the bottom pan gently heating, but not touching the bottom of the upper pot. Those fancy double boilers are always called for in curd making because indirect heat means the eggs won't scramble. I make my own double boiler by nesting a metal or glass bowl in a medium saucepan filled with 2 or 3 inches of bubbling water so the bottom of the bowl is *over,* but not touching, the water. A large bowl is easier to work with, and its rim should be larger than the diameter of the saucepan. Only metal or glass will conduct and disperse the heat to make the silkiest curd or custard.

BIRDSEED, CRUSHES, AND ROCKY ROAD GARNISHES

Garnishes add texture and flavor to both savory and sweet slab pies. You'll need about ½ cup to scatter over a pie or sprinkle in a 2-inch swath around the edges, and about 1 cup to cover a pie more thoroughly. See How to Toast Nuts, page 253, to toast the seeds.

BIRDSEED

Makes a little more than ½ cup

¼ cup (35 g) toasted sesame seeds

2 tablespoons toasted pepitas (pumpkin seeds)

2 tablespoons toasted sunflower seeds

1 tablespoon poppy seeds

1 teaspoon flaky salt, such as Maldon or *fleur de sel*

½ teaspoon crushed red pepper

1 teaspoon grated lemon zest

In a small bowl, stir together the seeds, salt, pepper, and zest. Store in a tightly closed jar in the refrigerator for one month.

CRUSHES

Makes 3 to 4 cups

Fritos, Doritos, Bugles, tortilla chips, or potato chips

Pick one. A 9-ounce bag will make plenty of crunchy topping. Crush the chips right inside the bag using a rolling pin (vent the bag first by cutting a small opening or the bag will go POW!).

THE POWER OF PIE CRUST

ROCKY ROAD

Makes 2 to 3 cups

Mini chocolate chips

Mini marshmallows, snipped into four pieces with lightly oiled scissors

Cracker Jack

Mini M&M's

Toffee bits

Tiny nonpareils

Toasted coconut flakes

Candied ginger

Candied orange peel

Chocolate espresso beans

Salted, even smoked, almonds

Valrhona chocolate pearls

Tiny caramels

Little peanut butter cups

Mix and match as many or as few of the items listed here as you like. It takes about 2 to 3 cups to thickly cover a pie. One cup will scatter across the top of a rich pie, such as Grande Mocha Cappuccino Slab Pie (page 297).

SWEET, NUTTY, OR SAVORY STREUSELS

Instead of a top crust, make a streusel. Buttery, nutty, cheesy—here are three options to add texture to a pie topper. All the streusels call for toasted nuts. See How to Toast Nuts (page 253).

Put the dry ingredients in the food processor and pulse until the mixture resembles pebbles, about 5 times. Remove the lid, scatter the butter over the dry ingredients, and pulse until the mixture looks like damp clumps. Empty the streusel into a large bowl and rub the pieces between your fingers to make large, buttery clumps. (If working without a food processor, opt for a textural streusel and break up the nuts by hand, rubbing the butter into the ingredients.)

To use, scatter the streusel over the pie for the final 25 minutes of baking. If it browns too quickly, tent with foil.

GRANOLA STREUSEL

Makes 1 cup

⅓ cup (40 g) all-purpose flour

¼ cup (25 g) rolled (not instant) oats

2 tablespoons packed light brown sugar

⅛ teaspoon ground cinnamon

½ teaspoon kosher salt

⅓ cup (37 g) toasted pecans, chopped

2 tablespoons (28 g) unsalted butter, cubed and chilled

THE POWER OF PIE CRUST

HOW TO BROWN BUTTER

Browning butter adds a nutty depth of flavor to streusel, changing the character from sweet to sultry. Brown the butter, then chill it hard before massaging it into the dry ingredients.

In a small saucepan, melt and then heat the butter until it foams and bubbles. Let the butter cook, on low, and continue to bubble until it is medium brown in color and smells heavenly, about 12 minutes. Watch it carefully and do not let brown butter blacken. If that happens, start over. There is no return from burnt. When butter is browned, most of the foam will have moved to the sides of the pan and there will be solids at the bottom of the pan, below the clear, nutty butter.

Use a spoon to lift and dispose of the foam from the surface. Pour the translucent liquid into a small bowl, leaving the solids behind. Refrigerate the brown butter until cooled and hardened, then use as directed in the streusel recipe.

NUTTY BROWN-BUTTER STREUSEL

Makes 2½ lightly packed cups

1 cup toasted hazelnuts (or any other nut), roughly chopped

⅔ cup (135 g) granulated sugar

¾ cup (90 g) all-purpose flour

¼ teaspoon kosher salt

8 tablespoons (113 g) butter, browned (see box), chilled, and cut into ¼-inch pieces

CACIO E PEPE SAVORY STREUSEL

Makes 2½ cups

1 cup toasted slivered almonds

1 cup grated Pecorino

½ cup (60 g) all-purpose flour

¼ cup (30 g) semolina (or additional all-purpose flour)

½ teaspoon kosher salt

2 teaspoons coarsely ground black pepper

8 tablespoons (113 g) cold unsalted butter, cut into ¼-inch pieces

BABY BISCUITS

Makes 24 1½-inch biscuits

Form small biscuits and layer them over a pie, touching cheek to cheek. Follow the biscuit baking instructions and add them to the already baking pie for the designated baking time. Use high-fat, low-water-content European butter if you can.

5 cups (600 g) all-purpose (not self-rising) flour, preferably White Lily, plus more for dusting

1 tablespoon baking powder

1 tablespoon kosher salt

8 tablespoons (113 g) unsalted butter, cubed and frozen for at least 20 minutes

1 cup (240 ml) buttermilk

2 tablespoons (28 g) unsalted butter, melted

In the bowl of the food processor, weigh the flour, then add the baking powder and salt. Set the bowl on the processor base, place the metal blade, and cut in the frozen butter, pulsing 12 times. Add the buttermilk all at once and process just until a shaggy dough forms, only a minute or so.

Empty the dough, floury bits, and loose flour from the processor work bowl onto the counter. Use a bench scraper to gather the dough, pressing along the sides and patting the top gently, lifting and folding the dough over and patting it down, and evening the sides with the bench scraper. Continue to fold and pat 4 or 5 times, until a cohesive mass emerges. Press it out to a ½-inch thickness using your fingertips or a well-floured rolling pin.

Cut out 24 biscuits with a 1½-inch round cutter, or use the bench scraper to make 1½-inch square biscuits. Discard the scraps.

To use, tuck the biscuits close together on the surface of the pie. Bake the biscuits at the highest temperature the pie will withstand (at least 400°F but as high as 450°F) for the last 8 to 10 minutes of baking, until layered with pale golden brown. Brush the tops with the melted butter as soon as the pie comes out of the oven.

CRUST-FREE TOPPERS

THE POWER OF PIE CRUST

After snipping lattice strips, stamping out hearts and stars, or simply taking a knife to the edge of the pie, there will always be odd bits of dough on the counter. Tuck the assembled pie in the freezer or refrigerator to chill while the oven heats and use the time to make some nibbles for the cook and her friends. Use the pie baking oven temperature—somewhere between 350°F and 425°F —and watch for browning to indicate the pastry is ready to snack on. Pie dough will need at least 20 minutes. Puff pastry is quicker, 10 to 12 minutes.

In a savory mood? Dip small shards or strips of uncooked pie dough in the egg wash, then roll in grated cheese, sprinkle with smoked paprika, or dredge in "everything bagel" mix.

(Make an everything mix yourself: Mix together 1 teaspoon each granulated onion, poppy seeds, sesame seeds, caraway seeds, and kosher salt.) Stretch and twist the dough into a rough corkscrew shape. Bake on a parchment-lined baking sheet while the pie is baking until toasty brown, about 20 minutes.

For those with a sweet tooth, use your fingertips to tap a pie dough scrap into a flat shape, spread jam or honey or cinnamon sugar on one side, and roll the dough up in a loose jelly roll. Or pinch a piece of pie dough around a chunk of semisweet or bittersweet chocolate. Brush with the egg wash and sprinkle with sugar. Bake on a parchment-lined baking sheet while the pie bakes until golden brown, 20 minutes or so.

Chapter Three

SAVOR A PIE

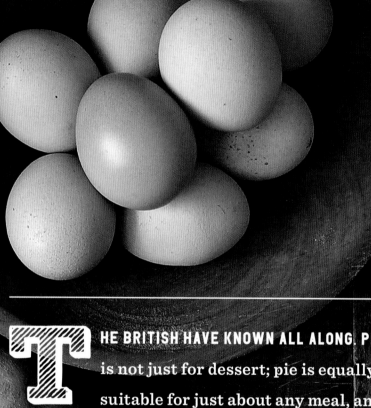

THE BRITISH HAVE KNOWN ALL ALONG. PIE is not just for dessert; pie is equally suitable for just about any meal, any time of day. Whether nibbles with a cocktail, the star of a light lunch, or part of a hearty supper, savory pies are just right. Here are vegetarian pies and meaty pies, appetizer pies and side dish pies. Breakfast pies with eggs, a pie that's a salad, pies made from leftovers, and pies that make great leftovers. Make slab pie part of your weekly dinner plan.

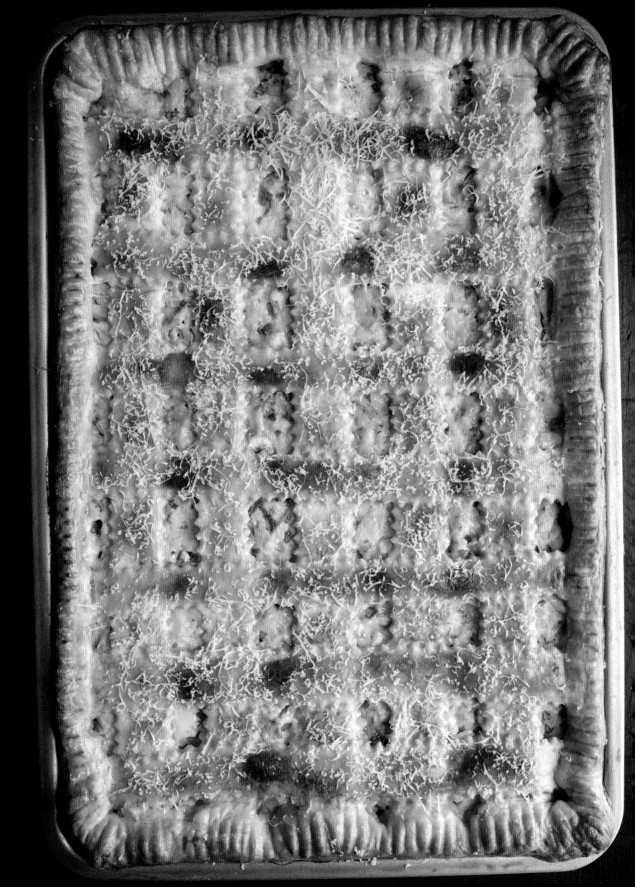

JUST-LIKE-ARTICHOKE-DIP SLAB PIE

WITH A CREAM CHEESE CRUST

Serves 15 to 24

We all have our comfort foods, and artichoke dip is mine. It's soothing and familiar and cheesy and goes with a rainy day and a Netflix binge. Next time, invite a few friends over, wrap that familiar combination in a tender cream cheese crust, and make a pie. Select artichokes packed in water, not marinated or in a vinegar brine. Chop the artichokes into small pieces, pressing the liquid out as you go. The drier the artichokes, the better the texture and flavor of the filling. Add a lattice or open-work crust that you dusted with cheese, cut the pie into tiny bite-sized pieces, and you have a fancy pass-around for a swanky cocktail party.

Make Ahead: Combine the filling ingredients up to one day ahead.

CREAM CHEESE CRUST

2½ cups plus
2 tablespoons (325 g)
all-purpose flour

8 tablespoons (113 g)
unsalted butter, cubed and
frozen for 20 minutes

8 tablespoons (113 g)
cream cheese, cubed and
refrigerated for 20 minutes

¼ teaspoon kosher salt

½ cup (120 ml) ice water

FILLING

2 (14-ounce) cans
artichoke hearts in water
(800 g), drained and
chopped

(Continued)

For the crust: In the food processor, pulse the flour, butter, cream cheese, and salt until the fats are in small pieces coated with flour, about 15 times. Add the water all at once and process until the mixture almost forms a ball. Form the dough into a 6- by 4-inch rectangle using plastic wrap and a bench scraper to firmly press the dough into a cohesive form. Wrap tightly and refrigerate a minimum of 4 hours.

Remove the dough from the refrigerator and allow it to warm slightly. Divide the dough into two pieces, one slightly larger than the other. Roll out the larger piece to 11 by 15 inches and place in the slab pie pan, pressing it into the corners of the pan and allowing the excess to drape over the sides. Refrigerate. Roll out the second piece of dough to 10 by 14 inches, place it on a lightly floured sheet of parchment, and refrigerate.

Heat the oven to 400°F; if you have one, place a baking stone, Baking Steel, or inverted baking sheet on the center rack to heat (see page 4).

(Continued)

SAVOR A PIE

¾ cup (170 g) mayonnaise
(not low-fat)

1 cup (100 g) grated
Parmigiano Reggiano

½ cup (30 g) chopped
fresh flat-leaf parsley

½ cup (30 g) snipped
fresh chives

2 garlic cloves, grated
or minced

Juice of 1 lemon

½ teaspoon freshly
ground pepper

1 egg yolk

1 tablespoon cold water

3 tablespoons finely grated
Parmigiano Reggiano

For the filling: Combine the artichokes, mayonnaise, 1 cup Parmigiano, the parsley, chives, garlic, lemon juice, and pepper and scoop into the chilled bottom crust. Cut lattice strips from the chilled top crust. Spread the filling evenly in the bottom crust and lattice the top.

Combine the egg yolk and water in a small bowl. Dip a pastry brush into the egg wash and lightly glaze the lattice. Scatter the 3 tablespoons Parmigiano over the surface of the pie. Slide the pie into the oven (on top of the steel, stone, or baking sheet, if using) and bake until the filling is bubbly and the crust is browned and glossy, 45 to 50 minutes. Cool slightly before serving.

Techniques: Cream Cheese Crust (page 37), Mixing and Rolling Out (page 14), Lattices, Cutouts, Stamps, and Shapes (page 26)

Swaps:

• Use an All-Butter (page 30) or Butter and Shortening Crust (page 33).

• Press in an Olive Oil Crust (page 56) with no upper crust.

• Add a small can of green chiles or small jar diced pimentos, drained, to the filling—or add both.

• Top with crushed Bugles.

NACHO SLAB PIE
WITH A CORNBREAD CRUST

Serves 12 to 15

Making this pie is a bit of a commitment, but it's a fantastic party in a pie and so worth the effort. To speed the pie-making process, make the carnitas well in advance. Because a pork shoulder will make more carnitas than needed for this pie, make the pie after a taco dinner, or enjoy leftover tacos later. Feel emboldened when it comes to fixings. Scatter the chewy, crisped carnitas over the cornbread batter, add your favorite nacho additions, and bake. For big parties, I make two pies—including one that's all beans and no meat for the vegetarians in the crowd. Don't skip the layering when adding the chips at the end; that's what makes the pie crunchy all the way through, like a big platter of nachos.

Make Ahead: The carnitas must be made in advance. They'll keep for a week in the refrigerator and three months in the freezer.

3 cups (680 g) Pork
Carnitas (recipe follows)

CORNBREAD CRUST

6 tablespoons (85 g)
unsalted butter, melted

¾ cup (90 g) all-purpose
flour

¾ cup (115 g) stone-
ground cornmeal

1½ teaspoons baking
powder

1 teaspoon baking soda

1 teaspoon kosher salt

1 cup (240 ml) buttermilk

2 large eggs, beaten

(Continued)

Place a rack in the upper third of the oven. Heat the oven to broil. Place the carnitas (including some of the fat) on a rimmed baking sheet, slide into the oven, and crisp until well browned, about 5 minutes. Move the rack to the center and set the oven to 400°F. If you have one, place a baking stone, Baking Steel, or inverted baking sheet on the center rack to heat (see page 4).

For the crust: Heat oven to 400°F. Brush a slab pie pan with 1 tablespoon of the melted butter, especially in the corners and up the sides. In a deep bowl, whisk the flour and cornmeal with the baking powder, baking soda, and salt. In another bowl, whisk together the remaining 5 tablespoons butter, the buttermilk, and eggs. Add the egg mixture to the flour mixture and, using no more than a fork, quickly incorporate it. Lumps are okay. Pour all but ½ cup into the pan. (Do not pour all the batter in the pan or it will spill over. Guaranteed. Butter a ramekin and pour that extra bit in to bake up for a cook's snack. Bake it next to the pie for 23 to 25 minutes, until browned and pulling away from the edge of the ramekin.)

(Continued)

SAVOR A PIE

FILLING

½ cup (50 g) thinly sliced scallions, white and green parts (about 4)

11 ounces (314 g) ripe fresh tomato, diced (about 1½ cups)

1 (15-ounce) can black beans (425 g), rinsed and well drained

TOPPINGS

8 ounces (225 g) cheddar or Monterey Jack cheese, or a combination, grated (about 2 cups)

10 ounces (285 g) white or yellow corn tortilla chips, crushed (about 4 cups)

12 slices fresh or pickled jalapeño for garnish, optional

GARNISHES

1 cup (225 g) sour cream or Mexican crema

6 fat radishes, sliced

3 avocados, peeled, pitted, and cubed

Pico de gallo and hot sauce for serving

To fill the pie: Layer on top of the cornbread batter in this order: carnitas, scallions, tomato, and black beans. Sprinkle half the cheese evenly across the pie, top with half the crushed chips, another layer of cheese, and another layer of chips. Garnish with jalapeños, if desired. Slide the pie into the oven (on top of the steel, stone, or baking sheet if using) and bake for 23 to 25 minutes, until the cheese is bubbling and the cornbread is pulling away from the edges of the pan.

Decorate this pie with a flourish. Drizzle sour cream and scatter radishes and avocados across the surface. Serve pico de gallo and hot sauce on the side.

Techniques: Cornbread Crust (page 68), Crushes (page 81)

Swaps:

- Fully cooked shredded chicken, turkey, or brisket can substitute for the carnitas.
- Omit the meat altogether and add refried beans, pintos, or more black beans.
- Use crushed Fritos, Doritos, or Bugles instead of tortilla chips.

PORK CARNITAS

Makes about 4½ cups

A whole bone-in pork shoulder is party food that serves an army. I reserve those Flintstone-sized pieces for barbecue champions. My preferred shoulder cut is the Boston butt—a strong-muscled cut about half the weight of a whole shoulder—boneless because it's easier to cube. The shoulder meat is dense with a firm, white fat cap that bastes the meat as it slowly cooks. There's no babysitting, nothing to do but wait for the glorious, velvety, flavorful meat. Stuff carnitas in tacos, scatter some on a bowl of grains or greens, or make enchiladas or burritos. Freeze the meat (before crisping, in 3-cup portions) for a weeknight slab pie dinner ready in under an hour.

PORK CARNITAS

3 pounds (1.5 kg) boneless Boston butt

2 tablespoons kosher salt

3 cups (710 ml) cool water

1 large white onion (175 g), quartered

1 navel orange, quartered

6 garlic cloves, peeled

2 bay leaves

2 cinnamon sticks

1 tablespoon Mexican oregano

Cut the pork into 2-inch cubes, or some close approximation. Resist the urge to cut away the fat and rest easy knowing it will melt and moisturize the meat while it cooks. Rub the salt into the pork pieces, cover, and refrigerate for 2 hours (or overnight).

Heat the oven to 275°F. In a deep, wide, enameled, and lidded 5-quart cast iron pot (like Le Creuset) in which all the meat will easily fit, add the pork, water, onion, orange, garlic, bay leaves, cinnamon, and oregano and place over high heat. Bring the liquids to a boil, cover the pot, and slide the pot onto the center rack of the oven. Cook until the meat falls away with a fork, 3½ to 4 hours.

Discard the orange, onion, bay leaves, and cinnamon sticks. Cool the pork in the liquid, then refrigerate until ready to serve. The fat will rise to the surface, but do not discard it. The carnitas will need to crisp up in some of that fat.

To prepare the carnitas for the Nacho Slab Pie, or for tacos, or any other application, heat the oven to broil, placing a rack close to the heat source. Spoon the meat, including some of the fat, onto a baking sheet, spreading it out so there is plenty of surface area to crisp. Slide the pan under the broiler and watch carefully. Do not turn your back. It will brown, bronze, and even blacken a little on the edges in about 5 minutes. Now they are carnitas.

The cooked pork, before crisping, may be frozen in its liquid and fats for 3 months. Defrost in the refrigerator before finishing the preparation under the broiler.

VARIATION

Carnitas may also be made in a slow cooker: Place all the ingredients in the slow cooker. Start on high until the liquid is simmering, then reduce the heat to low, cover, and cook for 6 to 8 hours, until the meat falls away with a fork.

LOADED BAKED POTATO SLAB PIE

WITH A CARAMELIZED ONION CRUST

Serves 12 to 20

There are times when a fully loaded baked potato is all I want. Fill 'er up with all the good/bad things. Bacon and scallions. Chives and cheddar. Sour cream. How could this get better? Wrap it up in a caramelized onion crust. Add broccoli because we all need something green. This pie is a loaded potato skin appetizer that serves a crowd or a divine side dish when roast beef is on the menu. There are some steps involved, but do them over a day or two—baking the potatoes, making the crust—and assemble the pie in no time at all. Or use the time the potatoes are in the oven to put together the rest of the filling.

Make Ahead: Bake the potatoes, cook the bacon, and grate the cheese up to 3 days ahead. Blanch the broccoli only at the last minute or it will develop a skunky broccoli scent. Alternatively, use frozen broccoli, direct from the package, no cooking ahead required.

CARAMELIZED ONION CRUST

2½ cups plus
2 tablespoons (325 g)
all-purpose flour

16 tablespoons (225 g)
Onion Butter (page 44)

½ teaspoon kosher salt

½ cup (120 ml) ice water

FILLING

2¼ pounds (1 kg) russet
potatoes (about 4 medium)

8 ounces (225 g) bacon,
chopped (about 1½ cups)

(Continued)

For the crust: In the food processor, pulse the flour, onion butter, and salt until the butter is in small pieces coated with flour, about 15 times. Add the water all at once and process until the mixture almost forms a ball. Form the dough into a 6- by 4-inch rectangle using plastic wrap and a bench scraper to firmly press the dough into a cohesive form. Wrap tightly and refrigerate a minimum of 4 hours.

Remove the dough from the refrigerator and allow it to warm slightly. Divide the dough into two pieces, one slightly larger than the other. Roll out the larger piece to 11 by 15 inches and place in the slab pie pan, pressing it into the corners of the pan and allowing the excess to drape over the sides. Refrigerate. Roll out the second piece of dough to 10 by 14 inches, place it on a lightly floured sheet of parchment, and refrigerate.

Heat the oven to 350°F.

For the filling: Wash the potatoes and pierce with a sharp knife in 3 or 4 places. Place the potatoes directly on the oven rack and bake for 1 to 1½ hours, until soft all the way through. Slice the potatoes open lengthwise and squeeze together at the two ends to vent the steam. This makes for a fluffier potato. Once the steam has dispersed,

12 ounces (340 g) bite-size broccoli florets (about 4 cups)

1 cup (225 g) sour cream

½ cup (50 g) thinly sliced scallions, white and green parts (about 4)

¼ cup (10 g) snipped chives

2 large eggs, beaten

1 teaspoon salt

½ teaspoon freshly ground pepper

6 ounces (170 g) extra sharp cheddar cheese, grated (about 1½ cups)

a minute or two, use a table fork to fluff and scrape the potato flesh out of the peel into a large bowl; you should have about 3 cups of potato. Dispose of the potato skins or slather them with butter and sour cream and have a snack.

The oven should still be at 350°F. Prepare a plate with a double layer of paper towels. On a baking sheet, spread out the chopped bacon, slide the pan into the oven, and bake until the bacon is crisp, 20 to 25 minutes. Using a slotted spoon, transfer the bacon to the paper towels to drain.

Set up a large bowl with ice water. Add 2 inches of water to a pan large enough to hold all the broccoli. Once the water is boiling, add the broccoli; as soon as the water returns to a boil, cover the pot and cook, gently shaking the pan from time to time to move the florets from top to bottom, until they are all bright green and barely fork-tender, 3 to 5 minutes. (Alternatively, you can microwave the broccoli in a scant ¼ cup water, covered, for 2 or 3 minutes.) Drain the water and shock the florets in ice water to stop the cooking and retain their bright color. Remove the broccoli from the ice bath when it is cool, drain well and thoroughly, and set aside.

Increase the oven temperature to 425°F; if you have one, place a baking stone, Baking Steel, or inverted baking sheet on the center rack to heat (see page 4). Gently stir together the potato, sour cream, scallions, chives, eggs, salt, and pepper with a fork. The mixture should be combined but still lumpy. Gently incorporate the bacon, broccoli, and cheese. Fill the bottom crust with the filling. Do not pack it down, but leave some air pockets. Cover with the top crust, crimp, and slash. Bake (on top of the steel, stone, or baking sheet if using) for 20 minutes and reduce the temperature to 375°F. Bake an additional 30 to 40 minutes, until the crust is toasty brown and the filling is hot all the way through. Serve warm.

Techniques: Caramelized Onion Crust (page 42), Mixing and Rolling Out (page 14), Crimp and Slash (page 24)

Swaps:

• Press in a Pretzel Crust (page 62) and cut back on the salt in the filling.

• Use an Olive Oil Crust (page 56).

• Squiggle sour cream and sprinkle chives over the baked pie.

PAN-ROASTED MUSHROOM AND KALE SLAB PIE

WITH AN ALL-BUTTER CRUST

Serves 12 to 15

I learned to pan-roast mushrooms while watching Chef Patrick O'Connell at his emerald green cooker at the Inn at Little Washington. Sauté them in a pan that's as hot as possible in hot, hot oil. Be bold and don't touch them until they release from the pan readily and are deeply bronzed, not wrinkled or desiccated, then do the same on their other side. What emerges are sturdy, meaty mushrooms, a key ingredient in this pie, with their woodsy flavor and substantial texture. This is a slim, quiche-like slab full of flavor and texture, the kale's vegetal addition balancing the filling's rich, onion-studded custard. Cut this pie into small pieces as a pass-around appetizer, or serve larger pieces—with a salad—for Sunday brunch, weekday lunch, or light supper fare.

Make Ahead: Pan-roast the mushrooms a day ahead. This pie reheats very well.

ALL-BUTTER CRUST

2½ cups plus
2 tablespoons (325 g)
all-purpose flour

16 tablespoons (225 g)
unsalted butter, cubed and
frozen for 20 minutes

¼ teaspoon kosher salt

½ cup (120 ml) ice water

FILLING

¼ cup (60 ml) olive oil

6 ounces (170 g) shiitake
mushrooms, stemmed
and thickly sliced (about
3½ cups)

¼ teaspoon kosher salt

(Continued)

For the crust: In the food processor, pulse the flour, butter, and salt until the butter is in small pieces coated with flour, about 15 times. Add the water all at once and process until the mixture almost forms a ball. Form the dough into a 6- by 4-inch rectangle using plastic wrap and a bench scraper to firmly press the dough into a cohesive form. Wrap tightly and refrigerate a minimum of 4 hours.

Remove the dough from the refrigerator and allow it to warm slightly. Divide the dough into two pieces, one slightly larger than the other. Roll out the larger piece to 11 by 15 inches and place in the slab pie pan, pressing it into the corners of the pan and allowing the excess to drape over the sides. Refrigerate. Roll out the second piece of dough to 10 by 14 inches, place it on a lightly floured sheet of parchment, and refrigerate.

For the filling: Pour 1½ tablespoons of the olive oil into a wide skillet and set over high heat until the oil shimmers. Add the shiitake mushrooms and push them around into a single layer. Sprinkle with half the salt and red pepper flakes and leave the pan alone until one mushroom, tested, can be lifted easily without sticking, a good 6 to

¼ teaspoon red pepper flakes

6 ounces (170 g) cremini mushrooms, stemmed and sliced (about 3½ cups)

2 tablespoons dry sherry, optional

2 medium onions (285 g), sliced in ¼-inch-thick half-moons

1 teaspoon fresh thyme leaves

3 cups (426 g) frozen chopped kale, thawed and squeezed dry; or 5 cups (426 g) finely chopped stemmed fresh kale

1 cup (240 ml) whole milk

2 large eggs plus 1 egg white

¾ teaspoon kosher salt

½ teaspoon freshly ground pepper

4 ounces (113 g) Gruyère cheese, grated (about 1 cup)

1 egg yolk

1 teaspoon water

¼ teaspoon kosher salt

9 minutes. Be brave: The mushrooms will smoke, snap, and sizzle. Turn all the mushrooms quickly and cook until the other side is equally browned, another couple of minutes. Transfer the shiitakes to a bowl. Repeat the pan-roasting process with another 1½ tablespoons oil, the cremini mushrooms, and salt and red pepper. Return the shiitakes to the pan. If using sherry, add to the pan and cook over high heat until the scent of alcohol has diminished and most of the liquid has evaporated. Remove the mushrooms to a bowl.

To the pan, add the remaining 1 tablespoon olive oil. Reduce the heat to medium-high and add the onions and thyme, stirring to coat with warm oil. Reduce the heat to medium and cook gently until the onions are soft and golden brown, about 15 minutes. Stir in the kale and remove from the heat.

Heat the oven to 400°F; if you have one, place a baking stone, Baking Steel, or inverted baking sheet on the center rack to heat (see page 4).

Scatter the mushrooms along the bottom crust, add the kale and onions, and gently push the filling around and into the corners of the crust.

Whisk the milk, eggs, and egg white together with the salt and pepper. Pour the eggs over the filling and distribute the grated cheese across the whole beautiful thing. Drape the top crust across the pan. Crimp and slash. Whisk the egg yolk and water in a small bowl. Use a pastry brush to paint the top of the crust. Sprinkle with salt. Chill for 20 minutes, if you have time. Otherwise, slide it into the oven (on top of the steel, stone, or baking sheet if using) and bake until a knife inserted into the pie comes out clean, 45 to 50 minutes.

Cool for at least 10 minutes before portioning. Refrigerate leftovers and bring them back to room temperature to serve, or wrap in foil and reheat at 350°F for 15 to 20 minutes.

Techniques: All-Butter Crust (page 30), Mixing and Rolling Out (page 14), Crimp and Slash (page 24)

Swaps:

- A Cream Cheese Crust (page 37) makes this pie tender and sweet and perfect for brunch.

- Trade in spinach for the kale.

- Get wild with mushrooms, adding chanterelles, morels, or oyster.

- Switch up the Gruyère with cheddar, pepper Jack, or fontina.

- Go ahead, add cubed ham.

- Is there truffle salt in your pantry? Sprinkle a tiny amount over the egg-washed top crust before baking.

SPINACH, GORGONZOLA, AND WALNUT SLAB PIE

WITH A CREAM CHEESE CRUST

Serves 12 to 24

Slab pies turn out to be the perfect solution for cocktail hour. Inspired by a phyllo filling from *The Silver Palate Cookbook*, I first combined spinach, gorgonzola, and walnuts in my early 20s when I decided to have a cocktail party. I made so much, I spent five days filling and freezing tiny phyllo appetizers. They were devoured and everyone was amazed, but I never did it again. Since then, I've shied away from large fussy projects and tend toward simplification. Pie is all that. And this pie is all that and more.

Make Ahead: The pie may be assembled and baked several hours in advance and reheated from room temperature: Cover in foil and heat for 20 minutes at 350°F, then 5 to 10 minutes uncovered, until warmed through.

CREAM CHEESE CRUST

2½ cups plus
2 tablespoons (325 g)
all-purpose flour

8 tablespoons (113 g)
unsalted butter, cubed and
frozen for 20 minutes

8 tablespoons (113 g)
cream cheese, cubed and
refrigerated for 20 minutes

¼ teaspoon kosher salt

½ cup (120 ml) ice water

FILLING

24 ounces (680 g) fresh
baby spinach leaves (about
6 cups, firmly packed)

2 tablespoons olive oil

(Continued)

For the crust: In the food processor, pulse the flour, butter, cream cheese, and salt until the fats are in small pieces coated with flour, about 15 times. Add the water all at once and process until the mixture almost forms a ball. Form the dough into a 6- by 4-inch rectangle using plastic wrap and a bench scraper to firmly press the dough into a cohesive form. Wrap tightly and refrigerate a minimum of 4 hours.

Remove the dough from the refrigerator and allow it to warm slightly. Divide the dough into two pieces, one slightly larger than the other. Roll out the larger piece to 11 by 15 inches and place in the slab pie pan, pressing it into the corners of the pan and allowing the excess to drape over the sides. Refrigerate. Roll out the second piece of dough to 10 by 14 inches, place it on a lightly floured sheet of parchment, and refrigerate.

Heat the oven to 400°F; if you have one, place a baking stone, Baking Steel, or inverted baking sheet on the center rack to heat (see page 4).

(Continued)

1 medium onion (142 g), diced (about 1 cup)

2 shallots (70 g), diced (about ½ cup)

½ teaspoon kosher salt

½ teaspoon freshly ground black pepper

1 (12-ounce) jar (340 g) sliced roasted red peppers, drained

6 ounces (170 g) gorgonzola, crumbled (about 1½ cups)

6 ounces (170 g) toasted walnuts, chopped (about 1½ cups)

1 egg yolk

1 tablespoon cool water

½ teaspoon flaky sea salt, such as Maldon or *fleur de sel*

For the filling: Place the spinach in a microwave-safe bowl, cover loosely, and microwave for 2 minutes. (If you do not have a microwave, steam the spinach briefly until just wilted.) Squeeze out any moisture.

Warm the olive oil in a medium skillet over medium heat until shimmering. Add the onion and cook until translucent. Add the shallots and continue cooking until both the shallots and onion have wilted; the entire process will take about 10 minutes. Stir in the spinach, salt, and pepper and coat everything in the oil. Taste and add more salt or pepper if you wish, keeping in mind the cheese is salty and there will be salt on the top crust as well. Scrape the spinach mixture into the prepared crust and sprinkle the roasted peppers, cheese, and walnuts on top of the greens.

Cut strips from the rolled-out top crust and drape them diagonally over the filling, or form a lattice, or top the pie with any other open form crust until the surface is mostly, but not completely, covered. To replicate the look in the photo (page 108), roll out the top crust and place it on a sheet of parchment. Chill well, then stamp out the squares with a cookie cutter, holding the cutouts aside. Drape the top crust over the filling, then replace the cutouts. Stir the egg yolk and water together and, using a pastry brush, paint the top crust with egg wash. Scatter flaky salt over the surface.

Bake (on top of the steel, stone, or baking sheet if using) for 40 to 45 minutes, until the filling is bubbling and the surface is golden brown. Cool on a rack for at least 10 minutes. Slide the entire pie out of the pan onto a large board. Cut the pie into smallish squares and serve with a cocktail.

Techniques: Cream Cheese Crust (page 37), Mixing and Rolling Out (page 14), Crimp and Slash (page 24), Lattices, Cutouts, Stamps, and Shapes (page 26), How to Toast Nuts (page 253)

Swaps:

• It's only natural to fill a phyllo crust (see page 70) with this savory, nutty, cheesy mixture.

• Or press in an Olive Oil Crust (page 56).

• Use 24 ounces fresh kale or Swiss chard instead of the spinach.

• Try goat cheese or feta instead of gorgonzola.

• Use pecans or hazelnuts instead of walnuts.

ASPARAGUS, FONTINA, AND PANCETTA SLAB PIE
WITH A LARD CRUST

Serves 10 to 20

Pair a rich, flaky crust with tender spring asparagus, salty pancetta, and gooey cheese for the best little pre-dinner bite or a savory brunch entree. It's not truly a quiche because there's only a whisper of custard, just enough to keep the asparagus from rolling around. Fontina cheese is sweet and young and creamy and melts into the custard. Be diligent scraping the asparagus spears to reveal the tender center and make a gloriously appealing pie, a celebration of everything spring.

Make Ahead: Prep the pancetta and asparagus hours in advance.

LARD CRUST

1⅓ cups (160 g)
all-purpose flour

6 tablespoons (85 g)
rendered lard or leaf lard,
cubed and frozen for
20 minutes

2 tablespoons (28 g)
unsalted butter, cubed and
frozen for 20 minutes

⅛ teaspoon kosher salt

¼ cup (60 ml) ice water

FILLING

1 pound (450 g) asparagus,
preferably thick spears

1 cup (225 g) diced
pancetta

5 large eggs

(Continued)

For the crust: In the food processor, pulse the flour, lard, butter, and salt until the fats are in small pieces coated with flour, about 15 times. Add the water all at once and process until the mixture almost forms a ball. Form the dough into a 6- by 4-inch rectangle using plastic wrap and a bench scraper to firmly press the dough into a cohesive form. Wrap tightly and refrigerate a minimum of 4 hours.

Remove the dough from the refrigerator and allow it to warm slightly. Roll out the dough to 11 by 15 inches and place in the slab pie pan. Crimp the edges. Using a fork, poke the bottom of the crust until it is dotted with holes. This is called docking and it will help to keep the crust from rising up as it bakes. Line the crust with parchment paper or foil. If there is time, chill for 30 minutes. Fill the parchment-lined crust with uncooked dried beans or rice or pie weights. Bake for 20 minutes, remove the paper and pie weights, and bake the crust for an additional 5 minutes to dry it out. Cool on a wire rack.

Heat the oven to 400°F; if you have one, place a baking stone, Baking Steel, or inverted baking sheet on the center rack to heat (see page 4).

(Continued)

½ cup (120 ml)
heavy cream

¾ teaspoon kosher salt

½ teaspoon freshly ground
black pepper

8 ounces (225 g)
fontina cheese, grated
(about 2 cups)

½ cup (50 g) thinly slivered
scallions, white and green
parts (about 4)

½ cup (20 g) fresh basil
leaves, stacked and
slivered

¼ cup (10 g) snipped
fresh chives

For the filling: Trim the asparagus stalks to 10 inches. If the asparagus are large or at all tough, use a vegetable peeler to scrape the base down to the more tender center. Heat a small skillet over medium heat and cook the pancetta until crisped. Remove from the pan and drain on paper towels. Whisk the eggs, cream, salt, and pepper until frothy. Deftly scatter the pancetta and half the fontina across the crust, then scatter all the scallions, basil, and chives over the cheese. Place the asparagus, head to tail, on top of the herbs, and add the remaining cheese. Pour in the egg mixture. Slide the pan into the oven (on top of the steel, stone, or baking sheet if using) and bake until the custard is set, 25 to 30 minutes.

Cool for a moment before slicing and serving warm.

Techniques: Lard or Leaf Lard Crust (page 45), Mixing and Rolling Out (page 14), Crimp and Slash (page 24), Blind Baking (page 29)

Swaps:

• Single-crust All-Butter (page 30), Butter and Shortening (page 33), and Rye Crusts (page 48) are all delicious.

• With a rye crust, add a dab of Dijon mustard to the custard.

SOUTHERN-STYLE TOMATO SLAB PIE

WITH A CHEDDAR CHEESE CRUST

Serves 12 to 16

I like this pie best when it's cooled to room temperature, but friends of mine like it piping hot. Either way, you'll be happy with the summertime taste in this flaky, juicy, sweet take on a classic tomato pie. While I think it's perfect with a crackly cheddar cheese crust, the tomatoes will tuck into a grocery store crust beautifully, just in case you're still suffering from *doughphobia*.

Make Ahead: The entire pie may be made several hours in advance and reheated from room temperature: Cover in foil and heat for 20 minutes at 350°F, then for 5 to 10 minutes uncovered, until warmed through and bubbling here and there.

CHEDDAR CHEESE CRUST

4 ounces (113 g) extra sharp cheddar cheese, preferably orange, cold

2½ cups plus 2 tablespoons (325 g) all-purpose flour

16 tablespoons (225 g) unsalted butter, cubed and frozen for 20 minutes

¼ teaspoon kosher salt

½ cup (120 ml) ice water

FILLING

½ cup (100 g) mayonnaise

2 pounds (900 g) ripe tomatoes (about 5 medium), sliced ½ inch thick

(Continued)

For the crust: Grate all but 1 ounce of cheese on the large holes of a box grater. Chop the remaining cheese into small chunks. In the food processor, pulse the flour, butter, and salt until the butter is in small pieces coated with flour, about 15 times. Add the grated and chopped cheese and water and process until the mixture almost forms a ball. Form the dough into a 6- by 4-inch rectangle using plastic wrap and a bench scraper to firmly press the dough into a cohesive form. Wrap tightly and refrigerate a minimum of 4 hours.

Remove the dough from the refrigerator and allow it to warm slightly. Divide the dough into two pieces, one slightly larger than the other. Roll out the larger piece to 11 by 15 inches and place in the slab pie pan, pressing it into the corners of the pan and allowing the excess to drape over the sides. Refrigerate. Roll out the second piece of dough to 10 by 14 inches, place it on a lightly floured sheet of parchment, and refrigerate at least 20 minutes.

Heat the oven to 400°F; if you have one, place a baking stone, Baking Steel, or inverted baking sheet on the center rack to heat (see page 4).

(Continued)

1 cup (100 g) sliced scallions, white and green parts (about 8)

6 ounces (170 g) extra sharp cheddar cheese, grated (about 1½ cups)

1 teaspoon kosher salt

½ teaspoon freshly ground pepper

1 egg yolk

1 tablespoon cool water

½ teaspoon flaky salt, such as Maldon or *fleur de sel*

For the filling: Slather the bottom crust with the mayonnaise. Place the tomatoes from edge to edge, touching, to fill the crust in one layer. Scatter the scallions and the cheese over the tomatoes. Sprinkle the salt and pepper across the filling.

Cut strips from the top crust and twist each one gently two or three times before draping it diagonally over the filling leaving space between the strips. Place twisted strips in the opposite direction for a Lazy Lattice (see page 26). Crimp all the way around. Stir the egg yolk and water together and, using a pastry brush, paint the strips with egg wash. Finally, scatter flaky salt over the surface.

Bake (on top of the steel, stone, or baking sheet if using) for 40 to 45 minutes, until the filling is bubbling and the surface is golden brown. Cool on a rack for at least 10 minutes.

Techniques: Cheddar Cheese Crust (page 39), Mixing and Rolling Out (page 14), Lattices, Cutouts, Stamps, and Shapes (page 26), Crimp and Slash (page 24)

Swaps:

- Use a crust from the grocery store (see page 69), or an All-Butter (page 30), Cream Cheese (page 37), or Butter and Shortening Crust (page 33).
- Trade blue cheese for the cheddar.
- The mayo is a must.

ZUCCHINI, FETA, AND KALAMATA OLIVE SLAB PIE

WITH A PUFF PASTRY CRUST

Serves 12

This summer-loving slab pie is delightful as an appetizer, perfect for brunch or lunch, and a suitable side for a backyard grilling party. The bright sweet squash is offset by salty olives and cheese. I like to use a mandoline to make paper-thin slices, but clever knife skills work, too. Floating above and below are the buttery lofty layers of puff pastry. Look for small, firm squash as they will be less watery.

Make Ahead: The filling may be made up to 3 days ahead. Bring to room temperature before adding to the pie. The crust and toppers may be prepared up to 2 hours ahead. Keep refrigerated until ready to use.

2 sheets (396 g) puff pastry (14 ounces), defrosted in the refrigerator overnight

2 tablespoons olive oil, plus extra for brushing the crust

2 small sweet onions (210 g), sliced in thin half-moons (about 1½ cups)

2 small green zucchini (140 g), quartered lengthwise and thinly sliced (about 2 cups)

2 small yellow summer squash (140 g), quartered lengthwise and thinly sliced (about 2 cups)

½ teaspoon dried oregano

½ teaspoon kosher salt

(Continued)

Remove the puff pastry from the refrigerator at the last minute, allowing the sheets to warm only for one or two minutes. Unroll the sheets of puff pastry one at a time. Press one sheet of puff pastry out slightly with a rolling pin, tidying any breaks from the folds. Pierce the dough all over with a fork, every 2 inches or so, going right through to the pan below. Trim 1-inch strips from each edge to make raised edges (a wall) around the entire pastry. Refrigerate. Roll out the second sheet of puff pastry and stamp out twelve 2-inch-square toppers, one for each serving. Or make triangles or circles or stars. Adorable! Set the cutouts on a piece of lightly floured parchment and refrigerate until ready to use.

In a large skillet, warm the olive oil over medium-low heat. Add the onions and cook until wilted, translucent, and beginning to brown on the edges, about 25 minutes. Turn the heat to high and add the zucchini, squash, oregano, and salt. Do not stir or disturb the squash, cooking them until browned, about 8 minutes. Stir and brown the other sides, another 5 minutes or so. Stir in the black pepper, olives, and zest. Taste the filling: It should be slightly salty and assertively flavored. Cool the filling before proceeding.

(Continued)

½ teaspoon freshly
ground pepper

½ cup (70 g) pitted
Kalamata olives, roughly
chopped

1 teaspoon grated
lemon zest

2 tablespoons
tomato paste

1 tablespoon warm water

1 cup (113 g) feta cheese,
crumbled

Heat the oven to 400°F; if you have one, place a baking stone, Baking Steel, or inverted baking sheet on the center rack to heat (see page 4).

Stir together the tomato paste and warm water and brush across the bottom pastry, avoiding the border. Pile the filling into the pastry shell and gently smooth the surface with a tablespoon or an offset spatula. Sprinkle the top with feta and place the cutout toppers on the pie, one for each serving.

Bake (on top of the steel, stone, or baking sheet if using) for 25 minutes, until the filling is bubbling and the toppers are nice and bronzed and flaky. Cool 5 minutes before cutting and serving warm.

Techniques: Puff Pastry (page 72), Lattices, Cutouts, Stamps, and Shapes (page 26)

Swaps:

- Blind bake (see page 29) an Olive Oil Crust (page 56) and top with Savory Streusel (see page 86).

- Eggplant can stand in for the squash and zucchini; or half zucchini and half eggplant makes this a ratatouille pie.

- Instead of feta, try ricotta salata. Alternatively, Bel Paese or fontina cheese, draped across the filling under the toppers, is gooey and scrumptious.

- Pile on white anchovies (under the toppers) to take this pie right over the top.

NIÇOISE-STYLE TUNA AND SPRING GREENS SLAB PIE
WITH A PRETZEL CRUST

Serves 8

I've taken some liberties in calling this a pie. In reality, it's nothing more than a composed salad set attractively atop a salty, satisfying pretzel plate. Putting this pie together takes some pre-planning, and the actual construction is a little bit fussy, but it's a clever way to serve a salad at a party. Look for the freshest eggs, with deep yellow-orange yolks, and tiny, divine, perfect vegetables: Potatoes the size of cherry tomatoes; thin, new, bright green beans. Assemble a blend of tender greens with sharp, bitter ones: I like arugula, baby kale, edible flowers, squash blossoms, dandelion greens, mâche, frisée, or a fresh young spring mix from a local farmer. Find high-quality, sustainably fished tuna packed in olive oil, often sold in glass jars and imported from Italy or Spain, and the little white anchovies packed in oil. If all the Tinkertoy layering is too fussy, toss the salad together and pile it on top of the baked crust.

Make Ahead: Make the crust up to several hours ahead but assemble the salad as close to the last minute as possible. Make the dressing up to a week ahead. There will be dressing remaining—you'll find many opportunities to use it.

PRETZEL CRUST

½ pound (225 g) fat pretzels, knots, or rods (about 2 cups crushed)

8 tablespoons (113 g) unsalted butter, cubed, at room temperature

SALAD FILLING

1 teaspoon white vinegar

2 large eggs, at room temperature

½ pound (225 g) tiny Yukon Gold potatoes

(Continued)

For the crust: Heat the oven to 350°F; if you have one, place a baking stone, Baking Steel, or inverted baking sheet on the center rack to heat (see page 4). Place the pretzels in a ziptop bag and bash them with a rolling pin until they are in crumbs and small shards but not powdered. Pour the crumbs into a medium bowl, add the butter cubes, and knead the mixture until a cohesive dough forms. Press the dough into the corners and up the sides and across the bottom of the slab pie pan. Bake the crust (on top of the steel, stone, or baking sheet if using) for 20 to 25 minutes, until browned in the corners and edges. Cool on a rack.

For the eggs: Prepare a bowl of ice water. Fill a small saucepan two-thirds with cool water, add the vinegar, and bring to a rolling boil. Add the eggs and cook for 8 minutes at a boil. Drain and plop the eggs in the ice water. As soon as you can bear to have your hands

1 teaspoon kosher salt

½ pound (225 g) tiny green beans (haricot verts), stem end trimmed

1 teaspoon minced shallot

¼ teaspoon kosher salt

3 tablespoons sherry vinegar or apple cider vinegar

⅓ cup (80 ml) best-quality olive oil

¼ cup (35 g) pitted Kalamata olives, minced

1 tablespoon honey

¼ teaspoon kosher salt

4 anchovies (preferably white), optional

4 tablespoons (56 g) unsalted butter, softened

2 tablespoons lemon juice

¼ teaspoon kosher salt

¼ teaspoon freshly ground black pepper

1 baguette

8 cups (140 g) young tender salad greens

2 (10-ounce) jars tuna in olive oil (560 g), drained

in the icy bowl, peel the eggs underwater. Drain the eggs on paper towels and set aside.

For the potatoes and beans: Prepare another bowl of ice water. Fill a medium saucepan with potatoes and enough water to cover. Add the salt, bring to a boil, and cook the potatoes until fork-tender, anywhere from 8 to 12 minutes depending on the size of the potatoes. Scoop the potatoes from the water with a slotted spoon and set aside to cool. Immediately add the green beans to the boiling water. As soon as the water returns to a boil, taste test a bean for tenderness. When they're tender, scoop the beans into the ice bath until cooled.

For the dressing: In a small covered jar, combine the shallot, salt, and vinegar and let the shallot pickle for 3 minutes. Add the olive oil, olives, honey, and salt, cover the jar, and shake the dressing until creamy.

For the toasts: Heat the oven to 350°F or use a toaster. With a fork, break up and combine the anchovies (if using) and butter, add the lemon juice, and blend thoroughly, making the anchovy butter as chunky or smooth as you wish. Add the salt and black pepper. Slice the baguette on the diagonal into 8 slabs and toast until warmed and slightly golden. Spread the anchovy butter thickly across the warm baguette slices.

Mix the salad greens with half the dressing and taste before adding more dressing. Pile the greens onto the pretzel crust. Quarter the eggs lengthwise and place them, along with potatoes, beans, and tuna, on top of the greens. Plate the toasts separately and serve with the salad or tuck each buttered toast in with the salad, resting on the edge of the pan. Serve immediately.

Techniques: Press-In Crusts (page 55), Cracker Crumb Crusts (page 61)

Swaps:

- Any Cracker Crumb Crust (page 61) will work here.
- A single-crust Olive Oil Crust (page 56) made with a fruity, young, green oil is sensational.
- Swap in barely steamed asparagus for the green beans.
- Use tofu cubes, chicken, or shrimp instead of tuna.
- Add slivered radishes, carrots, or young turnips.
- Use your favorite dressing.
- Omit the anchovies, if you must.

SUMAC-SCENTED EGGPLANT SLAB PIE

WITH A PHYLLO CRUST

Serves 12 to 15

Slab pies are not only for hot, humid summer days in the backyard. This is the little black dress of slab pies, dressed up and ready for the holiday sideboard. It's elegant, it's refined, it's complex, and it's vegetarian. Crackly phyllo wraps around a bold, sweet and sour eggplant filling tinged with citrusy sumac. If sumac is unavailable, shower the pie with lemon zest and carry on. To make this dish entirely vegan, omit the yogurt topping and substitute olive oil for the melted butter used for brushing the phyllo.

Make Ahead: The filling may be made up to 3 days ahead, or frozen for up to a month. Defrost in the refrigerator before using.

½ cup (120 ml) olive oil

2 garlic cloves, peeled

2 pounds (1 kg) firm purple Italian eggplant, peeled and cut into ½-inch cubes (about 5 cups)

1 (28-ounce) can crushed tomatoes (about 3 cups)

1 tablespoon ground sumac

¾ teaspoon kosher salt

½ teaspoon freshly ground black pepper

2 to 3 tablespoons pomegranate molasses, plus extra for garnish

½ cup (50 g) chopped scallions, white and green parts (about 4)

(Continued)

In a deep, wide skillet or Dutch oven, heat the olive oil over medium heat until shimmering. Add the garlic cloves and reduce the heat to medium-low. Cook the garlic, without browning, until the oil is scented, about 5 minutes. Remove and discard the garlic. Pour off ¼ cup of the oil and reserve for the phyllo.

Increase the heat under the pan until the oil is hot and shimmering. Add the eggplant in batches so they are not crowded, tossing and browning the cubes until browned and softened. Give this process time to allow the eggplant to take on some color, about 10 or 15 minutes total. It will seem as though there is not enough oil but there is.

Turn down the heat and add the tomatoes, sumac, salt, and pepper and let the sauce bubble slowly until thick, 15 to 20 minutes. Stir in 2 tablespoons of the pomegranate molasses. Stir in the scallions, cilantro, and mint. Taste and adjust the seasoning, adding more pomegranate molasses if desired. It should be a little textural, chunky even, with a tangy, assertive, slightly salty finish. Let the filling cool.

Stir the reserved garlic oil and melted butter together until combined. Unroll the phyllo sheets and immediately cover with a sheet of plastic wrap and a slightly damp, clean kitchen towel. Brush the slab pie pan with the butter mixture. Peel off a sheet of phyllo, taking care

½ cup (30 g) chopped fresh cilantro, plus extra for garnish

½ cup (30 g) chopped fresh mint, plus extra for garnish

4 tablespoons (56 g) unsalted butter, melted

4 ounces (113 g), phyllo pastry, defrosted in the refrigerator overnight

½ cup (120 ml) full-fat or Greek yogurt

to cover the stack of phyllo sheets not in use. Settle the sheet into the pan with the excess overhanging the edges. Brush the phyllo sheet with the butter mixture and continue to layer the phyllo and butter until there are six buttered sheets in the pan.

Spread the cooled eggplant filling across the buttered, stacked phyllo. Place a phyllo sheet on top of the filling and dab with the butter mixture, continuing to layer with five additional sheets, each brushed with the buttery oil. Once the pie has been covered, trim the overhanging pieces, tucking in the phyllo along the edges. Brush the surface well with the remaining butter mixture. Chill the pie for 20 minutes.

Heat the oven to 375°F; if you have one, place a baking stone, Baking Steel, or inverted baking sheet on the center rack to heat (see page 4).

Using a sharp knife, cut through the top layers of phyllo to mark the serving portions (these cuts are critical—without them serving the pie is impossibly challenging). Slide the pie in the oven (on top of the steel, stone, or baking sheet if using) and bake until the top is bronzed and the filling is bubbling, 45 to 50 minutes. Cool for at least 10 minutes before serving—or even longer; the flavor only gets better. Serve warm or at room temperature. Top each slice with a dollop of yogurt, a dot or two of pomegranate molasses, and a pinch of fresh cilantro and mint leaves.

Technique: Phyllo (page 70)

Swaps:

- Use an Olive Oil Crust (page 56).

- Add a handful of golden raisins and chopped toasted almonds to the filling.

CHEESY CAULIFLOWER RAREBIT SLAB PIE

WITH A RYE CRUST

Serves 10 to 12

Cheesy cauliflower is always a welcome addition to dinner, so why not put it into a pie? Here is a slab-ified riff on rarebit, celebrating fall with the earthy flavors of cauliflower cloaked in a hoppy sauce. Look for cauliflower when it shows up at farmers' markets in displays overflowing with multicolored heads the size of dinner plates. I'm fond of the orange and bright white varieties and even the green; but note that the purple makes this a strange-looking pie. Porter beer is traditional and tasty, but any dark, bitter beer will add zip to the filling.

Make Ahead: Cook the cauliflower filling up to 4 hours in advance.

RYE CRUST

1¾ cups plus 1 tablespoon (225 g) all-purpose flour

1 cup (100 g) rye flour

8 tablespoons (113 g) butter, cubed and frozen for 20 minutes

8 tablespoons (113 g) Spectrum or other vegetable shortening, cubed and frozen for 20 minutes

½ teaspoon kosher salt

½ cup (120 ml) ice water

1½ teaspoons ice cold vodka, optional

(Continued)

For the crust: In the food processor, pulse the flours, butter, shortening, and salt until the fats are in small pieces coated with flour, about 15 times. Add the water and vodka (if using) all at once and process until the mixture almost forms a ball. Form the dough into a 6- by 4-inch rectangle using plastic wrap and a bench scraper to firmly press the dough into a cohesive form. Wrap tightly and refrigerate a minimum of 4 hours.

Remove the dough from the refrigerator and allow it to warm slightly. Divide the dough into two pieces, one slightly larger than the other. Roll out the larger piece to 11 by 15 inches and place in the slab pie pan, pressing it into the corners of the pan and allowing the excess to drape over the sides. Refrigerate. Roll out the second piece of dough to 10 by 14 inches, place it on a lightly floured sheet of parchment, and refrigerate.

Heat the oven to 425°F; if you have one, place a baking stone, Baking Steel, or inverted baking sheet on the center rack to heat (see page 4).

(Continued)

FILLING

3 tablespoons olive oil

1½ cups (160 g) sliced shallots (about 5)

6 stalks fresh thyme

1 medium cauliflower (1 pound, 455 g), cut into small florets (about 5 cups)

½ cup (120 ml) dark beer, such as Guinness

¼ cup (15 g) finely chopped fresh flat-leaf parsley

½ teaspoon kosher salt

¼ teaspoon freshly ground black pepper

½ cup (120 ml) whole milk

3 large eggs

2 tablespoons Worcestershire sauce

½ teaspoon Coleman's mustard powder

10 ounces (283 g) extra sharp cheddar cheese, coarsely grated (2½ cups)

1 egg yolk

1 tablespoon water

¼ cup (25 g) finely grated Parmigiano Reggiano

For the filling: Heat the olive oil in a deep skillet over medium-high heat until it shimmers. Add the shallots and thyme and cook until the shallots are browned on the edges. Fish out and discard the thyme. Add the cauliflower and stir to coat with oil. Increase the heat to medium-high, pour in the beer, and bring to a boil. Reduce the heat, cover, and steam the cauliflower until fork-tender, about 7 minutes. Uncover and cook until all the liquid has evaporated, another 5 minutes. Remove the pan from the heat and stir in the parsley, salt, and pepper. Cool to room temperature.

Fill the bottom crust with the cauliflower filling. Whisk together the milk, eggs, Worcestershire, and mustard in a small bowl until the eggs are thoroughly incorporated. Pour over the cauliflower filling, sprinkle with the cheddar cheese, and cover with the top crust. Crimp and slash.

Combine the egg yolk and water and use a pastry brush to paint it on the top crust from edge to edge. Sprinkle with the Parmigiano and slip the pie into the hot oven (on top of the steel, stone, or baking sheet if using). Bake for 20 minutes. Reduce the temperature to 375°F and bake until the crust is bronzed and the filling is bubbling, 35 to 40 minutes. Cool slightly before slicing into portions.

Techniques: Rye Crust (page 48), Mixing and Rolling Out (page 14), Crimp and Slash (page 24)

Swaps:

- Try an All-Butter (page 30), Butter and Shortening (page 33), Leaf Lard (page 45), or Hash Brown Crust (page 67).

- Use broccoli or a combination of cauliflower and broccoli.

- Cruciferous vegetable fans will embrace the sturdy flavor of Brussels sprouts instead of cauliflower.

- Add parboiled sliced carrots.

- Add diced smoked ham.

- Instead of a top crust, cover the surface with fresh rye bread crumbs.

SESAME SWEET POTATO SLAB PIE

WITH A GINGERSNAP CRUST

Serves 12 to 16

Searching for a side dish for the holidays? Look no further. This sweet potato pie is a far cry from the familiar marshmallow-topped casserole; it's shot through with miso and sesame oil for an umami-rich undercurrent offset by the spicy, sweet gingersnap crust (use a very basic cookie here, nothing fancy). Miso is a fermented soybean paste: White miso is sweet and delicate, the red and brown miso pastes are sturdier and saltier with a pushier flavor. Look for miso in Asian markets, health food stores, or in the refrigerated section of some grocery stores, near the tofu. Now that you have miso in the refrigerator, smear some on a piece of salmon or thick slices of eggplant before roasting, whisk a small amount into salad dressing, or dissolve a spoonful in boiling water, toss in some tofu, scallions, and fresh herbs for miso soup that's better than takeout.

Make Ahead: Roast the sweet potatoes up to 3 days ahead. The pie may be made a day in advance, covered and refrigerated. Bring to room temperature before serving.

GINGERSNAP CRUST

35 gingersnaps, (8 ounces, 225 g), crushed to a fine powder (about 2 cups)

8 tablespoons (113 g) unsalted butter, melted

¼ teaspoon kosher salt

FILLING

1½ pounds (680 g) orange sweet potatoes (about 3)

½ cup packed (100 g) light brown sugar

3 tablespoons (42 g) unsalted butter, melted

2 tablespoons white miso

(Continued)

For the crust: Heat the oven to 350°F; if you have one, place a baking stone, Baking Steel, or inverted baking sheet on the center rack to heat (see page 4). Combine the gingersnap crumbs, melted butter, and salt in a medium bowl, pressing the mixture against the side of the bowl until it is cohesive and the crumbs are thoroughly buttered. Dump the wet crumbs into the slab pie pan and press the mixture evenly along the bottom. Take your time pressing the crust in, using the side of your hand or a metal measuring cup to form a good edge and a smooth base until the crust feels firm to the touch. Slide the pan into the oven (on top of the steel, stone, or baking sheet if using) and bake until lightly browned, about 20 minutes. The crust may emerge still damp, but as it cools it will firm up.

For the filling: Increase the oven temperature to 400°F. Roast the sweet potatoes on a parchment-lined baking sheet for 50 to 60 minutes, until fork-tender. Reduce the oven temperature to 375°F.

(Continued)

1 teaspoon toasted
sesame oil

½ teaspoon ground ginger

½ teaspoon kosher salt

½ teaspoon freshly ground
black pepper

3 large eggs, separated

1 cup (235 ml) full-fat
coconut milk

TOPPING

1 cup (227 g) sour cream
or *labne*

2 tablespoons Birdseed
(page 81) or toasted
sesame seeds

Slice the potatoes open to cool. Scoop out the flesh and smash with a fork or potato masher to remove most of the lumps; there should be about 1½ packed cups. Discard the potato peels.

Place the sweet potatoes, brown sugar, melted butter, miso, sesame oil, ginger, salt, and pepper together in the bowl of a stand mixer and combine using the whisk attachment. Add the egg yolks, one at a time, beating between each addition. Pour in the coconut milk and beat until smooth and light. Pour the mixture into a large mixing bowl. Clean the bowl from the stand mixer.

Place the egg whites in the bowl of a mixer fitted with the whisk attachment and beat until medium peaks form, 3 to 4 minutes. Spoon a small amount of the egg whites into the bowl with the sweet potato mixture and stir well to lighten. Add the remaining egg whites and fold in for a mousse-like texture. It's alright if a few white streaks remain.

Gently scrape the filling into the crust and carefully smooth the surface. Slide the pie into the oven and bake, rotating halfway through, until the filling is set but still wobbly in the center, 30 to 35 minutes. Transfer to a wire rack to cool.

For the topping: Once the pie has cooled completely, spread the sour cream across the surface with an offset spatula and sprinkle the sesame seeds around the edges. Store in the refrigerator and bring to room temperature before serving.

Techniques: Press-In Crusts (page 55), Cookie Crumb Crusts (page 65)

Swaps:

- Try a Pretzel (page 62) or Ritz Cracker Crust (page 61).

- Blind bake (see page 29) a single-crust All-Butter (page 30) or Rye Crust (page 48).

- Trade the sweet potato for about 1½ cups butternut or kabocha squash puree.

FRIED GREEN TOMATO SLAB PIE

WITH A RITZ CRACKER CRUST

Serves 12

Do you hear the slam of the screen door? Smell the charcoal grill? It's lightning bug season and time to serve a cheesy, crunchy, tart, and juicy slab pie. It smells so good when sidled up alongside a pile of barbecue chicken or a platter of grilled sausages; it's my everything: Spicy pimento cheese bubbles below crispy fried tomatoes on a sweet and salty crust.

Frying can be scary, but use a deep pot, a deep-fry or candy thermometer, and only enough oil to cover the tomatoes (about 3 inches), and it's not quite so terrifying. Yes, it makes a bit of a mess, but it's so worth it. Monitor the temperature of the oil so the coating doesn't burn or blacken. If it does burn, discard the oil and replace it before continuing.

Make Ahead: The tomatoes may be fried 2 hours ahead and placed in a single layer on a paper towel–lined baking sheet. When cool, cover loosely with a clean kitchen towel, but do not refrigerate.

RITZ CRACKER CRUST

60 Ritz crackers (225 g, about 2 cups crushed)

8 tablespoons (113 g) unsalted butter, cubed, at room temperature

(Continued)

For the crust: Heat the oven to 350°F; if you have one, place a baking stone, Baking Steel, or inverted baking sheet on the center rack to heat (see page 4).

Mix the Ritz crumbs and butter together using your hands or a firm spatula. Knead the mixture until it is cohesive and the crumbs are thoroughly buttered. Dump the wet crumbs into the slab pie pan and press them evenly across the bottom, but not up the sides of the pan. Press down using a metal cup measure or the flat bottom of a glass until the crust feels collected and firm to the touch. Slide the pan into the oven (on top of the steel, stone, or baking sheet if using) and bake until lightly browned, 12 to 15 minutes. Remove from the oven to a wire cooling rack. The crust will appear loose until it is completely cooled.

For the filling: Stir the pimento cheese to loosen it; set aside ½ cup. Dab the rest across the cooled crust, leaving a 1-inch border all the way around. Lightly spread it across the crust using an offset spatula.

(Continued)

FILLING

1½ cups (440 g)
Classic Pimento Cheese
(recipe follows), at room
temperature

1 cup (120 g)
all-purpose flour

½ cup (69 g) stone-ground
cornmeal

2 large eggs

1 teaspoon salt

½ teaspoon coarsely
ground black pepper

½ teaspoon cayenne,
optional

3 medium green tomatoes
(750 g), cored and cut into
¼-inch slices

About 3 cups (710 ml)
peanut or vegetable oil

2 tablespoons chopped
fresh flat-leaf parsley

Getting a good coating on green tomatoes is challenging but possible. To be successful, you're going to have to dirty some dishes. And remember this mantra: *Left hand, dry ingredients; right hand, wet ingredients.* Set up a three-part "dredging station" in front of you. I use two baking sheets or dinner plates and a wide, shallow bowl between them. Divide the flour between the baking sheets and pour all the cornmeal on the baking sheet on the right. Crack the eggs into the bowl in the center and whip them with a fork until frothy. Season all three stations with salt, pepper, and cayenne.

Pat the tomato slices dry with paper towels. With your left hand, dredge a tomato slice in flour, turning to coat, then drop it into the egg. With your right hand, turn to coat then lift the tomato slice from the egg and deposit it in the cornmeal and flour mixture. With your left (still dry) hand, pick up flour and cornmeal mixture and sprinkle over the tomato, pressing it into the surface. Lift the coated tomato with your left hand, shake off the excess, and set aside until ready to fry.

Clean off and line one of the baking sheets with paper towels. Pour the peanut oil to about a 3-inch depth into a straight-sided pot, such as a Dutch oven. Turn the heat to high and heat until the oil is shimmering. Test for temperature (375°F) by dropping a small piece of bread in the hot oil. When it's ready, the bread will bubble, sizzle, and rise to the surface instantly. Add the tomatoes to the oil 3 or 4 at a time (do not crowd), and adjust the heat as necessary to keep the oil at 375°F. When the tomatoes are lowered into the oil, if it is hot enough, each slice will rise to the surface. When the tomatoes are golden brown, about 4 minutes, flip them and continue frying until toasty brown all over, another 3 minutes or so. Lift with a slotted spoon and transfer to the paper towels to drain. Repeat until all the slices are fried, bringing the oil back to temperature between batches. Watch the temperature carefully. As the tomatoes are added, it will decrease, but when it comes back to 375°F, reduce the heat and do not let it go higher. Remove the pan from the heat if it does, to cool the oil, so that the tomatoes will not burn.

Set the oven broiler to High. Place the tomatoes on top of the pimento cheese–coated crust. Using the remaining pimento cheese, add a dollop on top of each tomato slice. Slide the pie into the oven and broil until the cheese is bubbling and the edges of the tomatoes are browning, 3 to 5 minutes. Watch carefully so it doesn't burn. Cool slightly before garnishing with parsley and serving.

SAVOR A PIE

Techniques: Press-In Crusts (page 55), Cracker Crumb Crusts (page 61)

Swaps:

- Try a Saltine Crust (page 61).
- Swap in port wine spread or horseradish cheddar spread for the pimento cheese.
- Fry eggplant, onion rings, or zucchini.

CLASSIC PIMENTO CHEESE

Makes 1½ cups

6 ounces (170 g) extra sharp cheddar cheese, preferably orange

2 ounces (56 g) mild cheddar cheese, preferably white

4 tablespoons (56 g) cream cheese

1 (4-ounce jar) diced pimentos (114 g), drained

3 tablespoons mayonnaise, preferably Duke's

½ teaspoon smoked paprika

½ to 1 teaspoon Sriracha or another fruity hot sauce, depending on personal preference for heat

If pimento cheese isn't on your radar, try this recipe and become a member of the Forever Club, the club that cannot—will not—live without pimento cheese. The ground rules: Tempting as it might be to buy the already grated cheese, please don't. Most pre-grated, pre-packaged shredded cheeses have added cornstarch so the pieces won't clump. Cornstarch has no place in pimento cheese. Cold cheese is easier to grate than warm cheese, so a little time in the freezer (20 minutes will do) makes the process easier. I prefer and will only use the South's own Duke's mayonnaise in my pimento cheese—but I won't judge if you have another mayonnaise in your refrigerator.

Grate the two cheddar cheeses on the largest holes of a box grater into a large, wide bowl. Add the cream cheese, pimentos, mayonnaise, paprika, and Sriracha and stir by hand until well combined. Chill for at least 4 hours to let the flavors develop.

If not layering this cheese into the Fried Green Tomato Slab Pie, it's delicious served in celery boats.

CHRISTINE'S SMOKY FISH SLAB PIE
WITH A CARAMELIZED ONION CRUST

Serves 12 to 15

After making dozens upon dozens of pies as primary recipe tester for this book, Maine-based Christine Burns Rudalevige created this slab pie full of seaside flavors. She writes:

I'd never eaten fish pie until I lived in Norwich, England, where the coast was only a 30-minute drive in three directions. There were as many pubs in the county as there were days of the week and on most Fridays there was fish pie on offer. I've taken the best ideas from many and combined them into this one pie. Because saltiness varies from one smoked fish to another, I suggest tasting the filling before adding the salt. This is a pie designed to be enjoyed hot, so have your eaters sitting at the table when it's time to pull it out of the oven.

Make Ahead: Nothing about fish pie should be made ahead.

CARAMELIZED ONION CRUST

2½ cups plus
2 tablespoons (325 g)
all-purpose flour

16 tablespoons (225 g)
Onion Butter (page 44)

½ teaspoon kosher salt

½ cup (120 ml) ice water

WHITE FISH

1½ pounds (680 g) fresh flaky white American-caught fish (Atlantic cod, black cod, haddock, hake, or pollock are all good choices)

3 cups (710 ml) whole milk

2 bay leaves

12 black peppercorns

(Continued)

For the crust: In the food processor, pulse the flour, onion butter, and salt until the butter is in small pieces coated with flour, about 15 times. Add the water all at once and process until the mixture almost forms a ball. Form the dough into a 6- by 4-inch rectangle using plastic wrap and a bench scraper to firmly press the dough into a cohesive form. Wrap tightly and refrigerate a minimum of 4 hours.

Remove the dough from the refrigerator and allow it to warm slightly. Divide the dough into two pieces, one slightly larger than the other. Roll out the larger piece to 11 by 15 inches and place in the slab pie pan, pressing it into the corners of the pan and allowing the excess to drape over the sides. Refrigerate. Roll out the second piece of dough to 10 by 14 inches, place it on a lightly floured sheet of parchment, and refrigerate.

Heat the oven to 400°F; if you have one, place a baking stone, Baking Steel, or inverted baking sheet on the center rack to heat (see page 4).

(Continued)

SAVOR A PIE

6 fresh flat-leaf parsley
stalks

SAUCE

4 tablespoons (56 g)
unsalted butter

½ cup (60 g)
all-purpose flour

½ teaspoon smoked
paprika

1 cup (240 ml) heavy cream

4 ounces (113 g) mild
cheddar cheese, grated
(about 1 cup)

Kosher salt

Freshly ground black pepper

FILLING

8 ounces (227 g) hot
smoked salmon, skin
removed and meat flaked
into bite-sized chunks

1 pound (455 g) peeled
large (21 to 30 per pound)
American-caught shrimp,
thawed if frozen

1 pound (455 g) russet
potatoes, scrubbed, cut
into ½-inch dice, and
steamed until tender

1 cup (128 g) frozen peas

¼ cup (15 g) chopped
fresh flat-leaf parsley

1 tablespoon drained
capers

1 egg yolk

1 tablespoon cold water

½ teaspoon kosher salt

For the white fish: Place the white fish in a 3-inch-deep baking dish and cover with the milk. Add the bay leaves, peppercorns, and parsley stalks. Bake, uncovered, until the milk is hot and the fish is opaque, 12 to 15 minutes. Strain the liquid into a measuring cup and break the fish into bite-sized pieces.

For the sauce: Melt the butter in a medium saucepan. When it foams, add the flour and paprika and whisk until a smooth roux develops. Continue cooking, stirring all the while, until the roux has browned slightly and the flour smell goes away, about 2 minutes longer. Slowly whisk the warm liquid used to cook the fish into the roux. Keep whisking until the sauce has thickened slightly, 2 or 3 minutes longer. Remove from the heat. Stir in the cream and cheese and whisk until the sauce is smooth. Taste, season with salt and pepper as needed, and cool the sauce before proceeding.

To fill the pie: Pull the chilled bottom crust out of the refrigerator. Scatter the flaked cooked white fish across the bottom crust, followed by the salmon, shrimp, potatoes, peas, chopped parsley, and capers. Pour the sauce over the filling.

To replicate the decorated top crust in the photo, use a cookie cutter to make cutouts on the cold crust. (P.S. Do this before placing the crust on the pie.) Crimp and slash, if not using cutouts. Cover the pie with the top crust. Mix the egg yolk, water, and salt together. With a pastry brush, paint the crust generously with the salty egg wash. Slide the pie into the oven (on top of the steel, stone, or baking sheet if using) and bake for 20 minutes. Lower the temperature to 350°F and bake for an additional 30 to 35 minutes. Serve hot.

Techniques: Caramelized Onion Crust (page 42), Mixing and Rolling (page 14), Lattices, Cutouts, Stamps, and Shapes (page 26)

Swaps:

• Use an All-Butter Crust (page 30).

• Swap in a can of smoked oysters or mussels for the smoked salmon.

• Adding quartered hard-boiled eggs would be a very English thing to do.

FAVORITE TURKEY CHILI FRITO SLAB PIE

WITH A CORNBREAD CRUST

Serves 12 to 18

When the neighbors are gathered to watch a parade or celebrate a particularly beautiful day, I like to pull out this pie filled with familiar flavors. It's delicious hot out of the oven, but stands up at room temperature, too. While this is a kid-friendly pie, chipotles in adobo carry serious zing, so be confident, but cautious, depending on the crowd. If it's a group of heat seekers, include not only the tangy adobo sauce, but a chipotle, too, minced. Word to the wise: If all the cornbread batter is scraped into the pan, it will pour over the sides and spill to the bottom of the oven. It's inevitable you will do this at least once if you make this recipe more than a few times.

Make Ahead: The filling may be made up to 2 days in advance or frozen for up to 3 months.

TURKEY CHILI

2 tablespoons neutral oil like safflower, canola, or grapeseed

1 medium onion (142 g), diced (about 1 cup)

1½ pounds (680 g) ground turkey, half light and half dark meat

¾ cup (180 ml) water

2 tablespoons tomato paste

1 tablespoon sauce from chipotle in adobo (see headnote)

2 teaspoons chili powder (ancho chile powder, if available)

(Continued)

For the chili: In a large, straight-sided skillet over medium heat, warm the oil until it shimmers. Add the onions and cook until translucent. Add the turkey and cook, breaking it up with two wooden spoons, until browned. Add the water, tomato paste, adobo sauce (and minced chipotle if using), chili powder, salt, paprika, cumin, and cinnamon. Bring to a boil, reduce the heat to low, and cook until no pink remains in the meat, about 8 minutes. Stir in the scallions and cilantro and remove the pan from the heat. Let the chili cool while making the cornbread crust.

For the crust: Heat the oven to 400°F; if you have one, place a baking stone, Baking Steel, or inverted baking sheet on the center rack to heat (see page 4). Brush a slab pie pan with 1 tablespoon of the melted butter, especially in the corners and up the sides. In a deep bowl, whisk the flour and cornmeal with the baking powder, baking soda, and salt. In another bowl, whisk together the remaining 5 tablespoons melted butter, buttermilk, and eggs. Add the egg mixture to the flour mixture and using no more than a fork, quickly incorporate. Lumps are okay. Scoop about ½ cup of the batter into a buttered ramekin and bake this extra bit of batter as a cook's snack. (Don't use all the batter

SAVOR A PIE

1 teaspoon kosher salt

½ teaspoon smoked paprika

½ teaspoon ground cumin

¼ teaspoon ground cinnamon

½ cup (50 g) chopped scallions, white and green parts (about 4)

¼ cup (15 g) chopped fresh cilantro

CORNBREAD CRUST

6 tablespoons (85 g) unsalted butter, melted

¾ cup (90 g) all-purpose flour

¾ cup (115 g) stone-ground cornmeal

1½ teaspoons baking powder

1 teaspoon baking soda

1 teaspoon kosher salt

1 cup (235 ml) buttermilk

2 large eggs, beaten

TOPPINGS AND GARNISHES

4 ounces (113 g) Monterey Jack or sharp cheddar cheese, or a mix of the two, coarsely grated (about 1 cup)

6 ounces (170 g) Fritos, slightly crushed (about 3 cups)

Minced fresh cilantro

Lime wedges

in the pan or it will spill over.) Pour the remaining batter into the buttered pan.

To fill and top the crust: Scatter the turkey chili evenly across the cornmeal batter, cover with grated cheese, and top with Fritos. Don't fret. It's all going to come together.

Slide the pie into the oven (on top of the steel, stone, or baking sheet if using) and bake until the cornbread is pulling away from the corners and the Fritos are golden brown, about 22 minutes. Serve hot, warm, or at room temperature. Set out the garnishes and let everyone choose their favorite.

Techniques: Cornbread Crust (page 68), Birdseed, Crushes, and Rocky Road Garnishes (page 81)

Swaps:

- Make your vegetarian friends happy by using Vegetarian Black Bean Chili (recipe follows).

- Trade ground beef, venison, pork, or any combination for the turkey.

- Doritos for the Fritos? You might, I would never. I stand firmly with Frito pie tradition.

Sour cream or Mexican crema

Fresh or pickled jalapeño slices

Hot sauce

VEGETARIAN BLACK BEAN CHILI

3 tablespoons neutral oil like safflower, canola, or grapeseed

1 medium onion (142 g), diced (about 1 cup)

1 sweet potato (225 g), peeled and diced (about 1½ cups)

2 zucchini (225 g), peeled and diced (about 1½ cups)

1 (15-ounce) can black beans (425 g), rinsed and drained (about 2 cups)

¾ cup (180 ml) water

2 tablespoons tomato paste

1 tablespoon chipotle in adobo, adobo sauce only

2 teaspoons chili powder, (ancho chile powder, if available)

1 teaspoon kosher salt

½ teaspoon smoked paprika

½ teaspoon ground cumin

¼ teaspoon ground cinnamon

½ cup (50g) chopped scallions, white and green parts (about 4)

2 tablespoons cilantro, finely minced

VEGETARIAN BLACK BEAN CHILI

Serves 12 to 15

This hearty vegetarian version of the filling for my chili Frito slab pie will please even the carnivores. It's spicy and nuanced and full of texture. Carefully chop all the vegetables to the same size (½-inch dice is my preference) to make sure every bite has a bit of this and a bit of that.

Over medium heat, warm oil in a large, wide skillet with straight sides. When the oil begins to shimmer, cook the onions until translucent, add sweet potato, toss to coat with oil and cook for 2 to 3 minutes. Add zucchini, toss to coat in the oil and cook until the zucchini begins to soften, about 5 minutes, and add the beans, water, tomato paste, adobo sauce, chili powder, salt, paprika, cumin, and cinnamon. Bring to a boil, reduce heat and cook on low until the vegetables are cooked through but not mushy, about 15 to 20 minutes. Stir in the scallions and cilantro and remove the pan from the heat. Let the mixture cool. Continue with the Frito Slab Pie recipe (page 141).

POBLANO AND CHORIZO SLAB PIE

WITH A HASH BROWN CRUST

Serves 8 to 12

Mexican style fresh chorizo—spicy and porky—is the basis for this piquant, entirely gluten-free slab pie full of fruity poblano peppers and showered with crispy chips, herbs, and cheese. The potato crust is a hearty base that complements the tingle of the chiles. While this pie is scrumptious on its own, gild the lily by topping each serving with a sunny-side-up egg and a swath of hot sauce. Wait for the moment when the runny yolk hits the crunchy, cheesy, chile-laced pie. That's pie-happiness.

Make Ahead: The filling may be made up to 3 days ahead. The crust may be baked several hours in advance of filling and baking the pie.

HASH BROWN CRUST

2 tablespoons neutral oil like canola or grapeseed

1 medium onion (142 g), peeled

1½ pounds (680 g) medium russet potatoes (about 4), scrubbed but not peeled

1 large egg plus 1 egg white, beaten

1 teaspoon kosher salt

½ teaspoon coarsely ground black pepper

FILLING

2 large (285 g), plump poblano peppers

1 pound (455 g) spicy fresh chorizo sausage

(Continued)

For the crust: Heat the oven to 425°F; if you have one, place a baking stone, Baking Steel, or inverted baking sheet on the center rack to heat (see page 4). Use a pastry brush to paint 1 tablespoon of the oil into the corners, up the sides, and across the bottom of the slab pie baking sheet.

Grate the onion on the medium holes of a box grater or use a food processor's grating disk (my preference). Place the onions in a medium mixing bowl. Grate the potatoes on the large holes of the box grater or with the food processor. Take a handful of shredded potatoes, squeeze them over a small bowl to capture the liquid, and place the potato shreds in the bowl with the onions. Continue until all the potatoes have been grated and their liquid squeezed out. Work quickly to keep the potatoes from turning pink and brown.

Let the potato liquid sit for about 5 minutes, until the starch and liquid separate. Pour off the liquid, keeping the starchy white paste at the bottom of the bowl. That's potato starch and we love it. Add the starch to the grated onions and potatoes, then add the egg and egg white, salt, and pepper. Mix well (I use my hands). Firmly press the potato mixture into the prepared pan. Brush the surface of the potatoes with the remaining 1 tablespoon oil. Bake (on top of the steel, stone,

1 (15-ounce) can
(425 g) fire roasted diced
tomatoes

2 teaspoons dried Mexican
oregano or dried marjoram

½ teaspoon kosher salt

TOPPING

1 cup (100 g) thinly sliced
scallions, white and green
parts (about 8)

4 ounces (113 g) cotija
cheese, crumbled or finely
diced (about 1 cup)

½ cup (30 g) roughly
chopped fresh cilantro
leaves and stems

4 ounces (113 g) white or
yellow corn tortilla chips,
crushed (about 1½ cups)

or baking sheet if using) for 45 minutes, until toasted brown at the edges and across the surface.

For the filling: Heat the oven to broil. Wearing gloves, halve the poblanos lengthwise and remove and discard the stem, core, and seeds. Place the peppers, skin side up, on a parchment-lined baking sheet. Broil until the peels blister and blacken, 8 to 12 minutes. Remove the pan from the oven and cover the peppers with a kitchen towel to steam them. (Throw that towel in the wash afterwards, to avoid transferring chile heat.) As soon as it's possible to handle the peppers, wearing gloves slip off the blistered peel and slice the peppers into thin strips to make about 2 cups.

Set the oven temperature to 400°F. Split the casings on the sausage, empty the sausage meat into a large skillet, and discard the casings. Turn the heat to medium and break the meat apart using two wooden spoons. Cook low and slow until the meat has crumbled and is no longer pink, 7 or 8 minutes. Pour off and discard as much of the fat as possible. Add the poblano strips, tomatoes, oregano, and salt to the pan. Increase the heat to medium-high. When the mixture boils, reduce the heat to low and keep it bubbling low until thickened, about 20 minutes. Cool the filling.

To fill and top: Combine the scallions, cheese, and cilantro in a small bowl. Pour the cooled sausage filling into the potato crust and smooth it, filling up the corners. Sprinkle the surface with the scallion-cheese mixture and top with the crushed chips. Bake for 20 minutes, or until the filling is bubbling, the cheese is melting, and the chips are browned.

Slice and serve warm.

Techniques: Press-In Crusts (page 55), Hash Brown Crust (page 67), Birdseed, Crushes, and Rocky Road Garnishes (page 81)

Swaps:

- Sweet potatoes can stand in for the russets.
- For a vegetarian pie, trade the chorizo for a can of pinto beans, well drained.
- For a spicy option, swap in 2 small cans of diced Hatch chiles, drained, instead of roasting the poblanos.
- Substitute feta cheese for the cotija.
- Doritos (nacho cheese flavor) are wicked good as a topper.

ITALIAN SAUSAGE AND PEPPER SLAB PIE

WITH AN ALL-BUTTER CRUST

Serves 8 to 12

My favorite calzone is piquant and rich with the sweet, grassy addition of spinach and fennel-laced zesty sausage. That is how I dreamed up an open-faced, saucy calzone slab. The spinach should be squeezed bone dry or you risk a soupy filling. Serve it to the soccer team after practice. They'll be so grateful.

Make Ahead: The sausage filling may be made up to 3 days ahead. The bottom crust may be blind baked several hours ahead.

ALL-BUTTER CRUST

1⅓ cups (160 g)
all-purpose flour

8 tablespoons (113 g)
unsalted butter, cubed and
frozen for 20 minutes

⅛ teaspoon kosher salt

¼ cup (60 ml) ice water

FILLING

1 pound (455 g) fresh
spinach leaves; or 10
ounces (285 g) thawed
frozen chopped spinach

1 pound (455 g) bulk Italian
sausage, mild or spicy

1 medium onion (142 g),
diced (about 1 cup)

2 garlic cloves, slivered

1 (28-ounce) can (794 g)
crushed tomatoes

(Continued)

For the crust: In the food processor, pulse the flour, butter, and salt until the butter is in small pieces coated with flour, about 15 times. Add the ice water all at once and process until the mixture almost forms a ball. Form the dough into a 3- by 4-inch rectangle using plastic wrap and a bench scraper to firmly press the dough into a cohesive form. Wrap tightly and refrigerate a minimum of 4 hours.

Heat the oven to 400°F; if you have one, place a baking stone, Baking Steel, or inverted baking sheet on the center rack to heat (see page 4). Remove the dough from the refrigerator and allow it to warm slightly. Roll out to 11 by 15 inches and place in the slab pie pan, pressing it into the corners of the pan and allowing the excess to drape over the sides. Refrigerate. Dock the surface of the dough and crimp the edges. Refrigerate for at least 20 minutes. Blind bake the crust (on top of the steel, stone, or baking sheet if using) for 20 minutes. Decrease the oven temperature to 350°F.

For the filling: If using fresh spinach, place in a microwavable bowl and sprinkle ½ teaspoon water over the top. Cover and microwave for 1 minute. Let the spinach cool for a few minutes. Squeeze out as much water from the cooked spinach or thawed frozen spinach as you can using your hands or pressing the cooked leaves against the sides of a colander with a stiff spoon or spatula. Chop roughly.

(Continued)

½ teaspoon kosher salt

½ teaspoon freshly ground black pepper

½ cup (60 g) basil leaves, stacked and sliced into ribbons

1 (8-ounce) jar roasted peppers (225 g), drained and sliced into ribbons

4 ounces (113 g) grated shaved Parmigiano Reggiano (about ½ cup)

Heat a large, wide, straight-sided skillet over medium heat. Add the sausage and cook, breaking up the meat until the pink is gone, just 4 or 5 minutes. Remove the sausage using a slotted spoon and set aside. Pour off all but about 2 tablespoons of the oil in the pan, add the onions, and cook until translucent, about 10 minutes. Add the garlic and cook until fragrant but not burned, about 30 seconds. Add the sausage back to the pan, then add the tomatoes, salt, and pepper. Stir well. Bring to a slight boil, more of a burble, and cook, uncovered, until the sauce is quite thick, about 30 minutes. Cool to room temperature before assembling the pie.

Scatter the spinach over the crust. Pour in the sausage sauce and scatter the basil over the sauce. Top with the peppers and cheese. Slide the pie into the oven and bake until the filling is bubbling, the cheese has melted and browned slightly, and the pie smells amazing, 30 to 35 minutes.

Cool about 5 minutes. Serve with a bright green salad.

Techniques: All-Butter Crust (page 30), Mixing and Rolling Out (page 14), Blind Baking (page 29)

Swaps:

- Put a top crust on it.
- Opt for an Olive Oil Crust (page 56) and top with Cacio e Pepe Savory Streusel (page 86).
- Any bulk sausage will do, or skip the sausage and add diced eggplant or cremini mushrooms.
- Substitute tiny cooked meatballs for the sausage.
- A few pinches of fresh mozzarella are welcome.

CURRIED CHICKEN SLAB PIE

WITH A CARAMELIZED ONION CRUST

Serves 12 to 18

A splendidly rich and exotic-tasting pie, full of texture and a little bit of heat. Add the seeds from the jalapeño for more zing, or remove the chile pepper altogether to keep the filling on the mild side. Curry powders are combinations of spices and the flavors can vary widely, so it's good to find one you like (and replace it frequently as old curry powder has no punch whatsoever). The recipe calls for 1 to 3 tablespoons curry powder: Taste the filling for flavor and add more as needed, remembering once cloaked in crust, the filling should be assertively spiced to get noticed. Try a turmeric-tinted Madras-style curry with cumin, coriander, ginger, cardamom, and chiles, or change the flavor entirely with garam masala, in which cinnamon, bay, and cloves play with cumin, coriander, and cardamom.

Make Ahead: The curry filling may be made up to 3 days ahead and refrigerated, or frozen for 3 months. Defrost overnight in the refrigerator.

CARAMELIZED ONION CRUST

2½ cups plus
2 tablespoons (325 g)
all-purpose flour

16 tablespoons (225 g)
Onion Butter (page 44)

½ teaspoon kosher salt

½ cup (120 ml) ice water

FILLING

3 tablespoons canola,
grapeseed, or vegetable oil

2 medium onions
(285 g), sliced into
half-moons (about 3 cups)

(Continued)

For the crust: In the food processor, pulse the flour, onion butter, and salt until the butter is in small pieces coated with flour, about 15 times. Add the water all at once and process until the mixture almost forms a ball. Form the dough into a 6- by 4-inch rectangle using plastic wrap and a bench scraper to firmly press the dough into a cohesive form. Wrap tightly and refrigerate a minimum of 4 hours.

Remove the dough from the refrigerator and allow it to warm slightly. Divide the dough into two pieces, one slightly larger than the other. Roll out the larger piece to 11 by 15 inches and place in the slab pie pan, pressing it into the corners of the pan and allowing the excess to drape over the sides. Refrigerate. Roll out the second piece of dough to 10 by 14 inches, place it on a lightly floured sheet of parchment, and refrigerate.

For the filling: In a large, heavy Dutch oven, heat the oil over medium-high heat until it shimmers. Add the onions and cook low and slow for about 30 minutes, stirring from time to time, until soft, browned, and sweet. Stir in the minced chile. Transfer the onions to

1 jalapeño or serrano
chile, seeds removed and
minced

2 tablespoons (28 g)
unsalted butter

2 pounds (900 g) boneless
skinless chicken breasts,
cut into 1-inch chunks

1 teaspoon kosher salt

½ teaspoon ground black
pepper

3 tablespoons all-purpose
flour

1 cup (235 ml) chicken
stock or water

1 cup (235 ml) coconut milk

1 to 3 tablespoons curry
powder

¾ pound (355 g)
cauliflower florets from
a medium head (about
3 cups)

½ pound (225 g) carrots,
diced (about 3 cups)

½ pound (225 g) sugar
snap peas, cut into 2 or 3
pieces each (about 1 cup)

½ cup (30 g) roughly
chopped fresh cilantro
leaves and stems

a bowl and set aside. Add the butter to the pot and increase the heat to medium-high. When the butter foams, add the chicken, salt, and pepper and cook, tossing everything around in the pan, just until the pink is gone. Do not overcook (it will continue to cook in the sauce). Reduce the heat, sprinkle the flour over the chicken, and stir everything around until slightly browned and the flour smell is gone, 4 or 5 minutes. Stir in the stock, coconut milk, and curry powder. Add the cauliflower and carrots and bring the mixture to a boil. Reduce the heat until it's slowly bubbling. Cover and cook for 10 to 12 minutes, until the cauliflower is barely fork-tender but not mushy. Stir in the snap peas and cilantro and remove the pan from the stove. Cool to room temperature before filling the pie.

Heat the oven to 425°F; if you have one, place a baking stone, Baking Steel, or inverted baking sheet on the center rack to heat (see page 4).

Fill the bottom crust with the cooled filling. Drape the top crust over the filling and trim the overhang. Crimp and slash, using a sharp paring knife on the cold upper crust (before placing it on the pie) and slice a stack of semicircular smiles, as in the photograph. Bake (on top of the steel, stone, or baking sheet if using) for 20 minutes. Reduce the temperature to 375°F and continue to bake for another 40 to 45 minutes, until toasty brown and smelling sensational.

Remove to a cooling rack and let it settle down for a few minutes before digging in. Serve with mango chutney and lime pickle.

Techniques: Caramelized Onion Crust (page 42), Mixing and Rolling Out (page 14), Crimp and Slash (page 24)

Swaps:

• Use an All-Butter Crust (page 30).

• Make it vegetarian by omitting the chicken and doubling the cauliflower or adding broccoli, zucchini, mushrooms, butternut squash, corn, or small cooked potatoes.

• Use about 3 cups of cubed or shredded leftover rotisserie chicken (add after cooking the filling).

CHICKEN POT SLAB PIE
WITH AN ALL-BUTTER CRUST

Serves 10 to 12

Herbes de Provence and leeks make a decidedly French-ified filling, and a generous dash of fresh thyme keeps it grassy and fresh. This hearty pie makes great use of whatever leftovers are around after a roast chicken dinner. Because there is never enough leftover chicken in this house, I usually roast two chickens, to make sure I can make a pie, too. I'm partial to a lumpy, bumpy top crust, but puff pastry cutouts, one per serving, are party-worthy.

Make Ahead: The filling may be made a day or two ahead.

ALL-BUTTER CRUST

2½ cups plus
2 tablespoons (325 g)
all-purpose flour

16 tablespoons (225 g)
unsalted butter, cubed
and frozen for 20 minutes

¼ teaspoon kosher salt

½ cup (120 ml) ice water

FILLING

¼ cup (60 ml) olive oil

2 medium leeks (170 g),
white and pale green parts
only, sliced into ½-inch
disks (about 2 cups)

2 medium carrots
(170 g), peeled, cut in half
lengthwise, and sliced into
½-inch half-moons (about
1½ cups)

(Continued)

For the crust: In the food processor, pulse the flour, butter, and salt until the fats are in small pieces coated with flour, about 15 times. Add the water all at once and process until the mixture almost forms a ball. Form the dough into a 6- by 4-inch rectangle using plastic wrap and a bench scraper to firmly press the dough into a cohesive form. Wrap tightly and refrigerate a minimum of 4 hours.

Remove the dough from the refrigerator and allow it to warm slightly. Divide the dough into two pieces, one slightly larger than the other. Roll out the larger piece to 11 by 15 inches and place in the slab pie pan, pressing it into the corners of the pan and allowing the excess to drape over the sides. Refrigerate. Roll out the second piece of dough to 10 by 14 inches, place it on a lightly floured sheet of parchment, and refrigerate.

For the filling: Heat the olive oil in a deep, wide skillet or Dutch oven over medium heat. Add the leeks and cook until translucent, about 8 minutes. Add the carrots, celery, thyme, and herbes de Provence. Stir well to coat in oil and cook until the vegetables are slightly tender, 4 or 5 minutes. Splash in the wine and cook until the pan is nearly dry, about 3 minutes.

(Continued)

3 stalks celery (85 g),
sliced ½ inch thick
(about ¾ cup)

1 heaping teaspoon
fresh thyme leaves

1 teaspoon herbes de
Provence

¼ cup (60 ml) white wine
or water

4 tablespoons (56 g)
unsalted butter

¼ cup (30 g) all-purpose
flour

1½ cups (360 ml)
homemade or low-sodium
chicken stock

12 ounces (340 g)
cooked chicken, cubed
(about 2 cups)

6 ounces (170 g) frozen
petite peas

1½ teaspoons kosher salt

¾ teaspoon freshly ground
black pepper

Turn the heat to medium-high, add the butter, and cook until it is foaming. Sprinkle the flour over the buttery vegetables and cook, stirring, until the flour smell goes away and the roux (the paste created with butter and flour) has turned slightly golden, about 4 minutes. Pour in the stock and bring to a boil. Reduce the heat and let the stew bubble away until thickened, 5 or 6 minutes. Stir in the chicken, peas, salt, and pepper. Cool the filling for at least 30 minutes before filling the pie.

Heat the oven to 425°F; if you have one, place a baking stone, Baking Steel, or inverted baking sheet on the center rack to heat (see page 4). Bring the bottom crust out of the refrigerator, scrape in the filling, and spread it from edge to edge and into the corners. Place the top crust over the filling. Crimp and slash.

Bake the pie (on top of the steel, stone, or baking sheet if using) for 20 minutes. Reduce the temperature to 375°F and bake until the top is toasty brown and the filling is bubbling up out of the slashes, 40 to 45 minutes. Cool for 10 minutes before serving.

Techniques: All-Butter Crust (page 30), Mixing and Rolling Out (page 14), Crimp and Slash (page 24)

Swaps:

- Almost any crust can substitute for the All-Butter version here—Butter and Shortening (page 33), Leaf Lard (page 45), Cheddar Cheese (page 39), or Rye Crust (page 48).

- Trade 2 cans of white beans, drained, for the chicken and use vegetable stock, and this is a vegetarian pie.

- Try cutouts of puff pastry or Biscuits (page 87) instead of an upper crust, popping them on top of the pie after the first 30 minutes of baking.

AFTER-THANKSGIVING TURKEY SLAB PIE

WITH A BUTTER AND SHORTENING CRUST

Serves 8

There comes a time in every post-Thanksgiving home when leftovers are no longer interesting: The sandwiches have happened. The second-day plate with everything covered in gravy has been devoured. That's when I gather whatever is left and make pie. Because so much of what might be included in the filling may have been salted already, make the filling first, taste it, and add more salt and pepper only if needed.

Make Ahead: This pie is a study in make-ahead strategy. Every leftover has a place in this pie.

BUTTER AND SHORTENING CRUST

1⅓ cups (160 g) all-purpose flour

4 tablespoons (56 g) unsalted butter, cubed and frozen for 20 minutes

4 tablespoons (56 g) Spectrum or other vegetable shortening, cubed and frozen for 20 minutes

⅛ teaspoon kosher salt

¼ cup (60 ml) ice water

1½ teaspoons vodka, optional

FILLING

¼ cup (60 ml) olive oil

2 medium onions (285 g), sliced into ½-inch disks (about 3 cups)

(Continued)

For the crust: In the food processor, pulse the flour, butter, shortening, and salt until the fats are in small pieces coated with flour, about 15 times. Add the water and vodka (if using) all at once and process until the mixture almost forms a ball. Form the dough into a 3- by 4-inch rectangle using plastic wrap and a bench scraper to firmly press the dough into a cohesive form. Wrap tightly and refrigerate a minimum of 4 hours.

Remove the dough from the refrigerator and allow it to warm slightly. Roll out the crust to 11 by 15 inches and place in the slab pie pan, pressing it into the corners of the pan and allowing the excess to drape over the sides. Pierce the crust all over with the tines of a fork or a docking tool. Crimp the edge. Refrigerate.

Heat the oven to 425°F; if you have one, place a baking stone, Baking Steel, or inverted baking sheet on the center rack to heat (see page 4).

For the filling: Warm the olive oil in a deep, wide skillet or Dutch oven over medium-high heat until shimmering. Add the onions and cook until translucent, about 8 minutes. Add the carrots, celery, thyme, and sage. Stir well to coat the vegetables in oil and cook until slightly tender, 4 or 5 minutes. Splash in the wine and cook until the pan is nearly dry.

(Continued)

2 cups (170 g) cooked carrots or sweet potatoes; or 2 medium carrots, peeled, cut in half, and sliced into ½-inch half-moons

3 stalks celery (85 g), sliced ½ inch thick

1 heaping teaspoon fresh thyme leaves

½ teaspoon fresh sage leaves, minced

¼ cup (60 ml) white wine or water

4 tablespoons (56 g) unsalted butter

¼ cup (30 g) all-purpose flour

1 cup (240 ml) leftover gravy plus ½ cup (120 ml) water; or 1½ cups (360 ml) turkey or chicken stock

12 ounces (340 g) fully cooked turkey, cubed or shredded (about 2 cups)

¾ cup (85 g) cooked green beans or frozen petite peas

Kosher salt and freshly ground black pepper, if needed

3 cups leftover stuffing

4 tablespoons (56 g) unsalted butter, melted

Over medium-high heat, add the butter and cook until foaming. Sprinkle the flour over the vegetables and cook, stirring, until the flour smell goes away and the roux (the paste created with butter and flour) has turned golden, about 4 minutes. Pour in the gravy and water and bring to a boil. Reduce the heat and let the stew bubble away until thickened, 5 or 6 minutes. Stir in the turkey and green beans. Most of these ingredients will have been seasoned already, so taste and season judiciously with salt and pepper. Cool the filling for at least 30 minutes before filling the pie.

Place a sheet of parchment in the crust-lined pie pan, weight with pie weights, and blind bake the crust (on top of the steel, stone, or baking sheet if using) for 20 minutes. Remove the paper and weights and place the pan back in the oven for 5 more minutes to dry out the crust. Reduce the oven temperature to 375°F.

Spoon the filling into the crust, smoothing the surface. Pinch off walnut-sized pieces of stuffing and dot the top of the pie. Drizzle the stuffing nuggets with the melted butter and slide the pie back into the oven. Bake until the stuffing is toasty brown and the filling is bubbling, about 25 minutes longer. Serve hot.

Techniques: Butter and Shortening Crust (page 33), Mixing and Rolling Out (page 14), Crimp and Slash (page 24), Blind Baking (page 29)

Swaps:

• Both the All-Butter (page 30) and Leaf Lard Crust (page 45) are equally suitable for this single-crust pie.

• A Caramelized Onion Crust (page 42) adds another layer of flavor, like an onion kaiser roll.

• Almost anything left over from Thanksgiving will find a place in the pie filling. Scatter roasted Brussels sprouts, creamed onions, or roasted sweet potatoes over the filling. And if there are mashed potatoes left over, make a Potato Mash topper (page 77).

"THE REUBEN" SLAB PIE
WITH A RYE CRUST

Serves 12 to 18

Whenever I find myself having lunch at an old-fashioned delicatessen, the grilled sandwich of corned beef, sauerkraut, and Swiss cheese—the Reuben—calls to me. It seemed fitting to create a pie with similar leanings. While the triad of beef, cabbage, and cheese is what describes this beautiful sandwich, it's the sauce that makes it exceptional. "Russian" dressing, much maligned and sadly overlooked in recent years, with its midcentury mix of mayo and ketchup, is the ying to this yang. Deli corned beef is a little tangier, and corned beef from a boiled dinner is a little sweeter: Both are delicious. Use either, but be sure to taste the filling for salt. Some of the meat will include fat, which should be added to the pie filling (diced) or the filling will be dry. This rich, flavorful pie is an alternative for leftover corned beef hash, stretching what remains to feed more people.

Make Ahead: The filling may be made up to 3 days ahead.

RYE CRUST

1¾ cups plus 1 tablespoon (225 g) all-purpose flour

1 cup (100 g) rye flour

8 tablespoons (113 g) unsalted butter, cubed and frozen for 20 minutes

8 tablespoons (113 g) Spectrum or other vegetable shortening, cubed and frozen for 20 minutes

½ teaspoon kosher salt

½ cup (120 ml) ice water

3 teaspoons ice cold vodka, optional

(Continued)

For the crust: In the food processor, pulse the flours, butter, shortening, and salt until the fats are in small pieces coated with flour, about 15 times. Add the ice water and vodka (if using) all at once and process until the mixture almost forms a ball. Form the dough into a 6- by 4-inch rectangle using plastic wrap and a bench scraper to firmly press the dough into a cohesive form. Wrap tightly and refrigerate a minimum of 4 hours.

Remove the dough from the refrigerator and allow it to warm slightly. Divide the dough into two pieces, one slightly larger than the other. Roll out the larger piece to 11 by 15 inches and place in the slab pie pan, pressing it into the corners of the pan and allowing the excess to drape over the sides. Refrigerate. Roll out the second piece of dough to 10 by 14 inches, place it on a lightly floured sheet of parchment, and refrigerate.

Heat the oven to 425°F; if you have one, place a baking stone, Baking Steel, or inverted baking sheet on the center rack to heat (see page 4).

(Continued)

SAVOR A PIE

FILLING

½ cup (113 g) mayonnaise (not low-fat)

½ cup (113 g) ketchup

½ cup (113 g) sweet pickle relish

¼ cup (40 g) finely minced onion

½ teaspoon horseradish

½ teaspoon freshly ground black pepper

2 pounds (900 g) corned beef, chopped (about 5 cups)

2 cups (455 g) sauerkraut, well drained

Up to ½ teaspoon kosher salt, depending on the saltiness of the corned beef and sauerkraut

6 ounces (175 g) Swiss cheese, grated (about 1½ cups)

1 egg yolk

1 tablespoon cool water

1 tablespoon caraway seeds

For the filling: In a large bowl, combine the mayonnaise, ketchup, relish, onion, horseradish, and pepper for the "Russian" dressing. Add the corned beef and toss like a salad to keep the mixture light. Combine a spoonful of filling and a pinch of sauerkraut together and taste to evaluate the saltiness; salt only if needed. Spread the sauerkraut across the bottom crust. Spoon the corned beef filling over the sauerkraut and cover with an even layer of cheese. Drape the top crust over the filling. Crimp and slash.

Whisk the egg yolk and water until thoroughly blended. With a pastry brush, paint the top but not the edges of the crust. Scatter caraway seeds across the surface. Bake (on top of the steel, stone, or baking sheet if using) for 20 minutes. Reduce the temperature to 350°F and bake until the crust is deeply golden brown and the filling is hot all the way through, 40 to 45 minutes. Serve hot or at room temperature.

Techniques: Rye Crust (page 48), Mixing and Rolling Out (page 14), Crimp and Slash (page 24)

Swaps:

- The Rye Crust is the one that makes the most sense, but any crust will do, such as All-Butter (page 30) or Leaf Lard (page 45).

- If smoked meat is your thing, try pastrami instead of corned beef.

BEEFY EMPANADA SLAB PIE

WITH A CREAM CHEESE CRUST

Serves 10 to 12

Inside a flaky, blistered crust lies a generous layer of meaty *picadillo*, a traditional dish served across Central America. The base is usually ground beef (an 80:20 meat-to-fat ratio is ideal), seasoned with tomatoes, olives, raisins, and herbs and spices that are regionally specific. This recipe reveals my admiration of both olives and raisins, but it calls for only a moderate quantity of each; if you are a fan, add more. If raisins aren't your thing, add another dried fruit like apricots or chopped raw apple instead. It's the sweet and salty harmony that is essential.

Make Ahead: The filling may be made up to 3 days ahead and refrigerated, or frozen up to 3 months.

CREAM CHEESE CRUST

2½ cups plus
2 tablespoons (325 g)
all-purpose flour

8 tablespoons (113 g)
unsalted butter, cubed
and frozen for 20 minutes

8 tablespoons (113 g)
cream cheese, cubed and
refrigerated for 20 minutes

¼ teaspoon kosher salt

½ cup (120 ml) ice water

(Continued)

For the crust: In the food processor, pulse the flour, butter, cream cheese, and salt until the fats are in small pieces coated with flour, about 15 times. Add the water all at once and process until the mixture almost forms a ball. Form the dough into a 6- by 4-inch rectangle using plastic wrap and a bench scraper to firmly press the dough into a cohesive form. Wrap tightly and refrigerate a minimum of 4 hours.

Remove the dough from the refrigerator and allow it to warm slightly. Divide the dough into two pieces, one slightly larger than the other. Roll out the larger piece to 11 by 15 inches and place in the slab pie pan, pressing it into the corners of the pan and allowing the excess to drape over the sides. Refrigerate. Roll out the second piece of dough to 10 by 14 inches, place it on a lightly floured sheet of parchment, and refrigerate.

For the filling: In a wide, large skillet set over medium-high heat, add the ground chuck, breaking it up with two wooden spoons, and cook until the meat is browned and the pink goes away. Spoon the meat into a bowl and pour off and discard the remaining fat.

(Continued)

FILLING

2 pounds (900 g) ground chuck (beef)

3 tablespoons olive oil

3 medium (426 g) sweet or yellow onions, diced (about 3 cups)

2 garlic cloves, minced

2 tablespoons olive brine

1 tablespoon Worcestershire sauce

1 teaspoon dried oregano

1 teaspoon smoked paprika

1 teaspoon kosher salt, plus more for seasoning

½ teaspoon cumin seeds

1 (28-ounce) can (794 g) crushed tomatoes (about 3 cups)

½ cup (71 g) large pimento-stuffed green olives (about 15), sliced

¾ cup (125 g) golden raisins

1 egg yolk

1 teaspoon cold water

Scant ½ teaspoon kosher or finishing salt, optional

Wipe out the pan, add the olive oil, and warm until shimmering. Add the onions and cook until translucent and beginning to brown on the edges. Stir in the garlic and cook an additional 30 seconds. Add the olive brine, Worcestershire, oregano, paprika, teaspoon of salt, cumin seeds, and tomatoes to the pan. Increase the heat and cook the sauce until thick, saucy, and reduced by half, 15 to 18 minutes. Stir in the cooked beef, olives, and raisins and remove the pan from the heat. Taste and add salt and pepper, if needed, then cool completely.

Heat the oven to 425°F; if you have one, place a baking stone, Baking Steel, or inverted baking sheet on the center rack to heat (see page 4). Fill the bottom crust with the cooled filling. Cover with the top crust. Crimp and slash, with a calligraphic, bold E, if you wish, sliced into the cold top crust before placing it over the filling. Mix the egg yolk and water together. With a pastry brush, paint the crust generously with the egg wash, avoiding the crimped edges, and scatter the salt across the surface. Slide the pie into the oven (on top of the steel, stone, or baking sheet if using) and bake for 20 minutes. Reduce the temperature to 350°F and bake for an additional 35 to 40 minutes, until the crust is toasty brown and the filling is piping hot.

Techniques: Cream Cheese Crust (page 37), Mixing and Rolling Out (page 14), Crimp and Slash (page 24)

Swaps:

- A Cheddar Cheese (page 39) or All-Butter Crust (page 30) fits the flavor profile.

- Shredded fully cooked short ribs or brisket, or ground dark meat turkey can stand in for the ground beef.

- Make a vegetarian *picadillo* with a can of pinto beans and 1 or 2 sweet potatoes.

- Top with a Potato Mash (page 77).

COWBOY BEEF STEW SLAB PIE

WITH A LARD CRUST

Serves 12 to 15

Cowboy beef stew is differentiated from other stew recipes by the black coffee that flavors the gravy. I have always imagined this stems from some romantic notion of the Wild West—the campfire, covered wagons, and the last cup of coffee in the ever-present speckled coffee pot. For me, the provenance is not as important as the flavor, which is earthy and rich; every bite inspires the question, "What is that?" Cut the beef into bite-sized pieces to make this pie easier to serve and eat. Brown the cubes in a hot pan, quickly, to sear the meat and ensure a nice, tender, never mushy bite of meaty pie. The crust is flaky and sturdy at the same time, a proper foundation for this hearty dinnertime pie.

Make Ahead: The filling may be thoroughly cooked and refrigerated for up to 3 days or frozen for up to 3 months. Defrost in the refrigerator overnight.

LARD CRUST

2½ cups plus
2 tablespoons (325 g)
all-purpose flour

12 tablespoons (170 g)
rendered lard or leaf lard,
cubed and frozen for 20
minutes

4 tablespoons (56 g)
unsalted butter, cubed
and frozen for 20 minutes

½ teaspoon kosher salt

½ cup (120 ml) ice water

2 tablespoons vodka,
ice cold, optional

(Continued)

For the crust: In the food processor, pulse the flour, lard, butter, and salt until the fats are in small pieces coated with flour, about 15 times. Add the water and vodka (if using) all at once and process until the mixture almost forms a ball. Form the dough into a 6- by 4-inch rectangle using plastic wrap and a bench scraper to firmly press the dough into a cohesive form. Wrap tightly and refrigerate a minimum of 4 hours.

Remove the dough from the refrigerator and allow it to warm slightly. Divide the dough into two pieces, one slightly larger than the other. Roll out the larger piece to 11 by 15 inches and place in the slab pie pan, pressing it into the corners of the pan and allowing the excess to drape over the sides. Refrigerate. Roll out the second piece of dough to 10 by 14 inches, place it on a lightly floured sheet of parchment, and refrigerate.

For the filling: Slowly brown the bacon over low heat in a heavy-bottomed Dutch oven or a large, straight-sided skillet. When the bacon is beginning to brown, stir the flour and chili powder together in a large bowl, then toss the beef cubes in the seasoned flour to coat. When the bacon is crisp, transfer to a bowl with a slotted spoon

FILLING

½ pound (225 g) thick cut, smoked bacon, diced (about 1 cup)

¼ cup (30 g) all-purpose flour

1 tablespoon chili powder (ancho chile powder, if available)

1 pound (450 g) sirloin tips, cut into 1-inch dice

1 tablespoon olive oil, if needed

2 medium onions (285 g), diced (about 2 cups)

2 medium carrots (140 g), diced (about 1 cup)

2 stalks celery (140 g), diced (about 1 cup)

¾ teaspoon kosher salt

½ teaspoon freshly ground black pepper

½ cup (120 ml) strong black coffee

1½ cups (360 ml) beef stock

¼ cup (15 g) chopped fresh flat-leaf parsley

and turn up the heat. Working in small batches, shake the excess flour off the beef and brown the pieces in the bacon fat. Transfer the beef to the bowl with the bacon.

There should be sufficient bacon fat still in the pan, but if not, add the olive oil. Add the onions, turn the heat to medium, and cook until wilted and translucent. Add the carrots and celery and toss them around to coat with the oil. Salt and pepper are next, and stir again to keep coating the vegetables. Cook for 3 to 4 minutes, until the celery begins to soften.

Turn the heat to medium-high and pour in the black coffee. Scrape up all the brown bits in the bottom of the pan as the coffee bubbles away. Add the beef and bacon and the stock, stir well, and bring to a boil. Reduce the heat and cook uncovered and bubbling slowly for 30 minutes. Give it a lazy stir from time to time. Remove from the heat and stir in the parsley. Taste and add more salt or pepper, if needed, keeping in mind the seasoning should be assertive. Cool the stew thoroughly.

Heat the oven to 425°F; if you have one, place a baking stone, Baking Steel, or inverted baking sheet on the center rack to heat (see page 4).

Spoon the filling into the bottom crust and gently spread it out, pushing it into the corners. Drape the top crust over the filling. Crimp and slash. Bake the pie (on top of the steel, stone, or baking sheet if using) for 20 minutes. Reduce the temperature to 375°F and bake until the top is toasty brown and the filling is bubbling up out of the slashes, about 45 minutes longer. Cool slightly before serving.

Techniques: Lard or Leaf Lard Crust (page 45), Mixing and Rolling Out (page 14), Crimp and Slash (page 24)

Swaps:

- Use Butter and Shortening (page 33) or Caramelized Onion Crust (page 42).

- Substitute leftover roast beef, shredded cooked brisket, or browned ground beef.

- Cover with a Potato Mash (page 77) instead of a top crust.

SAVOR A PIE

MOROCCAN-STYLE SHEPHERD'S SLAB PIE

WITH AN OLIVE OIL CRUST

Serves 12 to 18

Spicy, minted ground lamb and carrots are cloaked in a cloud of mashed potatoes for a new take on shepherd's pie. The olive oil press-in crust means this meal is ready in under an hour with no rolling pin. The spice mix will make a little jar full of goodness, more than needed for the recipe, and such a good addition to the pantry. Harissa, a chile paste sold in tubes or jars (found in the international foods aisle, or near the ketchup, at many grocery stores) can have widely varying chile heat, so taste it before dolloping it into the sauce willy-nilly! It's a kicky chile heat-bomb that will find a happy place in your kitchen arsenal. Some people use it like ketchup, but I'm more likely to use it anywhere I might reach for tomato paste.

Make Ahead: The filling may be made a day ahead. The crust may be made several hours in advance and refrigerated. The potatoes may be boiled and mashed a day ahead. Whip them again before piling fluffy potato clouds all over the pie.

OLIVE OIL CRUST

1⅔ cups (200 g)
all-purpose flour

1½ teaspoons kosher salt

1½ teaspoons sweet
smoked paprika

⅔ cup (156 ml) mild
olive oil

2 tablespoons plus
2 teaspoons water

FILLING

2 pounds (900 g) ground
lamb, preferably from the
shoulder

(Continued)

For the crust: Heat the oven to 350°F; if you have one, place a baking stone, Baking Steel, or inverted baking sheet on the center rack to heat (see page 4). Stir together the flour, salt, and paprika in a medium bowl using a fork. With the same fork, whisk the olive oil and water in a small bowl until combined and smooth. Make a well in the flour mixture and pour in the oil mixture. Using the fork, draw the flour into the oil, turning the bowl at the same time. Be patient, it will come together as a wet dough. Gather the ball of dough with your hands and plop it into the slab pie pan.

Pinch off pieces of dough to first build the sides of the crust up. Make the edge about ¼ inch thick and as high as the sides of the pan. Work all the way around, then use the heel of your hand to spread the remaining dough along the bottom of the pan. Be deliberate. It takes time and patience to press the dough across the pan evenly. Blind bake the crust (on top of the steel, stone, or baking sheet if using) for 20 minutes; there is no need to pierce the dough or weight it.

(Continued)

2 medium onions (285 g), cut into ½-inch dice (about 2 cups)

3 garlic cloves, minced

1 teaspoon fresh ginger, grated

4 teaspoons Moroccan Spice Mix (recipe follows)

1 pound (450 g) carrots, cut into slim 2- by ½-inch sticks (about 2 cups)

2 tablespoons harissa

2 tablespoons tomato paste

1 teaspoon kosher salt

¼ cup (15 g) chopped fresh mint

TOPPING

2½ pounds (1.14 kg) russet potatoes, peeled and cut into chunks

1 teaspoon kosher salt, plus extra for boiling

3 tablespoons (42 g) unsalted butter, cubed

½ teaspoon coarsely ground black pepper

¼ cup (60 ml) whole milk

Increase the oven temperature to 400°F.

For the filling: Brown the lamb in a large skillet over medium-high heat, using two wooden spoons to break up any clumps. Spoon the meat into a bowl with a slotted spoon. Pour off and discard all but 3 tablespoons of the fat from the pan. Add the onions and cook until wilted, about 5 minutes. Stir in the garlic, ginger, and spice mix. Cook until the spices release their amazing scent, another minute or so. Add the carrots and stir them around in all the onions and spices. Cook for 2 or 3 minutes, then spoon in the harissa, tomato paste, and salt and blend well with a sturdy spoon. Return the lamb to the pan, reduce the heat, and let the filling simmer to mix the flavors together and soften the carrots, about 10 minutes. Remove from the heat and stir in the mint. Cool the filling.

For the topping: Add the potatoes to a medium saucepan and cover with cool water and a big pinch of salt. Place the cover on the pot and boil over high heat until the potatoes are fork-tender and soft, 12 to 15 minutes. Drain all the water from the pan, leaving the potatoes, un-cover, and let them steam for 5 minutes to dry out. Mash the potatoes with a stand mixer fitted with the whisk attachment, a hand mixer, or a good old handheld masher, adding the butter, salt, and pepper. Pour in the milk slowly, whipping all the time, until the potatoes are smooth and velvety and not too stiff.

Spoon the lamb filling into the crust and spread it out from edge to edge. Dollop the potato topping across the top. Gently spread the potatoes from edge to edge leaving none of the filling exposed. Slide the pie into the oven (on top of the steel, stone, or baking sheet if using) and bake for 40 minutes, until the peaks of the potato topping are beginning to brown. Serve warm.

Techniques: Press-In Crusts (page 55), Olive Oil Crust (page 56), Blind Baking (page 29), Potato Mash (page 77)

Swaps:

• Substitute ground beef for the ground lamb.

• Add mashed celery root to the potato topping.

• Switch it up and mash sweet potatoes instead.

MOROCCAN SPICE MIX

Makes about 5 tablespoons

1 tablespoon
coriander seeds

1 tablespoon cumin seeds

1 tablespoon anise or
fennel seeds

1 tablespoon ground
cinnamon

2 teaspoons turmeric

½ teaspoon cayenne

Moroccan spices hold the dusky scents of the *souk*, transforming the ordinary into a holiday. Sprinkle over scrambled eggs, yogurt, or avocado toast, or mix into a lamb and feta burger. If neither a spice grinder nor mortar and pestle is available, simply use the unground mixture, making sure to scoop both the ground and whole spices when measuring.

Dry toast the coriander, cumin, and anise seeds in a small skillet over high heat until fragrant, 3 or 4 minutes.

Grind the seeds in a spice grinder or crush in a mortar and pestle and transfer the powder to a glass jar. Add the cinnamon, turmeric, and cayenne, cover, and shake to blend. Store this mix in the jar, at room temperature, for up to 6 months.

LAMB VINDALOO SLAB PIE

WITH A CARAMELIZED ONION CRUST

Serves 12 to 15

Whenever I eat at an Indian restaurant, I may crave the belly-warming sauces and the sultry Indian spices, but it's the breads I devour. The flatbread naan, when studded with sweet, long-cooked onions, is one of my favorites. Like that lovely bread, the caramelized onion crust here complements the complex sweet and sour flavors of vindaloo. If you are lucky enough to have a butcher, request lamb shoulder; or, because the shoulder may be difficult to locate, lamb leg is a fine option. I'm partial to spicy fillings, particularly with this savory crust, so I add serrano to the filling with a casual devil-may-care attitude. You may wish to be more circumspect.

Make Ahead: The filling may be made and frozen up to 3 months ahead. Defrost in the refrigerator overnight. The vindaloo sauce may be made up to 1 week ahead. Keep refrigerated.

CARAMELIZED ONION CRUST

2½ cups plus
2 tablespoons (325 g)
all-purpose flour

16 tablespoons (225 g)
Onion Butter (page 44)

½ teaspoon kosher salt

½ cup (120 ml) ice water

FILLING

¼ cup vegetable oil

1 pound (455 g) lamb
shoulder or leg, cut into
1-inch chunks

Vindaloo Sauce
(recipe follows)

(Continued)

For the crust: In the food processor, pulse the flour, onion butter, and salt until the butter is in small pieces coated with flour, about 15 times. Add the water all at once and process until the mixture almost forms a ball. Form the dough into a 6- by 4-inch rectangle using plastic wrap and a bench scraper to firmly press the dough into a cohesive form. Wrap tightly and refrigerate a minimum of 4 hours.

Remove the dough from the refrigerator and allow it to warm slightly. Divide the dough into two pieces, one slightly larger than the other. Roll out the larger piece to 11 by 15 inches and place in the slab pie pan, pressing it into the corners of the pan and allowing the excess to drape over the sides. Refrigerate. Roll out the second piece of dough to 10 by 14 inches, place it on a lightly floured sheet of parchment, and refrigerate.

For the filling: Heat the oil in a large skillet over medium-high heat until it begins to shimmer. Add the lamb chunks a few at a time and turn them quickly to brown on all sides, 3 to 5 minutes per batch. Remove the lamb as it browns, place in a bowl, and add the vindaloo sauce.

(Continued)

1 medium onion (142 g), chopped (about 1 cup)

4 medium carrots (225 g), chopped (about 1 cup)

½ teaspoon minced seeded serrano chile, optional

1 cup (225 g) diced cooked potato (about 2 large russets)

1 cup (175 g) frozen peas

Add the onion to the pan and cook until translucent. Add the carrots, stir to coat, and cook until slightly tender, 5 or 6 minutes longer. Finally, add the lamb with the sauce and the serrano, if using. Bring the mixture to a boil and turn down until it's gently bubbling. Cook uncovered until thickened and saucy, about 30 minutes. Add the cooked potatoes and peas and stir well. Remove the pan from the heat and cool the filling completely.

Heat the oven to 425°F; if you have one, place a baking stone, Baking Steel, or inverted baking sheet on the center rack to heat (see page 4).

Bring the bottom crust out of the refrigerator. Spoon the filling into the bottom crust and spread it from edge to edge and into the corners, smoothing the surface. Place the top crust over the filling. Crimp and slash or stamp out three circles from the top crust before placing it over the filling.

Bake the pie (on top of the steel, stone, or baking sheet if using) for 20 minutes. Reduce the temperature to 375°F and bake until deeply browned and smelling sensational, 30 to 35 minutes more.

Techniques: Caramelized Onion Crust (page 42), Mixing and Rolling Out (page 14), Crimp and Slash (page 24)

Swaps:

- Use a single-crust All-Butter (page 30) or a Saltine Crust (page 61) with a potato chip crush topper.

- Go vegetarian with one 15-ounce can of chickpeas and one 15-ounce can of crushed tomatoes in place of the lamb.

- Trade cubed boneless, skinless chicken thighs for the lamb.

VINDALOO SAUCE

Makes about 1¼ cups

1 head plump garlic

1 tablespoon grapeseed oil

1 tablespoon water

2 tablespoons honey

1 tablespoon tomato paste

1 tablespoon smoked paprika

1 teaspoon salt

1 teaspoon ground ginger

1 teaspoon ground cinnamon

½ teaspoon ground cumin

¼ to ½ teaspoon cayenne pepper

⅛ teaspoon ground cloves

½ cup (120 ml) cider vinegar

¼ cup (60 ml) water

All of this sauce will be used in the lamb filling. Make more and try it with chicken, tofu, or fish.

Heat the oven to 350°F (if you have a toaster oven, use it). Slice the top off the head of garlic, exposing the tops of the cloves. Place the garlic on a sheet of foil and drizzle the oil and 1 tablespoon water over the cut surface. Wrap tightly in the foil. Bake until the individual garlic cloves are soft and fork-tender, about 45 minutes.

Carefully, because it will be hot, unwrap the head of garlic and squeeze the soft, sweet paste out into a large bowl. Discard the spent hulls. To the roasted garlic paste, whisk in the honey, tomato paste, paprika, salt, ginger, cinnamon, cumin, cayenne, and cloves to make a paste. Whisk in the vinegar and ¼ cup water and continue to whisk until the sauce is smooth and emulsified.

The sauce may be made up to 1 week in advance. Keep covered and refrigerated until ready to use.

HAM AND GRUYÈRE SLAB PIE

WITH AN ALL-BUTTER CRUST

Serves 10 to 20

A devilishly rich pie, a slimmer version of quiche with fewer eggs and more add-ins. It's perfect for brunch, lunch, or cocktail hour—whether cut in small squares or hearty servings. The custard is studded with sweet baked ham and nutty cheese and two ingredients that set it apart: a swipe of mustard on the bottom crust and a dab of honey in the custard.

Make Ahead: With the exception of the pie dough, this is a make-at-the-last-minute pie.

ALL-BUTTER CRUST

2½ cups plus
2 tablespoons (325 g)
all-purpose flour

16 tablespoons (225 g)
unsalted butter, cubed and
frozen for 20 minutes

¼ teaspoon kosher salt

½ cup (120 ml) ice water

(Continued)

For the crust: In the food processor, pulse the flour, butter, and salt until the fats are in small pieces coated with flour, about 15 times. Add the water all at once and process until the mixture almost forms a ball. Form the dough into a 6- by 4-inch rectangle using plastic wrap and a bench scraper to firmly press the dough into a cohesive form. Wrap tightly and refrigerate a minimum of 4 hours.

Remove the dough from the refrigerator and allow it to warm slightly. Divide the dough into two pieces, one slightly larger than the other. Roll out the larger piece to 11 by 15 inches and place in the slab pie pan, pressing it into the corners of the pan and allowing the excess to drape over the sides. Refrigerate. Roll out the second piece of dough to 10 by 14 inches, place it on a lightly floured sheet of parchment, and refrigerate.

Heat the oven to 375°F; if you have one, place a baking stone, Baking Steel, or inverted baking sheet on the center rack to heat (see page 4).

(Continued)

FILLING

5 large eggs

1 cup (240 ml) half-and-half

3 tablespoons honey

1 tablespoon snipped fresh chives

1 teaspoon fresh thyme leaves

1 teaspoon kosher salt

3 tablespoons Dijon mustard (smooth, grainy, or coarse)

8 ounces (225 g) sliced smoked ham, chopped

8 ounces (225 g) Gruyère cheese, grated (about 2 cups)

For the filling: Whisk the eggs and half-and-half until frothy. Add the honey, chives, thyme, and salt and whisk again. Spread the mustard thickly across the bottom crust. Scatter the ham and cheese evenly across the mustard, and pour in the egg mixture. Cover with the top crust and crimp and slash. Bake (on top of the steel, stone, or baking sheet if using) until a knife plunged into the center of the custard comes out clean, 40 to 45 minutes.

Techniques: All-Butter Crust (page 30), Mixing and Rolling Out (page 14), Crimp and Slash (page 24)

Swaps:

- Use an Olive Oil Crust (page 56) with no topper.

- Any melty cheese, any cooked vegetable, or any other protein may be substituted for the ham and cheese.

CARBONARA ZOODLE SLAB PIE

WITH AN OLIVE OIL CRUST

Serves 16 to 20

The spiralizer is a vegetable-transforming noodle-making kitchen gadget that converts zucchini (and more) into long curly strips that resemble noodles visually, but in no other way. A zoodle is not a noodle, but it is an entertaining way to present a vegetable, as are the beautiful slim sticks from a mandoline, or the thick ribbons from a vegetable peeler. There is delight, pleasure—and a good portion of personal satisfaction—in transforming a lowly green zucchini into something so adorable. In this pie, I've smothered the summer squash with the creamy, bacon-y, eggy, cheesy goodness of a classic carbonara sauce and baked it all in an olive oil crust. It's a brunch dish, a supper dish, a week of take-to-work-for-lunch meals.

Make Ahead: The crust may be made several hours ahead.

OLIVE OIL CRUST

1⅔ cups (200 g) all-purpose flour

1½ teaspoons kosher salt

⅔ cup (156 ml) mild olive oil

2 tablespoons plus 2 teaspoons water

FILLING

¾ pound (340 g) thick-sliced smoked bacon, chopped into 1-inch chunks

1¾ pounds (790 g) medium zucchini

3 tablespoons mild olive oil

(Continued)

For the crust: Heat the oven to 350°F; if you have one, place a baking stone, Baking Steel, or inverted baking sheet on the center rack to heat (see page 4).

Stir together the flour and salt in a large bowl with a table fork. Whisk the olive oil and water with the same fork. (I do this right in the measuring cup.) Make a well in the flour mixture and pour in the oil mixture. Using the fork, draw flour into the oil, turning the bowl at the same time. Once the dough starts to come together, switch to using your hands and gather the ball of dough and plop it into the slab pie pan.

Pinch off pieces of dough and build up the sides of the crust first. Make the edge about ¼ inch thick and as high as the sides of the pan. Work all the way around, then use a metal measuring cup or the heel of your hand to spread the remaining dough along the bottom of the pan, about ⅛ inch thick. Blind bake the crust for 20 minutes; there is no need to pierce the dough or weight it. Leave the oven on.

For the filling: Line a baking sheet with parchment to make cleanup easier and scatter the bacon pieces in a single layer. Bake the bacon for 20 to 30 minutes, until crisp. Transfer the crisped bacon with a slotted spoon to a large, deep mixing bowl. Do not obsess about

1 large shallot, minced (about 3 tablespoons)

8 ounces (225 g) Parmigiano Reggiano, finely grated (about 2 cups)

5 large eggs

1 cup (240 ml) whole milk

1 teaspoon kosher salt

1 teaspoon freshly ground black pepper

removing the bacon fat. In this case, whatever small amount clings to the crisped bacon flavors the filling.

Soak the whole zucchini in a bowl of ice water for 20 minutes. Trim the ends and use a spiral cutter to create long strands of zucchini noodles. If you don't have a spiral cutter, you can shred the zucchini on the largest holes of a box grater, use the grating disk on the food processor, peel swaths with a vegetable peeler, or use a mandoline's thick-julienne setting. I prefer the mandoline because the thick boxy pieces hold their shape and the eggy custard clings.

In a large, deep skillet, heat 1 tablespoon of the olive oil over medium heat until it shimmers. Add 1 tablespoon of the minced shallot. Cook, stirring for 1 minute. Add one-third of the zoodles to the pan and cook until just wilted, about 4 minutes. Scoop into the bowl with the bacon. Repeat this process twice until all the oil, shallot, and zucchini have been wilted. Cool, then scrape the zoodle bacon mixture into the baked crust and spread out to fill the corners. Sprinkle the cheese over the top.

Whisk the eggs, milk, salt, and pepper until frothy. Slowly, so it has time to disperse, pour the custard over and through the zoodle mixture. Slide the pan into the oven (on top of the steel, stone, or baking sheet if using) and bake until the custard is set and a knife plunged in the center comes out clean, 30 to 35 minutes. Once out of the oven, let the pie firm up for 5 minutes before slicing and serving.

Techniques: Press-In Crusts (page 55), Olive Oil Crust (page 56), Blind Baking (page 29)

Swaps:

- Blind bake (see page 29) a Leaf Lard (page 45) or Butter and Shortening Crust (page 33).

- Shred yellow squash, carrots, potatoes, or sweet potatoes instead of zucchini.

- Duck eggs are so rich and good in this (but you'll only need four).

- Amp up the authenticity factor with 1/2 pound of pancetta or guanciale instead of the bacon.

- Remove the bacon entirely for a vegetarian option; add a healthy pinch of smoked paprika to the egg mixture for a smoky flavor.

SAVOR A PIE

HAWAIIAN PIZZA SLAB PIE

WITH AN ALL-BUTTER CRUST

Serves 8 to 12

Why ask why? I love a good ham and pineapple pizza pie without reservation and I'll shout it from the rooftops. It's salty, it's sweet, it's textural, and...okay, it's too weird for many people. If you're on Team Hawaiian, jump into a lip-smacking pie with a buttery crust and plenty of cheese. Do I dare call it deep-dish slab pie?

Make Ahead: Make the sauce up to 3 days ahead. Bake the pie right before serving.

ALL-BUTTER CRUST

1⅓ cups (160 g) all-purpose flour

8 tablespoons (113 g) unsalted butter, cubed and frozen for 20 minutes

⅛ teaspoon kosher salt

¼ cup (60 ml) ice water

FILLING

¼ cup (60 ml) olive oil

2 garlic cloves, slivered

1 (25-ounce) can (709 g) crushed tomatoes

1 teaspoon dried oregano

1 teaspoon salt

½ teaspoon crushed red pepper

(Continued)

For the crust: In the food processor, pulse the flour, butter, and salt until the fats are in small pieces coated with flour, about 15 times. Add the water all at once and process until the mixture almost forms a ball. Form the dough into a rectangle 3 by 4 inches using plastic wrap and a bench scraper to firmly press the dough into a cohesive form. Wrap tightly and refrigerate a minimum of 4 hours.

Remove the dough from the refrigerator and allow it to warm slightly. Roll out the crust to 11 by 15 inches and place in the slab pie pan, pressing it into the corners and allowing the excess to drape over the sides. Refrigerate.

Heat the oven to 350°F; if you have one, place a baking stone, Baking Steel, or inverted baking sheet on the center rack to heat (see page 4).

For the filling: In a medium saucepan, warm the olive oil over medium heat until it shimmers. Add the garlic slivers and cook, stirring, for 30 seconds. Add the tomatoes, oregano, salt, and red pepper. Bring the mixture to a boil, reduce the heat, and cook the sauce with occasional bubbles on the surface until slightly thickened, about 20 minutes.

(Continued)

**2 cups (225 g) diced
smoked ham**

**2 cups (280 g) pineapple,
in rings or diced**

**8 ounces (225 g) fresh
mozzarella cheese, torn
into small pieces**

Scatter the ham and pineapple across the chilled crust and pour in the tomato sauce. Dot evenly with mozzarella. Bake the pie (on top of the steel, stone, or baking sheet if using) until the filling is hot, 35 to 40 minutes. Change the oven to broil (high) and broil until the top is blistered and browned, like a pizza, 4 to 7 minutes.

Serve hot.

Techniques: All-Butter Crust (page 30), Mixing and Rolling Out (page 14)

Swaps:

- Anything that works on a pizza works here: olives and artichokes; peppers and onions; pepperoni; more cheese.
- Spike the sauce with crushed red pepper.
- Top with piles of pan-roasted mushrooms or sausage or anchovies.

ENGLISH-STYLE PORK SLAB PIE

WITH A HOT WATER CRUST

Serves 16 to 20

Pork pie is so ubiquitous in Britain that a hat was modeled on its classic shape. Often served with pickles and mustard and appearing in butcher shops, on pub menus, and in Dorothy Sayers mysteries, these pies differ from an American meat pie in a few striking ways. The hot water crust is more sturdy than flaky, but it's gloriously shiny and incredibly easy to shape and crimp. Rolling it on a silicone baking pad (Silpat) or parchment will make the transfer to the pan much easier. In this case, the filling is raw when sealed inside the crust, and rather than a flour or cornstarch-based gravy, relies on the addition of gelatin after baking to form a seal around the filling, keeping the dough from becoming soggy. Because the gelatin is a distinct player in the pie, use excellent, preferably homemade, stock in the preparation. The crust is a little tricky and demands quick and efficient work to be successful, and pouring in the liquefied gelatin is not for the faint of heart (and you'll need a small funnel), but it's well worth the effort. The English know things about pie.

Make Ahead: The pie should be made in one fell swoop as it's hot crust touching raw meat; however, the pie is truly the most delicious the day after it's baked. The flavors develop after a rest, so make it at least a day ahead, or even two. The pie keeps very well for 3 or 4 days.

FILLING

2 pounds (900 g) ground pork

½ pound (225 g) thick-cut smoked bacon, finely chopped

1 medium onion (142 g), finely chopped (about 1 cup)

½ cup (30 g) fresh flat-leaf parsley, roughly chopped

(Continued)

Heat the oven to 400°F; if you have one, place a baking stone, Baking Steel, or inverted baking sheet on the center rack to heat (see page 4).

For the filling: Stir together the pork, bacon, onion, parsley, salt, pepper, and sage.

For the crust: Lightly dust a Silpat (silicone baking mat) or parchment paper with flour. Combine the flours and salt in a large, deep bowl. Rub the butter and lard into the flours with your floured fingertips until the mixture is coarse and sandy. Pour the boiling water over the mixture and beat with a firm wooden spoon. As soon as the dough is smooth, tip it out onto the Silpat. Form a ball and let it rest

1½ teaspoons kosher salt

1 teaspoon coarsely ground black pepper

½ teaspoon rubbed sage

HOT WATER CRUST

2¼ cups (265 g) all-purpose flour, plus more for dusting

½ cup (60 g) bread flour

1 teaspoon kosher salt

6 tablespoons (78 g) rendered lard or leaf lard, cubed and cold but not frozen

4 tablespoons (56 g) unsalted butter, cubed and cold but not frozen

½ cup (120 ml) boiling water

Egg yolk

1 tablespoon (7 g) (one ¼-ounce packet) plain, powdered gelatin

1 cup (240 ml) chicken stock, preferably homemade

until slightly cooler, about 5 minutes. If there are any flour lumps, knead it further. Divide the dough into two pieces, one slightly larger than the other.

Work quickly: If the dough cools, it will become stiff, brittle, and difficult. Roll the larger piece of dough to 11 by 15 inches. Transfer it to the slab pie pan and press into the corners allowing any excess to drape over the edges. Fill the bottom crust with the pork filling carefully and thoroughly, trying to pack the meat mixture into the pan and avoiding air pockets. Smooth the filling with an offset spatula. Beat the egg yolk and brush it over the edges of the bottom crust.

Roll out the top crust on the Silpat to 10 by 14 inches and transfer it to the pan, draping it over the filling. Trim the top and bottom crusts to ½ inch beyond the edge of the pan. Crimp, pinch, or otherwise get decorative with the edges, making certain the top and bottom crusts are completely sealed. Take the trimmings and make decorative pieces for the top of the pie. I like to put a leaf or a pair of leaves on each serving. Using a small (½-inch) cookie cutter or the bottom of a pastry tip or a chopstick, pierce a hole through the top crust for each portion of pie. Brush the top crust and edges generously with the rest of the egg yolk. Get that pie in the oven (on top of the steel, stone, or baking sheet if using). Bake for 50 minutes, until deeply golden brown and the filling is bubbling under the steam vents.

Cool the pie on a wire rack for no more than 5 or 10 minutes. Put the gelatin in the bottom of a heat proof measuring cup or another pitcher with a spout. Bring the stock to a boil and stir it into the gelatin. Using the funnel, gently pour about a teaspoon of the hot gelatin into each of the holes in the top crust. Allow the pie to cool, then chill for 2 hours, or overnight, before serving. Don't forget the mustard.

Techniques: Hot Water Crust (page 54), Crimp and Slash (page 24), Lattices, Cutouts, Stamps, and Shapes (page 26)

Swaps:

• There are no crust substitutions for an English-style pie.

• For a variation on this pie, with holiday-spiced filling, see the Christmas in London Slab Pie on page 188.

SAVOR A PIE

CHRISTMAS IN LONDON SLAB PIE

WITH A HOT WATER CRUST

Serves 12 to 16

Another proper British tradition is the Christmas pie. Similar to the Pork Slab Pie (page 185) in execution, but slightly different in the filling, this is redolent with herbs, spices, and meaty goodness. The Canadians give this concept a French twist with the holiday *tourtière*. The French make *pâté en croute*, a meaty filling surrounded by sturdy crust. Make this pie inspired by every tradition, then make a few of your own. I like to imagine serving a piece to Scrooge.

Make Ahead: Make this pie in one sitting. It will keep for 3 or 4 days, once cooked, and the flavors are best after resting for at least one day.

FILLING

¾ pound (355 g) russet potatoes, peeled (about 2)

Kosher salt

1½ pounds (680 kg) ground pork

1 pound (456 g) ground venison or lean beef or veal

1 medium onion (142 g), finely chopped (about 1 cup)

1 medium apple (112 g), cored but not peeled, finely chopped (about 1 cup)

2 carrots (170 g), finely chopped (about 1 cup)

½ cup (30 g) fresh flat-leaf parsley, roughly chopped

(Continued)

Heat the oven to 400°F; if you have one, place a baking stone, Baking Steel, or inverted baking sheet on the center rack to heat (see page 4).

For the filling: Cut the potatoes into large chunks. Fill a medium saucepan with water and add ½ teaspoon salt and the potatoes. Boil until fork-tender, about 12 to 15 minutes. Drain, mash in the pot (a few lumps never hurt the pie), and set aside. Combine the pork, venison, onion, apple, carrots, parsley, thyme, 1½ teaspoons salt, pepper, cinnamon, allspice, and mace in a large bowl.

For the crust: Lightly dust a Silpat (silicone baking mat) or parchment paper with flour. Combine the flours and salt in a large, deep bowl. Rub the butter and lard into the flours with your floured fingertips until the mixture is coarse and sandy. Pour the boiling water over the mixture and beat with a firm wooden spoon. As soon as the dough is smooth, tip it out onto the Silpat. Form a ball and let it rest until slightly cooler, about 5 minutes. If there are any flour lumps, knead it further. Divide the dough into two pieces, one slightly larger than the other.

(Continued)

2 teaspoons fresh thyme
leaves

1 teaspoon coarsely
ground black pepper

½ teaspoon ground
cinnamon

¼ teaspoon allspice

⅛ teaspoon mace

HOT WATER CRUST

2¼ cups (265 g)
all-purpose flour

½ cup (60 g) bread flour

1 teaspoon kosher salt

4 tablespoons (56 g)
unsalted butter, cubed and
cold but not frozen

6 tablespoons (65 g)
rendered lard or leaf lard,
cubed and cold but not
frozen

½ cup (120 ml) boiling
water

Egg yolk

1 tablespoon (7 g) (one
¼-ounce packet) plain,
powdered gelatin

1 cup (240 ml) beef stock

Work quickly: If the dough cools, it will become stiff, brittle, and difficult. Roll the larger piece of dough to 11 by 15 inches. Transfer it to the slab pie pan and press into the corners allowing any excess to drape over the edges. Fill the bottom crust with the filling, carefully and thoroughly trying to pack the meat mixture into the pan and avoiding air pockets. Smooth the filling with an offset spatula. Beat the egg yolk and brush it over the edges of the bottom crust.

Roll out the top crust on the Silpat to 10 by 14 inches and place it over the filling. Trim the top and bottom crusts to ½ inch beyond the edge of the pan. Crimp, pinch, or otherwise get decorative with the edges, making certain the top and bottom crusts are completely sealed. Take the trimmings and make decorative pieces for the top of the pie. I like to put a leaf or a pair of leaves on each serving. Using a small (½-inch) cookie cutter or the bottom of a pastry tip or a chopstick, pierce a hole through the top crust for each portion of pie. Brush the top crust and edges generously with the rest of the egg yolk. Get that pie in the oven (on top of the steel, stone, or baking sheet if using). Bake for 50 minutes, until deeply golden brown and the filling is bubbling under the steam vents.

Cool the pie on a wire rack for no more than 5 or 10 minutes. Put the gelatin in the bottom of a heatproof measuring cup or a pitcher with a spout. Bring the stock to a boil and add it to the gelatin. Stir well and, using a funnel, gently pour about a teaspoon of the hot gelatin into each hole in the top crust. Allow the pie to cool. Chill the pie for 2 hours, or overnight, before serving. Don't forget the mustard.

Techniques: Hot Water Crust (page 54), Crimp and Slash (page 24), Lattices, Cutouts, Stamps, and Shapes (page 26)

Swaps:

• Venison or elk make a splendid pie but lean ground beef is a good substitute.

SAVOR A PIE

EGGS FLORENTINE SLAB PIE

WITH A HASH BROWN CRUST

Serves 8 to 10

Sometime in the 1980s, I developed a deep and abiding love for eggs Florentine: It's the creamy spinach stirred together with a runny egg yolk. That sumptuous mixture was precisely the inspiration for this breakfast pie. It's what you want on a snowy morning—slightly wobbly coddled eggs basted with cream in a delicious roasted potato crust whose scent means carrying the pie from oven to table is a moment worthy of everyone's attention. Because nearly everyone likes bacon, scatter crispy bits across the top. All that, and it's gluten-free, too. Do not use a convection oven as a breeze wafting over the eggs results in a weird, rubbery texture.

Make Ahead: This pie is not suitable for making ahead of time.

½ pound (225 g) smoked bacon, chopped, optional

HASH BROWN CRUST

1 medium onion (142 g), peeled

1½ pounds (680 g) russet potatoes (about 4), scrubbed but not peeled

1 large egg plus 1 egg white, beaten

1 teaspoon kosher salt

½ teaspoon coarsely ground black pepper

2 tablespoons neutral oil like canola or grapeseed (if not using bacon fat)

(Continued)

Heat the oven to 350°F. Scatter the bacon across the slab pie pan, and bake for 15 to 20 minutes, until crispy. With a slotted spoon, transfer the bacon to a paper towel–lined plate and drain. Do not dispose of the bacon fat, but pour some into a small bowl and leave the rest in the pan. Increase the oven temperature to 425°F; if you have one, place a baking stone, Baking Steel, or inverted baking sheet on the center rack to heat (see page 4).

For the crust: Grate the onion on the medium holes of a box grater or a food processor's grating disk (my preference). Place the onions in a medium mixing bowl. Grate the potatoes on the large holes side of the box grater, and, taking a handful at a time, squeeze the shreds over a small bowl. As each handful is squeezed, place in the bowl with the onions. Continue until all the potatoes have been grated and their liquid squeezed out. Work quickly to keep the potatoes from turning brown. You should have about 4 cups of dry-ish potatoes in the end.

Let the potato liquid sit for about 5 minutes, until the starch and liquid separate. Pour off the liquid, keeping the starchy white paste at the bottom. That's potato starch and we love it. Add the starch to the grated onions and potatoes, then add the egg and egg white, salt, and

FILLING

1 (16-ounce) bag frozen chopped spinach (453 g), defrosted and the liquid squeezed out

4 tablespoons (56 g) unsalted butter

1 medium yellow onion (140 g), chopped into ½-inch dice (about 1 cup)

¼ teaspoon nutmeg

1 cup (240 ml) heavy cream

1 teaspoon salt

½ teaspoon freshly ground black pepper

8 large eggs (or see Swaps)

½ cup (120 ml) heavy cream

TOPPING

4 tablespoons grated Pecorino cheese

2 tablespoons chopped chives

pepper and stir with your hands. If bacon fat is not present on the baking sheet, brush the neutral oil into the corners and across the bottom of the pan. Firmly press the potato mixture into the pan using the sides of your hand and your knuckles. Brush the surface of the potatoes with bacon fat. Bake (on top of the steel, stone, or baking sheet if using) until the potatoes have started to turn brown, 35 to 45 minutes.

For the filling: Use your hands (or a colander and a firm wooden spoon) to squeeze the liquid out of the spinach. The drier the spinach, the less time is required to cook it, which keeps the flavor fresh and green and not metallic.

In a large, wide sauté pan, melt the butter over medium heat until frothy. Add the diced onions and cook until translucent, about 7 minutes. Turn up the heat, add the spinach, and cook until the mixture is nearly dry, another 5 to 7 minutes. Grate nutmeg over the spinach and add the cream, salt, and pepper. Cook, stirring over medium heat, until slightly thickened, 5 to 7 minutes more.

When the potato crust is baked and all crispy and browned, spread the spinach filling thickly over the top. Use the bottom of a ladle to form 8 wells in the spinach mixture and crack an egg into each divot. Spoon a tablespoon of cream over each egg.

Scatter the crispy bacon bits all across the pie. Slip the pan back in the oven and bake for 12 to 15 minutes, until the eggs' whites are cooked through. Remove the pan from the oven and sprinkle with the Pecorino and chives. Serve right away.

Technique: Hash Brown Crust (page 67)

Swaps:

- Eight large eggs fit easily. If you need to stretch to accommodate a crowd, you can fit ten small eggs or 18 quail eggs.

- Swap out half the russets for sweet potatoes. In a pinch, defrost frozen shredded potatoes.

- Instead of bacon, drape thin, translucent pieces of *jamon Iberico*, country ham, or prosciutto over the hot eggs when they emerge from the oven. Or opt for smoked salmon, trout, or fresh crab.

- To serve vegetarians, simply omit the hammy bits.

SAUSAGE AND BISCUIT SLAB PIE

WITH A RITZ CRACKER CRUST

Serves 12 to 24

I'm a fan of brunch at home, not out at a restaurant, and slab pies fit the brunch bill, especially when you'd rather be hanging out with your friends than spending time in the kitchen. Here is the classic Southern breakfast, sausage and biscuits, brought to the table in pie form. Use any favorite breakfast sausage. I choose one from a farmer I know—sweet, with a maple undercurrent. But from time to time, I'll opt for a zippy alternative, one full of sage and crushed red pepper. Whichever way your breakfast preferences lean, this slab is comforting and delicious.

Make Ahead: Make the cracker crust and the gravy ahead. Make the biscuits no more than 30 minutes ahead and refrigerate the pie until ready to bake.

RITZ CRACKER CRUST

60 Ritz crackers (about 2 cups crushed) (225 g)

8 tablespoons (113 g) unsalted butter or margarine, cubed, at room temperature

FILLING

1 pound (455 g) breakfast sausage, removed from the casings

3 tablespoons all-purpose flour

1 cup (240 ml) black coffee

1⅓ cups (320 ml) whole milk

1 teaspoon kosher salt

(Continued)

For the crust: Heat the oven to 350°F; if you have one, place a baking stone, Baking Steel, or inverted baking sheet on the center rack to heat (see page 4). Place the crackers in a ziptop bag and bash them with a rolling pin until they are in crumbs and small shards, but not powdered. Pour the crumbs into a medium bowl, add the butter cubes, and knead and work the cracker crumbs until a cohesive dough appears. Press the dough across the bottom of the slab pie pan and carefully into the corners and, if you have enough, up the sides. Bake the crust (on top of the steel, stone, or baking sheet if using) for 20 to 25 minutes, until browned in the corners and on the edges. Cool completely on a rack.

For the filling: In a large skillet, cook the sausage over medium heat, breaking it apart with two wooden spoons. When the pink is gone, scatter the flour over the meat and increase the heat to toast and brown the flour and the meaty bits. Keep stirring until the flour is well browned, about 3 minutes. Pour in the coffee and increase the heat to high while scraping up all the good bits stuck to the bottom of the pan. When the coffee has reduced by half, another 3 minutes or so, reduce the heat and add the milk and salt. Stir non-stop as the

BISCUITS

5 cups (600 g) White Lily flour (not self-rising), plus more for dusting

1 tablespoon baking powder

1 tablespoon kosher salt

8 tablespoons (113 g) unsalted butter, frozen

1 cup (240 ml) buttermilk, cold

2 tablespoons (28 g) melted butter

mixture comes to a boil and thickens, about 4 minutes more. When it is a saucy gravy, like heavy cream, remove the pan from the heat.

For the biscuits: Heat the oven to 475°F. Have a bench scraper close at hand and generously dust the counter with flour. In the bowl of the food processor, weigh the flour, then add the baking powder and salt. Set the bowl on the processor base, place the metal blade, and cut in the frozen butter, pulsing 12 times. Add the buttermilk all at once and process just until a shaggy dough forms, only a minute or so.

Empty the dough, floury bits, and loose flour from the processor work bowl onto the counter. Use a bench scraper to gather the dough, pressing along the sides and patting the top gently, lifting and folding the dough over and patting it down, and evening the sides with the bench scraper. Continue to fold and pat 4 or 5 times, until a cohesive mass emerges. Press it out to a ½-inch thickness using your fingertips or a well-floured rolling pin.

Cut out 24 biscuits with a 1½-inch round cutter, or use the bench scraper to cut one-and-a-half-inch square biscuits. Discard the scraps.

Spoon the sausage gravy over the cracker crust, smooth, and top with the biscuits. Slide into the oven (on top of the steel, stone, or baking sheet if using) and bake for 12 to 15 minutes, until the biscuits are good and brown.

As soon as the pie comes out of the oven, generously brush the tops of the biscuits with the melted butter. Serve the pie hot.

Techniques: Cracker Crumb Crusts (page 61), Blind Baking (page 29), Baby Biscuits (page 87)

Swaps:

- Try it with a blind-baked (see page 29) Leaf Lard Crust (page 45).

- Add a big pinch of crushed red pepper to the gravy with the milk.

- Trade out the breakfast sausage for Italian mild sausage and substitute white wine for the coffee.

- For lofty, flaky biscuits, White Lily flour is the best choice, but all-purpose flour may be substituted.

SAVOR A PIE

Chapter Four

SWEETIE PIES

A SLICE OF PIE FOR BREAKFAST ON THE MORNING AFTER
Thanksgiving is a given. In fact, who among us hasn't
said, "It's fruit!" while shamelessly tucking into a
portion of apple pie? Whether it's a slice after dinner, a sliver in
passing, or a perfectly sensible breakfast, sweet pie is an all-day
pleasure. Here are fruit pies, chocolate pies, pies filled with nuts,
custards, and creams—all served up in a slab pie pan. Gather your
people. Any time is the right time for pie.

ANY-SEASON RASPBERRY SLAB PIE

WITH AN ALL-BUTTER CRUST

Serves 12

Make this in February and dream of summertime. Frozen raspberries are my go-to for this pie because even if I'm picking raspberries in a patch swollen with fruit, I love them so much I've never made it home with enough fruit to fill a pie. Freeze any peeled, pitted fruit in the summer months, 3 cups (340 g) in a ziptop bag, and you'll be ready to make a pie when the snow flies. All frozen fruits work ideally for pie, but as the fruit defrosts, it adds substantial liquid to the filling. So you'll want to use an open-work crust, lattice, or cutouts to offset the added moisture. While constructing the pie, work quickly and don't worry if the surface is lumpy with frozen snowballs of fruit. It will all work out in the oven.

Make Ahead: Assemble the pie and freeze it, unbaked, for up to a month. Bake it frozen, do not defrost, and add 5 minutes to the total baking time.

ALL-BUTTER CRUST

2½ cups plus 2 tablespoons (325 g) all-purpose flour

16 tablespoons (225 g) unsalted butter, cubed and frozen for 20 minutes

¼ teaspoon kosher salt

½ cup (120 ml) ice water

FILLING

1 cup (200 g) granulated sugar

¼ cup (28 g) cornstarch

(Continued)

For the crust: In the food processor, pulse the flour, butter, and salt until the butter is in small pieces coated with flour, about 15 times. Add the water all at once and process until the mixture almost forms a ball. Form the dough into a 6- by 4-inch rectangle using plastic wrap and a bench scraper to firmly press the dough into a cohesive form. Wrap tightly and refrigerate a minimum of 4 hours.

Remove the dough from the refrigerator and allow it to warm slightly. Divide the dough into two pieces, one slightly larger than the other. Roll out the larger piece to 11 by 15 inches and place in the slab pie pan, pressing it into the corners of the pan and allowing the excess to drape over the sides. Refrigerate. Roll out the second piece of dough to 10 by 14 inches, place on a lightly floured sheet of parchment, and refrigerate.

Heat the oven to 400°F; if you have one, place a baking stone, Baking Steel, or inverted baking sheet on the center rack to heat (see page 4).

(Continued)

3 cups (680 g) frozen
raspberries

1 tablespoon lemon juice

¼ cup (60 ml) Grand
Marnier, orange liqueur, or
freshly squeezed orange
juice

1 egg yolk

1 tablespoon water

2 tablespoons sparkling
sugar

For the filling: In a large mixing bowl, stir together the sugar and cornstarch. Add the raspberries and stir to coat. They may still be in icy chunks and that's okay. Add the lemon juice and Grand Marnier. Scrape every ounce of the filling into the chilled crust, remembering that as it cooks and melts it will settle into the corners.

Stamp cutouts from the top crust or form a lattice and place on top of the frozen fruit, making sure each piece touches another and touches the edges of the bottom crust which will help avoid curling or sinking during baking. Stir together the egg yolk and water. Dab the cutouts with a pastry brush dipped in the egg wash and sprinkle the entire surface generously with sparkling sugar. Slide the pie into the oven (on top of the steel, stone, or baking sheet if using) and bake for 45 to 55 minutes, until the surface is shiny golden brown and the filling is bubbling.

Cool before serving.

Techniques: All-Butter Crust (page 30), Mixing and Rolling Out (page 14), Crimp and Slash (page 24), Lattices, Cutouts, Stamps, and Shapes (page 26)

Swaps:

• Use a grocery store crust (see page 69) for instant gratification.

• Fruit combinations can be thrilling: Try rhubarb and cherries, blueberries and nectarines, raspberries and white peaches.

• Of course, you can make this pie with fresh raspberries, too.

FREEZING FRESH FRUIT

If you are lucky enough to have a berry patch or fruit tree in the back yard, it's likely you know that frozen fruit can taste as fresh as the day it's picked. If there's no berry patch in the back, scour summer's farmers' markets, pick-your-own orchards, and roadside stands for the sweetest, ripest fruit at the peak of freshness and the best price. It takes only a few minutes to freeze and it's ready for pie (or smoothies, cobblers, yogurt toppings, and more) in the depths of winter.

IQF—Individual Quick Freezing—is a fancy name for a simple, sensible technique. When shopping for frozen fruits and vegetables, look for packages marked "IQF" to find perfectly sliced peaches or individual strawberries.

To IQF at home, peel fruit that needs to be peeled and pit fruit that needs to be pitted. Line a baking sheet with parchment paper and spread the fruit out and freeze thoroughly. Once frozen, pack the fruit into ziptop bags, remove the air, and label and date the bag. I freeze in portions appropriate for a pie, but IQF means it's possible to scoop out as much or as little fruit as needed for a recipe.

MOSTLY RHUBARB AND JUST A LITTLE STRAWBERRY SLAB PIE

WITH A BUTTER AND SHORTENING CRUST

Serves 12 to 16

There was a big patch of rhubarb that grew at the edge of the farm adjacent to my childhood home. It sat neglected, so everyone in the neighborhood claimed it; we would take a penknife or garden clippers or leverage our weight against the massive stalks and yank them hard until they came out fast and we tumbled to the ground. Harvesting a handful of stalks each week, my mother and I made compote or pie again and again through the season. Rhubarb hits all my happy spots—the pucker, the pink, the way it melts down into the most perfectly textured pie filling. A few truly local, freshly gathered strawberries are jewels in the crown. The iconic chef and cookbook author Edna Lewis paired nutmeg with rhubarb and I think she was so right.

Make Ahead: Freeze a pie's worth of fresh, sliced rhubarb in ziptop bags. A rhubarb pie in February is a beautiful thing.

BUTTER AND SHORTENING CRUST

2½ cups plus 2 tablespoons (325 g) all-purpose flour

8 tablespoons (113 g) unsalted butter, cubed and frozen for 20 minutes

8 tablespoons (113 g) Spectrum or other vegetable shortening, cubed and frozen for 20 minutes

¼ teaspoon kosher salt

(Continued)

For the crust: In the food processor, pulse the flour, butter, shortening, and salt until the fats are in small pieces coated with flour, about 15 times. Add the ice water and vodka (if using) all at once and process until the mixture almost forms a ball. Form the dough into a 6- by 4-inch rectangle using plastic wrap and a bench scraper to firmly press the dough into a cohesive form. Wrap tightly and refrigerate a minimum of 4 hours.

Remove the dough from the refrigerator and allow it to warm slightly. Divide the dough into two pieces, one slightly larger than the other. Roll out the larger piece to 11 by 15 inches and place in the slab pie pan, pressing it into the corners of the pan and allowing the excess to drape over the sides. Refrigerate. Roll out the second piece of dough to 10 by 14 inches, place it on a lightly floured sheet of parchment, and refrigerate.

(Continued)

½ cup (120 ml) ice water

3 teaspoons vodka, optional

FILLING

1¾ pounds (790 g) rhubarb, cut into ½-inch slices (about 4½ cups)

1 pint (250 g) strawberries, hulled and diced (about 1½ cups)

¾ cup (150 g) granulated sugar

¼ cup (28 g) cornstarch

½ teaspoon freshly grated nutmeg

Juice of 1 lemon

2 tablespoons (28 g) cold unsalted butter, cubed

1 egg yolk

1 tablespoon water

2 tablespoons sparkling sugar

Heat the oven to 425°F; if you have one, place a baking stone, Baking Steel, or inverted baking sheet on the center rack to heat (see page 4).

For the filling: Combine the rhubarb, strawberries, sugar, cornstarch, nutmeg, and lemon juice in a large bowl. Spoon the filling into the bottom crust and dot with the butter. With the top crust, build a lattice. I like a Brawny Lattice topper (see page 28) here. Trim the pieces of lattice with a sharp kitchen scissors. Crimp the crust all the way around.

Whisk the yolk and water together with a fork and use a pastry brush to lightly paint the lattice. Sprinkle with the sparkling sugar. If there is time, freeze the pie for half an hour or more. Slide the pie into the oven (on top of the steel, stone, or baking sheet if using) and bake for 20 minutes. Reduce the temperature to 375°F and bake an additional 40 to 45 minutes, until the crust is browned and the filling is bubbling.

Cool before slicing.

Techniques: Butter and Shortening Crust (page 33), Mixing and Rolling (page 14), Crimp and Slash (page 24), Lattices, Cutouts, Stamps, and Shapes (page 26)

Swaps:

• For an all-rhubarb pie, replace the strawberries with sliced rhubarb, cup for cup or gram for gram.

• Use an All-Butter (page 30) or Leaf Lard Crust (page 45).

• Try the Shortbread Crust (page 59) with a streusel topping (page 85).

FROSTED STRAWBERRY SLAB PIE

WITH A CREAM CHEESE CRUST

Serves 15 to 18

This sparkly, frosted treat is more Pop-Tart than pie. It's a glittery, berry-filled marvel that will delight children and children at heart. The cream cheese crust is a tender wrap for a tart, bright, fruity filling. The sweet frosting is essential to balance the tart filling. Strawberries are notoriously difficult to bake into a pie—so juicy they are hard to corral. These tips will provide a path to success: Use barely ripe berries, on the verge of perfect ripeness. If they're too ripe the filling will be runny and difficult to manage. Chop the berries into small pieces. Have all the ingredients assembled and work quickly; as soon as the sugar hits the strawberries, the juices start to flow, and sealing the edges of the pie becomes increasingly challenging. Be sure to freeze the pie hard before baking. And don't scrimp on the sprinkles. This pie doesn't make a good leftover. Go ahead, have another piece.

Make Ahead: Up to 2 months ahead, assemble and freeze the pie, well wrapped. Bake it directly from the freezer.

CREAM CHEESE CRUST

2½ cups plus
2 tablespoons (325 g)
all-purpose flour

8 tablespoons (113 g)
unsalted butter, cubed and
chilled

8 tablespoons (113 g)
cream cheese, cubed and
refrigerated for 20 minutes

¼ teaspoon kosher salt

½ cup (120 ml) ice water

(Continued)

For the crust: In the food processor, pulse the flour, butter, cream cheese, and salt until the fats are in small pieces coated with flour, about 15 times. Add the ice water all at once and process until the mixture almost forms a ball. Form the dough into a 6- by 4-inch rectangle using plastic wrap and a bench scraper to firmly press the dough into a cohesive form. Wrap tightly and refrigerate a minimum of 4 hours.

Remove the dough from the refrigerator and allow it to warm slightly. Divide the dough into two pieces, one slightly larger than the other. Roll out the larger piece to 11 by 15 inches and place in the slab pie pan, pressing it into the corners of the pan and allowing the excess to drape over the sides. Refrigerate. Roll out the second piece of dough to 10 by 14 inches, place it on a lightly floured sheet of parchment, and refrigerate.

(Continued)

SWEETIE PIES

FILLING

¾ cup (150 g) granulated sugar

¼ cup (28 g) cornstarch

1 tablespoon finely minced fresh mint

2 pounds (900 g) strawberries, slightly underripe

Juice of 1 lemon

2 tablespoons (28 g) cold butter, cubed

GLAZE

1 cup (113 g) powdered sugar

3 tablespoons cold milk

1 teaspoon vanilla extract

Multicolored sprinkles

For the filling: Stir the sugar, cornstarch, and mint together in a large bowl. Chop the strawberries into small pieces, none bigger than a blueberry. This takes dedication. If pressed for time, use the food processor, pulsing just two or three times until the berries are chopped but not puréed. Wait until all the fruit has been chopped before adding it to the sugar mixture, and then fold quickly three or four times to coat each piece of strawberry without crushing the fruit further.

Without delay, because the juices are going to start to flow, pile the filling into the bottom crust, squeeze the lemon juice over the filling, and dot with the butter cubes. Remove the top crust from the refrigerator and pierce all over with a docking tool or a sharp fork to make steam vents. Drape the top crust over the filling. Trim the excess dough with scissors, leaving about 1-inch overhang all the way around. Fold over 1 inch of the crust edge toward the center, all the way around, to seal. Fork crimp the edges with determination to keep the juices in. Check to make sure the docking or fork piercings are visible and, if not, poke a bamboo skewer through each one. This pie likes to leak and these escape valves are important. Put the pie in the freezer for at least 1 hour for the best baking result.

Heat the oven to 400°F; if you have one, place a baking stone, Baking Steel, or inverted baking sheet on the center rack to heat (see page 4). With a piece of parchment under the pan (to catch any mess), take the pie pan right from the freezer and place in the oven (on the stone, steel, or baking sheet if using). Bake for 45 to 50 minutes, until the top is browned and the juices are bubbling under the surface. Cool thoroughly on a wire rack.

For the glaze: Stir the powdered sugar, milk, and vanilla extract together in a small bowl, adding more sugar or more milk as needed to make a thick, spreadable frosting. With an offset spatula, smooth across the surface of the pie, leaving the forked edges bare. Scatter sprinkles thickly. Refrigerate to set the glaze, about 30 minutes, before serving.

(Continued)

Techniques: Cream Cheese Crust (page 37), Mixing and Rolling (page 14), Crimp and Slash (page 24)

Swaps:

• Try with an All-Butter (page 30) or Butter and Shortening Crust (page 33).

• Mix raspberries, blueberries, blackberries, and strawberries.

• Go for an egg wash and sparkling sugar instead of the frosting.

FRESH HERBS AND FRUIT PIES

One of the many things I learned by making jam and jelly was how herbs and spices liven up fruit, particularly dull fruit, particularly dull fruit that might have been purchased with enthusiasm and no real plan. Those mealy peaches, mushy plums, white-centered strawberries, and tasteless blueberries can come to life with some bright herbs, lemon juice, and the heat of the oven.

Using fresh mint with fruit enhances the flavor, adding a candy-like quality to even the most insipid fruit. Mint will thrive in a pot in the garden.

Lemon verbena remains my single favorite herb to pair with fruit. It's easy to grow in a pot in a sunny or semi-sunny location. Look for small plants at markets and garden centers in early summer. Some people dry it, but I like it best fresh, and when summer is gone so is verbena, until next year.

Genovese basil, Thai basil, thyme, lemon thyme, sweet cicely, and rosemary all mix with fruit. Use them judiciously—pie is about the fruit, after all. Mince the herbs into fine little pieces or place entire sprigs in the fruit mixture for an hour or so, then pluck them out and discard before filling the pie.

Herbs are not a necessary element, just an enhancement. If unavailable or unappealing, skip them.

SO VERY APRICOT SLAB PIE

WITH AN ALL-BUTTER CRUST

Serves 15 to 18

Apricots are one of my favorite summer fruits, but getting a ripe one without a mealy texture on the East Coast is nearly impossible. Fortunately, once cooked, any disappointing texture is no longer an issue; as the fruit softens and warms, the flesh becomes tender and sweet. Adding dried fruit not only absorbs excess fruit juices and gels the filling, it also adds a big punch of flavor. If you can't find *unsweetened* dried fruit, reduce the sugar in the filling by half. It's great to match fruits, but complementary flavors are equally compelling. Consider dried pears and fresh apples, dried cherries and fresh plums, or dried mango and fresh peaches. Or identical fruits, fresh and dried, as in this intensely apricot pie. A whisper of fresh thyme balances the tart, sweet combination with a grassy freshness.

Make Ahead: Stir the filling ingredients together up to 2 hours before baking. Assemble and refrigerate the pie up to 4 hours ahead or freeze up to 3 months ahead and bake directly from the freezer.

ALL-BUTTER CRUST

2½ cups plus
2 tablespoons (325 g)
all-purpose flour

16 tablespoons (225 g)
unsalted butter, cubed and
frozen for 20 minutes

¼ teaspoon kosher salt

½ cup (120 ml) ice water

FILLING

½ cup (100 g) plump dried
apricots

⅔ cup (135 g) granulated
sugar

(Continued)

For the crust: In the food processor, pulse the flour, butter, and salt until the butter is in small pieces coated with flour, about 15 times. Add the water all at once and process until the mixture almost forms a ball. Form the dough into a 6- by 4-inch rectangle using plastic wrap and a bench scraper to firmly press the dough into a cohesive form. Wrap tightly and refrigerate a minimum of 4 hours.

Remove the dough from the refrigerator and allow it to warm slightly. Divide the dough into two pieces, one slightly larger than the other. Roll out the larger piece to 11 by 15 inches and place in the slab pie pan, pressing it into the corners of the pan and allowing the excess to drape over the sides. Refrigerate. Roll out the second piece of dough to 10 by 14 inches, place it on a lightly floured sheet of parchment, and refrigerate.

(Continued)

SWEETIE PIES

1¾ pounds (790 g)
ripe apricots

Juice of 1 lemon

½ teaspoon finely minced
fresh thyme leaves,
optional

2 tablespoons cornstarch

2 tablespoons (28 g)
unsalted butter, cubed

1 egg yolk

1 tablespoon water

1 tablespoon sparkling or
granulated sugar

For the filling: In the food processor or a sturdy blender, whiz the dried apricots and sugar together until the apricots are in small pieces. If the fresh apricots are small enough, they may be halved and pitted; but if larger, pit and slice or cube the fruit. There is no need to peel them. In a large bowl, combine the apricot sugar with the fresh apricots, lemon juice, thyme, and cornstarch. Stir well to dissolve the sugar and coat the apricot slices in plenty of the lemony juices to discourage browning.

Heat the oven to 425°F; if you have one, place a baking stone, Baking Steel, or inverted baking sheet on the center rack to heat (see page 4).

Pour the fruit and every bit of the sugary syrup languishing in the bottom of the bowl into the bottom crust and push it around until evenly distributed. Dot with the cubes of butter. Place the top crust over the filling. Trim the excess dough with scissors. Crimp and slash. Stir the egg yolk and water together and, with a pastry brush, paint generously across the top crust, avoiding the crimped edges. Sprinkle with sugar. If there is time, freeze or refrigerate the pie one more time for at least 20 minutes.

Place the pie atop a sheet of parchment paper in the center of the oven (on the stone, steel, or baking sheet if using). Bake for 20 minutes. Reduce the temperature to 375°F and bake until the fruit juices are bubbling and the crust is toasty brown, 45 to 55 minutes. Place on a wire rack to cool for at least 3 hours before serving.

Techniques: All-Butter Crust (page 30), Mixing and Rolling Out (page 14), Crimp and Slash (page 24)

Swaps:

• Try a Butter and Shortening (page 33) or Rye Crust (page 48).

• Try a lattice or cutout topper.

• Use Nutty Brown-Butter Streusel (page 86) instead of a top crust.

• Substitute frozen fruit for fresh.

ABSOLUTELY PEACHY SLAB PIE

WITH AN ALL-BUTTER CRUST

Serves 12 to 15

This is my all-around fruit slab pie recipe and it works with everything from piles of blueberries, to sliced plums, to juicy blackberries, to succulent autumn pears. But it really sings with the queen of summer fruit—the peach. Cut the fruit into smaller pieces so the filling spreads out evenly, with fewer lumps, and every bite includes a piece of fruit. Almond paste, found in the baking aisle of the grocery store, is luscious and companionable. This is a party pie, with easy-to-cut portions. Make a Big Slab (see page 10) and win the potluck. Top with ice cream or whipped cream and say "Hello" to summertime!

Make Ahead: Stir the filling ingredients together up to 2 hours before baking. Assemble and refrigerate the pie up to 4 hours ahead or freeze up to 3 months ahead and bake directly from the freezer.

ALL-BUTTER CRUST

2½ cups plus
2 tablespoons (325 g)
all-purpose flour

16 tablespoons (225 g)
unsalted butter, cubed and
frozen for 20 minutes

¼ teaspoon kosher salt

½ cup (120 ml) ice water

FILLING

3 pounds (1.36 kg) ripe
peaches, peeled (see
box), or 2 pounds (900 g)
frozen peach slices (about
6 cups)

½ cup (100 g) granulated
sugar

(Continued)

For the crust: In the food processor, pulse the flour, butter, and salt until the butter is in small pieces coated with flour, about 15 times. Add the water all at once and process until the mixture almost forms a ball. Form the dough into a 6- by 4-inch rectangle using plastic wrap and a bench scraper to firmly press the dough into a cohesive form. Wrap tightly and refrigerate a minimum of 4 hours.

Remove the dough from the refrigerator and allow it to warm slightly. Divide the dough into two pieces, one slightly larger than the other. Roll out the larger piece to 11 by 15 inches and place in the slab pie pan, pressing it into the corners and allowing the excess to drape over the sides. Refrigerate. Roll out the second piece of dough to 10 by 14 inches, place it on a lightly floured sheet of parchment, and refrigerate.

For the filling: Cut the peaches into slim slices or bite-sized cubes. In a large bowl, mix together the peaches, sugar, cornstarch, lemon juice, and lemon verbena and stir well to dissolve the sugar and coat the peach slices in plenty of lemony juices to discourage browning. If time allows, cover and refrigerate up to 2 hours to let the flavors develop.

(Continued)

2 tablespoons cornstarch

Juice of 1 lemon

2 (3-inch) sprigs lemon
verbena, optional

6 ounces (168 g)
almond paste

1 egg yolk

2 tablespoons sparkling or
granulated sugar

Discard the lemon verbena from the fruit mixture. Pour the fruit and every bit of the sugary syrup languishing in the bottom of the bowl into the bottom crust and push it around until evenly distributed. Crumble the almond paste over the fruit. Heat the oven to 425°F; if you have one, place a baking stone, Baking Steel, or inverted baking sheet on the center rack to heat (see page 4).

Place the top crust over the filling. Trim the excess dough with scissors. Crimp and slash. Stir the egg yolk and sugar together and brush it generously across the top crust, avoiding the edges. If there is time, freeze or refrigerate the pie one more time for at least 20 minutes.

Place the pie on top of a piece of parchment, in the center of the oven (on the Baking Steel, stone, or baking sheet if using). Bake for 20 minutes. Reduce the temperature to 375°F and bake until the fruit juices are bubbling and the crust is toasty brown, 40 to 45 minutes more. Place on a wire rack to cool for at least 3 hours before serving.

This pie is best eaten the day it is made, but wrapped well, makes a superb breakfast.

Techniques: All-Butter Crust (page 30), Mixing and Rolling Out (page 14), Crimp and Slash (page 24)

Swaps:

- Try a Butter and Shortening (page 33) or Leaf Lard Crust (page 45).

- Gorgeous with a lattice topper (see page 26), or choose Nutty Brown-Butter Streusel (page 86) instead of a top crust.

- Substitute frozen fruit for fresh. Try apricots.

- Combine fruits into exotic and beautiful summer pairings: peach and blueberry, cherry and plum, strawberry and raspberry.

- Omit the almond paste and add 1 teaspoon vanilla extract to the filling.

HOW TO PEEL A PEACH (OR TOMATO)

Bring a 5-quart pot of water to a boil. Fill a bowl with ice water. Use a sharp paring knife to make an X in the bottom of each peach (or tomato). Working in batches, drop the peaches into boiling water. When the skin has begun to loosen and water eases into the space between the peel and the flesh, the peach will float to the top of the pot, 30 to 60 seconds, depending on size and ripeness. As they rise up to the surface, scoop the peaches out of the boiling water with a slotted spoon and transfer to the bowl of ice water.

Once cool, one at a time, lift the peach from the cold water and, using the X to get a handhold, peel the skin off in large swaths; if it does not peel easily, leave the next batch in the boiling water a little longer. A light touch with a paring knife or a vegetable peeler will remove any stubborn bits.

PEACH MELBA SLAB PIE
WITH AN ALL-BUTTER CRUST

Serves 12 to 15

This adult, satisfying, not-too-sweet pie has origins in *clafoutis*, the eggy, fruity, French concoction. I like to make the custard filling by hand with a big whisk and a deep bowl, but go ahead and pull out the stand mixer and use the whisk attachment if you want. For true ambrosia, make this with the perfumed white peaches of high summer. Lofty, creamy, and rich, surrounded by buttery crust—I think of peach-studded ice cream churned in high summer, scooped onto a cake cone, and carried down the boardwalk while ocean waves crash. In the depths of winter, with frozen fruit, this is one happy pie.

Make Ahead: Plan for at least 2 hours to chill the pie before serving.

ALL-BUTTER CRUST

2½ cups plus
2 tablespoons (325 g)
all-purpose flour

16 tablespoons (225 g)
unsalted butter, cubed and
frozen for 20 minutes

¼ teaspoon kosher salt

½ cup (120 ml) ice water

FILLING

1½ pounds (680 g) white
peaches, pitted, peeled,
and sliced (about 3 cups)

Juice of 1 lemon

1 cup (227 g) sour cream

¾ cup (150 g) granulated
sugar

½ teaspoon ground ginger

(Continued)

For the crust: In the food processor, pulse the flour, butter, and salt until the fats are in small pieces coated with flour, about 15 times. Add the water all at once and process until the mixture almost forms a ball. Form the dough into a 6- by 4-inch rectangle using plastic wrap and a bench scraper to firmly press the dough into a cohesive form. Wrap tightly and refrigerate a minimum of 4 hours.

Remove the dough from the refrigerator and allow it to warm slightly. Divide the dough into two pieces, one slightly larger than the other. Roll out the larger piece to 11 by 15 inches and place in the slab pie pan, pressing it into the corners of the pan and allowing the excess to drape over the sides. Refrigerate. Roll out the second piece of dough to 10 by 14 inches, place it on a lightly floured sheet of parchment, and refrigerate.

Heat the oven to 350°F; if you have one, place a baking stone, Baking Steel, or inverted baking sheet on the center rack to heat (see page 4).

For the filling: Stir together the sliced peaches and lemon juice, coating well and thoroughly to keep the peaches from browning. With a strong arm and a large whisk in a large bowl (or a stand or hand mixer), beat the sour cream and sugar together. Add the ginger and vanilla and combine until the wee black flecks of vanilla are well

½ teaspoon vanilla seeds (scraped from a vanilla bean) or 1 teaspoon vanilla extract

3 egg yolks

¼ cup (30 g) all-purpose flour

1 cup (125 g) ripe red raspberries

1 egg yolk

1 teaspoon granulated sugar

distributed. Scrape the bowl and add the egg yolks one at a time, whipping until the custard turns a beautiful light yellow, indicating the yolks are fully incorporated. Sprinkle the flour over the top of the custard and whisk in.

Spoon in the lemony peach slices into the chilled bottom crust and distribute them evenly from corner to corner. Pour the custard filling over the peaches. Scatter the raspberries over the custard. Slide the pie into the oven (on top of the steel, stone, or baking sheet if using) and bake for 20 minutes.

Stamp cutouts from the top crust. Stir together the egg yolk and sugar. Paint each cutout with egg wash. Remove the pie from the oven and quickly, like dealing cards, place the cutouts (glazed side up) across the surface of the pie. Return the pie to the oven and bake for another 40 minutes, until a knife plunged into the custard comes out clean and the cutout toppers are toasty brown and glistening.

Cool the pie on a wire rack for 1 hour. Chill the pie in the refrigerator for 2 hours. Serve cold.

Techniques: All-Butter Crust (page 30), Mixing and Rolling Out (page 14), How to Peel a Peach (page 217), Lattices, Cutouts, Stamps, and Shapes (page 26)

Swaps:

- Press in a Shortbread Crust (page 59) or Vanilla Wafer Crust (page 287).

- Strawberries, red currants, raspberries, and apricots are equally stupendous surrounded by the rich custard.

- A Granola Streusel (page 85) topping is a fine textural counterpoint.

YANKEE DOODLE DANDY SOUR CHERRY SLAB PIE

WITH AN ALL-BUTTER CRUST

Serves 12 to 15

I know it's not right to choose favorites, but cherry pie is mine. Pie cherries (also called sour or tart cherries), bright red and easy to pit, arrive at my Washington, D.C., farmers' market right around July 4th, in time for the most American of American pies. (I know: apple. But c'mon.) I never bring home fewer than 4 quarts, two for today's pie and two to pit and freeze for later. Spread out the newspaper, and start pitting. It's a task, sure, but find a pitter that you like (see Resources, page 310) and listen to podcasts or an audiobook and the time passes quickly. Cherry pie can be a little tricky—the fruit is especially juicy, so getting the filling to be gelled but not goopy is the goal. Here's where I rely on Instant ClearJel (see Resources, page 310), a cornstarch-based thickener that works like a charm. A lattice or cutout crust is essential for reducing the liquid in the filling.

Make Ahead: Stir the filling ingredients together, omitting the Instant ClearJel, up to 2 hours before baking. Add the Instant ClearJel right before assembling the pie. Refrigerate the unbaked pie up to 4 hours ahead of baking, or freeze up to 3 months ahead. Bake directly from the freezer.

ALL-BUTTER CRUST

2½ cups plus
2 tablespoons (325 g)
all-purpose flour

16 tablespoons (225 g)
unsalted butter, cubed and
frozen for 20 minutes

¼ teaspoon kosher salt

½ cup (120 ml) ice water

(Continued)

For the crust: In the food processor, pulse the flour, butter, and salt until the butter is in small pieces coated with flour, about 15 times. Add the water all at once and process until the mixture almost forms a ball. Form the dough into a 6- by 4-inch rectangle using plastic wrap and a bench scraper to firmly press the dough into a cohesive form. Wrap tightly and refrigerate a minimum of 4 hours.

Remove the dough from the refrigerator and allow it to warm slightly. Divide the dough into two pieces, one slightly larger than the other. Roll out the larger piece to 11 by 15 inches and place in the slab pie pan, pressing it into the corners of the pan and allowing the excess to drape over the sides. Refrigerate. Roll out the second piece of dough to 10 by 14 inches, place it on a lightly floured sheet of parchment, and refrigerate.

(Continued)

SWEETIE PIES

FILLING

2½ pounds (1.14 kg) tart, sour, or pie cherries, pitted over a bowl to capture the juices (about 2 quarts before pitting and 5 cups after pitting, including the juice)

¾ cup (150 g) granulated sugar

¼ cup (28 g) Instant ClearJel

½ teaspoon almond extract

2 tablespoons (28 g) unsalted butter, cubed

1 egg yolk

1 tablespoon cool water

1 tablespoon granulated sugar

For the filling: Combine the cherries and their juices with the sugar, Instant ClearJel, and almond extract in a bowl. Pour the fruit and every bit of the sugary syrup languishing in the bottom of the bowl into the bottom crust and push it around until evenly distributed. Dot the surface with the butter.

Retrieve the top crust from the refrigerator and stamp out as many rounds or other shapes as possible. Use different-sized cutters or make them all the same size, but make a lot of cutouts. Dot them across the surface of the pie filling, touching the edges and touching each other. Sometimes my pies are thoroughly covered and other times they are barely covered beyond the edges, but they will look beautiful no matter what you do. Cherries are like that. Stir the egg yolk, water, and sugar together and brush it generously across the cutouts, avoiding the edges. If there is time, freeze or refrigerate the pie one more time for at least 30 minutes.

Heat the oven to 425°F; if you have one, place a baking stone, Baking Steel, or inverted baking sheet on the center rack to heat (see page 4). Place the pie in the center of the oven (on a stone, steel, or baking sheet if using). Bake for 20 minutes. Reduce the temperature to 375°F and bake until the fruit juices are bubbling and the crust is toasty brown, about 45 minutes more. Place on a wire rack to cool for at least 3 hours before serving.

Techniques: All-Butter Crust (page 30), Mixing and Rolling Out (page 14), Lattices, Cutouts, Stamps, and Shapes (page 26)

Swaps:

- Use a Butter and Shortening (page 33) or Leaf Lard Crust (page 45).

- Granola Streusel (page 85) instead of a top crust.

- Substitute frozen or jarred fruit for fresh. Add a handful of dried cherries.

- Swap in 1 teaspoon vanilla extract for the almond extract.

BLUEBERRY STREUSEL SLAB PIE

WITH A SHORTBREAD CRUST

Serves 12 to 15

This is a quick-to-the-table pie to make after a day of berry picking, no rolling pin required. While fresh fruit makes a lovely pie, frozen fruit works in a pinch, so fruity pie is possible even in the dead of winter. Thaw frozen berries enough to break up the clumps before stirring in the cornstarch and sugar. The crumbly oat topping makes it a perfectly suitable breakfast pie, right? An open-plan streusel topping means the berries burst in the heat of the oven for a juicy, intense fruit filling. Pay attention to building up the sides of the crust to create a dam to hold back those purple juices.

Make Ahead: The crust may be pressed into the pan and refrigerated one day ahead, until ready to bake. The streusel may be made one day ahead and refrigerated until ready to use.

SHORTBREAD CRUST

6 tablespoons (85 g) unsalted butter, at room temperature

⅓ cup (67 g) granulated sugar

1 egg yolk

1½ cups (180 g) all-purpose flour

¼ teaspoon kosher salt

FILLING

1 pound (455 g) blueberries, picked over, stems and green berries discarded

(Continued)

For the crust: Using a stand mixer, hand mixer, or strong wooden spoon, beat the butter and sugar until smooth, lightened, and fluffy, about 5 minutes with the stand mixer. Add the egg yolk and beat until fully incorporated. Add the flour and salt and stir until a crumbly dough is formed.

Dump the dough into the slab pie pan and, with pieces no larger than a walnut, press the dough up the sides and well into the corners of the pan before worrying about the bottom. Use a metal cup measure or a flat-bottomed glass to press the remaining dough as uniformly as possible to an approximate ¼-inch thickness. Decorate the top edge using a table knife, fork, or another tool, making slight indentations all the way around. Chill the crust for at least 20 minutes.

Heat the oven to 350°F; if you have one, place a baking stone, Baking Steel, or inverted baking sheet on the center rack to heat (see page 4).

(Continued)

¾ cup (150 g)
granulated sugar

3 tablespoons cornstarch

⅛ teaspoon freshly grated
nutmeg

Juice of 1 lemon

STREUSEL

⅓ cup (40 g)
all-purpose flour

¼ cup (25 g) rolled
(not instant) oats

2 tablespoons packed
light brown sugar

⅛ teaspoon ground
cinnamon

½ teaspoon kosher salt

2 tablespoons (28 g)
unsalted butter, cubed
and chilled

⅓ cup (37 g) toasted
pecans, chopped

For the filling: Gently stir the berries, sugar, cornstarch, nutmeg, and lemon juice together in a large bowl. Scrape the berry filling into the chilled crust.

For the streusel: In a medium bowl, combine the flour, oats, brown sugar, cinnamon, and salt. Pinch in the butter, mixing it with the dry ingredients until the streusel resembles coarse meal. Stir in the pecans. Scatter the streusel mixture evenly across the filling. Slide the pie into the oven (on top of the steel, stone, or baking sheet if using) and bake until the edges are slightly browned and the filling is bubbling, 25 to 35 minutes.

This pie is best eaten warm, the day it is made, but if wrapped well it will reheat for a superb breakfast. Try it with a spoonful of plain yogurt on the side.

Techniques: Press-In Crusts (page 55), Shortbread Crust (page 59), How to Toast Nuts (page 253), Granola Streusel (page 85)

Swaps:

- Blind bake (see page 29) a single-crust All-Butter (page 30), Butter and Shortening (page 33), or Cream Cheese Crust (page 37) and top with a lattice.

- Raspberry, olallieberry, marionberry, blackberry, cranberry, huckleberry, or a combination of all the berries—any berry but strawberry—works here. (The structure of strawberries is different than other berries, and they do not so much burst but wrinkle and desiccate.)

- Change the pecans out for almonds, walnuts, or pine nuts.

BLACKBERRY, SWEET CORN, AND BASIL SLAB PIE

WITH A RYE CRUST

Serves 15 to 18

There is something delightfully textural about this pie. It came to me in a dream, the thought of sweet and tart berries and creamy corn balanced by the tangy sour of a rye crust. It is everything I hoped. This pie screams summer breakfast or afternoon snack. Gloriously tempered with a hearty crust, it's very nearly health food.

Make Ahead: This pie holds well. Make it a day before, if need be.

RYE CRUST

1¾ cups plus 1 tablespoon (225 g) all-purpose flour

1 cup (100 g) rye flour

8 tablespoons (113 g), unsalted butter, cubed and frozen for 20 minutes

8 tablespoons (113 g) Spectrum or other vegetable shortening, cubed and frozen for 20 minutes

½ teaspoon kosher salt

½ cup (120 ml) ice water

3 teaspoons ice cold vodka, optional

(Continued)

For the crust: In the food processor, pulse the flours, butter, shortening, and salt until the fats are in small pieces coated with flour, about 15 times. Add the water and vodka (if using) all at once and process until the mixture almost forms a ball. Form the dough into a 6- by 4-inch rectangle using plastic wrap and a bench scraper to firmly press the dough into a cohesive form. Wrap tightly and refrigerate a minimum of 4 hours.

Remove the dough from the refrigerator and allow it to warm slightly. Divide the dough into two pieces, one slightly larger than the other. Roll out the larger piece to 11 by 15 inches and place in the slab pie pan, pressing it into the corners of the pan and allowing the excess to drape over the sides. Refrigerate. Roll out the second piece of dough to 10 by 14 inches, place it on a lightly floured sheet of parchment, and refrigerate.

Heat the oven to 425°F; you have one, place a baking stone, Baking Steel, or inverted baking sheet on the center rack to heat (see page 4).

(Continued)

FILLING

2 cups fresh corn,
cut from 2 ears

5 cups (650 g) fresh
blackberries

¾ cup (150 g)
granulated sugar

¼ cup (32 g) Instant
ClearJel

¼ cup (15 g) fresh basil
leaves, stacked and
slivered

Juice of 1 lemon

2 tablespoons (28 g)
unsalted butter

1 egg yolk

1 tablespoon water

2 tablespoons sparkling
sugar

For the filling: Pulse the corn in a blender or mini-processor until it is in very small pieces suspended in a liquid-y paste. In a large bowl, gently stir the corn puree, blackberries, sugar, ClearJel, basil, and lemon juice to combine. Spoon the berry mixture and every bit of the sugary syrup in the bottom of the bowl into the bottom crust, pushing it into all the corners. Dot with the butter. Unfold the top crust over the filling. Trim the excess dough with scissors. Crimp and slash. Stir the egg yolk and water together and brush it generously across the top crust, avoiding the edges. Sprinkle with the sparkling sugar. If there is time, freeze or refrigerate the pie one more time for at least 20 minutes.

Place the pie atop a sheet of parchment paper in the center of the oven (on the stone, steel, or baking sheet if using). Bake for 20 minutes. Reduce the temperature to 375°F and bake until the fruit juices are bubbling and the crust is gloriously shiny and golden, 40 to 45 minutes. Place on a wire rack to cool for at least 3 hours before serving.

Techniques: Rye Crust (page 48), Mixing and Rolling Out (page 14), Crimp and Slash (page 24)

Swaps:

- For the traditionalist, use an All-Butter Crust (page 30).

- Blueberries work beautifully.

- Add 1 cup chopped crisp bacon to the filling.

- Instant ClearJel (see Resources, page 310) helps corral the berries' juiciness, ensuring a good firm set in the filling, easier slicing, and no gumminess—but ¼ cup of cornstarch or tapioca pearls will also work.

SWEETIE PIES

CONCORD GRAPE SLAB PIE

WITH AN ALL-BUTTER CRUST

Serves 12

Concord grapes have been a part of the New England landscape since Colonial days, so much so that ancient vines grow willy-nilly behind many of the homes in the region. It's a wine grape that ripens in autumn. The Concord's skin is thicker than table grapes and the pulp houses three significant seeds. The season is short, influenced by rain, heat, and fewer hours of daylight, so grab the grapes when you see them because this is one unforgettable pie. A Concord pie explodes with the foxy grape-y-ness of these fall harbingers, bubbling below the top crust. Making it is time consuming, messy, fussy, and all around annoying until you taste it and, eventually, like so much of life, the pain is forgotten. A food mill is a must. Admittedly, it's an odd recipe that seems like it shouldn't work, but it does: It's as old as those vines and just as reliable.

Make Ahead: Up to 2 hours ahead, separate the grape skins and pulp, cook the pulp, and remove the seeds.

ALL-BUTTER CRUST

2½ cups plus
2 tablespoons (325 g)
all-purpose flour

16 tablespoons (225 g)
unsalted butter, cubed and
frozen for 20 minutes

¼ teaspoon kosher salt

½ cup (120 ml) ice water

FILLING

2 quarts (3½ pounds,
1.5 kg) Concord grapes,
stemmed

(Continued)

For the crust: In the food processor, pulse the flour, butter, and salt until the butter is in small pieces coated with flour, about 15 times. Add the water all at once and process until the mixture almost forms a ball. Form the dough into a 6- by 4-inch rectangle using plastic wrap and a bench scraper to firmly press the dough into a cohesive form. Wrap tightly and refrigerate a minimum of 4 hours.

Remove the dough from the refrigerator and allow it to warm slightly. Divide the dough into two pieces, one slightly larger than the other. Roll out the larger piece to 11 by 15 inches and place in the slab pie pan, pressing it into the corners of the pan and allowing the excess to drape over the sides. Refrigerate. Roll out the second piece of dough to 10 by 14 inches, place it on a lightly floured sheet of parchment, and refrigerate.

(Continued)

1 cup (200 g)
granulated sugar

¼ cup (28 g) cornstarch

Juice of 1 lemon

⅛ teaspoon allspice

1 egg yolk

1 tablespoon water

2 tablespoons sparkling
sugar

Heat the oven to 425°F; if you have one, place a baking stone, Baking Steel, or inverted baking sheet on the center rack to heat (see page 4).

For the filling: Set up one bowl for the grape skins and a medium saucepan for the grape pulp. One by one, squeeze the pulp from the skin of the grape and deposit in the bowl or saucepan, according to plan. Once this is over, congratulate yourself, remembering this is a once-a-year pie. Mash the pulp in the saucepan and place over medium heat. Bring the pulp to a boil, remove from the heat and pour the warm pulp into a food mill or a medium sieve set over the bowl of grape skins. Mill the pulp to remove the grape seeds.

Stir the sugar, cornstarch, lemon juice, and allspice into the grape skin and pulp mixture and mix well. Scrape the filling into the bottom crust. Drape the top crust over the filling. Crimp and slash. Whisk the egg yolk and water with a fork until thoroughly blended. Dip a pastry brush into the egg wash and paint it across the surface of the top crust. Sprinkle generously with the sparkling sugar.

Slide the pie into the oven with a protective sheet of parchment under the pan and atop the Baking Steel, stone, or baking sheet if using. (This pie always bubbles up and over.) Bake for 20 minutes. Reduce the heat to 375°F and continue baking for 45 to 55 minutes, until the top crust is deeply golden brown and the juices are bubbling up through the slashes.

Techniques: All-Butter Crust (page 30), Mixing and Rolling Out (page 14), Crimp and Slash (page 24)

Swaps: There are no substitutions. It's too perfect the way it is.

EASY-AS-PIE APPLE SLAB PIE

WITH AN ALL-BUTTER CRUST

Serves 12 to 16

Too often, *doughphobia* keeps even the most accomplished cook from making a pie. It's been said that Nora Ephron, an excellent cook by all reports, refused to make her own pie crust when store-bought versions were available. My goal is to encourage pie-baking, whether dough-making or not. The right pie for a novice pie-maker, this spicy, sweet pie is made with mostly pantry ingredients and my sure-fire pie dough recipe. I'll try to understand if you must buy the pie crust and I've even provided instructions for using one (see page 69). But whatever you do, make this pie—it's made to eat out of hand and great for kids' parties or picnics.

Make Ahead: Freeze the unbaked pie, wrapped tightly in plastic and then in foil, for up to 1 month. Bake straight from the freezer.

ALL-BUTTER CRUST

2½ cups plus
2 tablespoons (325 g)
all-purpose flour

16 tablespoons (225 g)
unsalted butter, cubed and
frozen for 20 minutes

¼ teaspoon kosher salt

½ cup (120 ml) ice water

FILLING

2 pounds (900 g) apples,
about 4 large

⅓ cup packed (75 g)
light brown sugar

2 tablespoons all-purpose
flour

(Continued)

For the crust: In the food processor, pulse the flour, butter, and salt until the butter is in small pieces coated with flour, about 15 times. Add the ice water all at once and process until the mixture almost forms a ball. Form the dough into a 6- by 4-inch rectangle using plastic wrap and a bench scraper to firmly press the dough into a cohesive form. Wrap tightly and refrigerate a minimum of 4 hours.

Remove the dough from the refrigerator and allow it to warm slightly. Divide the dough into two pieces, one slightly larger than the other. Roll out the larger piece to 11 by 15 inches and place in the slab pie pan, pressing it into the corners of the pan and allowing the excess to drape over the sides. Refrigerate. Roll out the second piece of dough to 10 by 14 inches, place it on a lightly floured sheet of parchment, and refrigerate.

Heat the oven to 400°F; if you have one, place a baking stone, Baking Steel, or inverted baking sheet on the center rack to heat (see page 4).

(Continued)

SELECTING APPLES FOR PIE

In autumn, I hover over the baskets of apples at the farmers' market or roadside stand, choosing one from here and one from there. I read the cards, talk to the grower, and lean toward the ones with exquisite names. Newtown Pippin, anyone? But when I want to make an apple pie at the drop of a hat, I mix and match different grocery store varieties, remembering Granny Smith is sturdy and tart, Pink Lady is bright and crisp, Braeburn is winey and firm, Gala is sweet, Fuji is floral. Macintosh is saucy. You can't go wrong with any of them, but a combination adds complexity to a pie.

1 tablespoon lemon juice

½ teaspoon ground cinnamon

½ teaspoon ground ginger

½ teaspoon freshly grated nutmeg

¼ teaspoon kosher salt

2 tablespoons (28 g) cold unsalted butter, cubed

1 tablespoon heavy cream or whole milk

2 tablespoons sparkling, raw, or granulated sugar

For the filling: Line a large bowl with a threadbare, impeccably clean cotton kitchen towel or a double layer of cheesecloth. Place a box grater in the bowl and grate the apples, including the peel, right down to the core, right into the towel. Dispose of the cores. Twist the towel for a powerful squeeze, extracting the juice. This helps avoid a wet-bottomed pie. Capture all the delicious apple juice in a glass and drink up after all that hard work.

Empty the squeezed, grated apples out of the towel into the bowl. Add the brown sugar, flour, lemon juice, cinnamon, ginger, nutmeg, and salt. Stir well (or mix with your hands).

Take the bottom crust out of the refrigerator. Pile the filling into the center and gently tap the apples to fit. The filling will be about 1½ to 2 inches deep. Scatter the butter over the top of the filling. With scissors, trim the crust to about ½ inch over the edge of the pan. Tuck the bottom crust edge up and over the top crust, and fork crimp. Chill for 20 minutes.

Brush the surface of the pie with the cream and dust liberally with the sparkling sugar. Slash one or two vents and slide the pan into the hot oven (on top of the steel, stone, or baking sheet if using). Bake for 40 to 45 minutes, until the filling is bubbling and the crust is deeply browned. If the crust gets too dark, tent the pie with foil.

Cool for 10 minutes or more before slicing and serving. Top with cinnamon or caramel ice cream.

Techniques: All Butter Crust (page 30), Mixing and Rolling Out (page 14), Crimp and Slash (page 24)

Swaps:

- Try a Cream Cheese (page 37) or Cheddar Cheese Crust (page 39).

- Use firm pears instead of apples.

- Add 3 tablespoons chopped toasted pecans to the filling.

NOT-SO-OLD-FASHIONED APPLE SLAB PIE

WITH A CHEDDAR CHEESE CRUST

Serves 12 to 15

Initially, I thought I would call this Old-Fashioned Apple Slab Pie—but a few things happened along the way. I started thinking about how much I love cheese and apples together, so I added a Cheddar Cheese Crust. And apples made me think about New England and fall, and before I knew what was happening, maple syrup and maple sugar had found a home. This may not be Norman Rockwell's apple pie, but I bet he'd pull up a chair and dig right in.

Make Ahead: Stir together the filling several hours or up to 1 day in advance.

CHEDDAR CHEESE CRUST

2½ cups plus 2 tablespoons (325 g) all-purpose flour

16 tablespoons (225 g) unsalted butter, cubed and frozen for 20 minutes

4 ounces (113 g) extra sharp cheddar cheese, preferably orange, cold, half grated and half roughly chopped into almond-sized pieces

¼ teaspoon salt

½ cup (120 ml) ice water

(Continued)

For the crust: In the food processor, pulse the flour, butter, cheese, and salt until the butter and cheese are in small pieces coated with flour, about 15 times. Add the ice water all at once and process until the mixture almost forms a ball. Form the dough into a 6- by 4-inch rectangle using plastic wrap and a bench scraper to firmly press the dough into a cohesive form. Wrap tightly and refrigerate a minimum of 4 hours.

Remove the dough from the refrigerator and allow it to warm slightly. Divide the dough into two pieces, one slightly larger than the other. Roll out the larger piece to 11 by 15 inches and place in the slab pie pan, pressing it into the corners of the pan and allowing the excess to drape over the sides. Refrigerate. Roll out the second piece of dough to 10 by 14 inches, place it on a lightly floured sheet of parchment, and refrigerate.

Heat the oven to 425°F; if you have one, place a baking stone, Baking Steel, or inverted baking sheet on the center rack to heat (see page 4).

(Continued)

FILLING

½ cup (100 g) granulated sugar

¼ cup (56 g) maple sugar or 2 tablespoons maple syrup

¼ cup (30 g) all-purpose flour

1 tablespoon ground cinnamon

¼ teaspoon kosher salt

Juice of 1 lemon

3 pounds (1.5 kg) mixed apples, peeled, cored, and sliced ½ inch thick (about 6 large apples)

2 tablespoons (28 g) cold unsalted butter, cubed

1 tablespoon water

3 tablespoons maple sugar or sparkling sugar

For the filling: In a large bowl, mix together the granulated sugar, maple sugar, flour, cinnamon, and salt. Add the lemon juice and sliced apples and stir gently. I like to use my hands for this. Scrape the filling into the crust in the slab pie pan and top with the dots of butter. Place the top crust over the filling, trim, crimp, and slash.

With a pastry brush, paint the water across the surface of the pie, avoiding the edges. Sprinkle the maple sugar across the top of the pie.

Bake (on top of the steel, stone, or baking sheet if using) for 20 minutes. Reduce the heat to 350°F and bake an additional 40 to 45 minutes. If the top gets too dark, tent with foil. The pie is done when the filling is bubbling through the slashes.

Cool the pie thoroughly before serving. But if a warm pie is your heart's content, slip the cooled pie in a hot 350°F oven for 10 minutes before slicing.

Techniques: Cheddar Cheese Crust (page 39), Selecting Apples for Pie (page 234), Mixing and Rolling Out (page 14), Crimp and Slash (page 24)

Swaps:

• Trade in Cheddar Cheese Crust for an All-Butter Crust (page 30) or a heartier option like the Rye Crust (page 48).

• Add a handful of chopped candied ginger to the filling.

HOW TO PREPARE APPLES
(AND PEARS) FOR PIE

Every bite of a fruit pie should have fruit, every slice should cook evenly, and the pie, when cut, should be pretty. I love the slow meditation of preparing fruit for a pie. I have a favorite method for apples. It's quick and precise and uses tools. What's not to like?

As a clever teacher once told me, conquer one task at a time. First, peel all the apples or pears using a vegetable peeler. Try to keep it in one long piece: This game will keep you occupied through a few apples. Take those long, beautiful peels, push them in a jar, and cover them with bourbon. Put the jar in the closet and bring it out in a month for apple (or pear) bourbon cocktails. But I digress.

Next, remove the center core, any remaining peel and stem, and any brown spots with a melon baller. Finally, place the apple flat side down on the cutting board and slice horizontally from top to bottom, keeping the slices about ½ inch thick. Place in a bowl and coat with lemon juice to discourage browning.

PEAR AND FRANGIPANE SLAB PIE

WITH A PUFF PASTRY CRUST

Serves 8

——————

Warm squares of buttery pastry, rich pears, and the nutty sweetness of almonds. Frangipane, an almond custard, sounds fancy, doesn't it? It's surprisingly easy. The base for this classic filling is almond paste, found in the baking section of the grocery store. Usually layered into fruit tarts, frangipane works here as a pillow for spiced pears set atop store-bought puff pastry. The simplicity of the recipe relies on some pre-planning: Practice by placing the pears on a piece of parchment before putting them on the puff pastry. Depending on their size, they may have to be head to tail, or they may snuggle in with the chubby bottoms in the center and the slim tips facing the edge of the pan. I prefer Bosc pears, but Bartletts run a close second. Pink peppercorns are sweet and tingly but they can be omitted if you can't find them.

Make Ahead: Simmer the pears up to a week ahead and store them in the refrigerator, covered in the syrup. Make the frangipane no more than a few hours ahead.

1 sheet puff pastry (7 to 10 ounces, 200 to 285 g), defrosted if frozen, but still cold

4 firm pears, identical in size and shape

4 cups (960 ml) water

2 cups (400 g) granulated sugar

1 whole star anise pod

½ teaspoon pink peppercorns, optional

¼ cup (50 g) granulated sugar

(Continued)

Unfold the puff pastry and lightly roll it out until it fits in the slab pie pan, more or less. It is likely to be wider than needed, so trim a small piece from each side and stack it along the edge of the puff, forming a tiny raised wall. Refrigerate.

Peel the pears, halve vertically, core (use a melon baller for a pretty presentation), and remove both the stem and blossom end. Heat the water, sugar, star anise, and peppercorns (if using) in a saucepan until boiling. Boil for 10 minutes, reduce the heat, and add pears. Cook them over low heat for 20 to 30 minutes, until fork-tender. Let the pears cool and steep in the syrup for 1 hour or more.

Remove the pears from the syrup with a slotted spoon. (Save the syrup to gloss over the pears before baking, but also to add to a glass of seltzer water or champagne.) Place the pears on a cutting board with the cored side down and, using a sharp knife, cut into ½-inch slices crosswise across the pear, keeping the slices together.

(Continued)

4 tablespoons (56 g) unsalted butter, at room temperature

3 tablespoons (50 g) almond paste, at room temperature

1 egg, lightly beaten

3 tablespoons all-purpose flour, sifted

Heat the oven to 400°F; if you have one, place a baking stone, Baking Steel, or inverted baking sheet on the center rack to heat (see page 4). Beat the sugar, butter, almond paste, egg, and flour together to make the frangipane. Using a cookie scoop or a tablespoon, place 2 tablespoons frangipane in 8 spots on the pastry. You may have some left over. Nestle a sliced pear, head to tail and cored side down, atop each mound of frangipane. Press lightly so the pear slices spread out. With a pastry brush, paint a swath of syrup over the pears. Slide the pan into the oven (on top of the steel, stone, or baking sheet if using) and bake for 25 minutes, until the pastry is deeply browned and the frangipane is bubbling.

Use kitchen shears to snip the pie into 8 servings. Serve warm. This pie screams for ice cream.

Techniques: Puff Pastry (page 72), How to Prepare Apples (and Pears) for Pie (page 239)

Swaps:

- Blind bake (see page 29) a single-crust All-Butter Crust (page 30).

- Use pears in syrup, straight from the can, drained well, and sliced. They won't have the spice, but still will be delicious.

LEFTOVER CRANBERRY SAUCE SLAB PIE

WITH A SHORTBREAD CRUST

Serves 12 to 20

Every year, I go a little crazy making cranberry sauce at Thanksgiving. It's so pretty—a glorious ruby red—and tart and sweet and seasonal and my enthusiasm leaves me with cranberry sauce languishing in the refrigerator long after the last bite of turkey has been consumed. Meet the pie that solves my problem. Based on *fregolotta*, a classic Italian jam tart, this slab pie is quick to put together, even if Thanksgiving cooking has been going on long enough.

Make Ahead: Make the cranberry sauce up to 1 month ahead and freeze.

SHORTBREAD CRUST

12 tablespoons (170 g) unsalted butter, at room temperature

⅔ cup (130 g) granulated sugar

2 egg yolks

¼ teaspoon almond extract

3 cups (360 g) all-purpose flour

½ teaspoon kosher salt

(Continued)

For the crust: Heat the oven to 350°F; if you have one, place a baking stone, Baking Steel, or inverted baking sheet on the center rack to heat (see page 4).

Using a stand mixer, hand mixer, or strong wooden spoon, beat the butter and sugar together until lightened and fluffy. Add the eggs yolks one at a time and beat until fully incorporated. Mix in the extract. Add the flour and salt and mix on a low speed until a crumbly dough is formed. Divide the dough into two portions, one twice as large as the other. Wrap the smaller portion in plastic wrap and chill while assembling the rest of the pie.

Turn out the larger portion of the dough into the slab pie pan and, pinching off walnut-sized pieces, press the crust into the sides, corners, and edges and across the bottom of the pan. Use your knuckles, the side of your hand, a metal cup measure, or a flat-bottomed glass to press the crust firmly and as uniformly as possible to about a ¼-inch thickness.

(Continued)

FILLING

1½ cups (440 g) cranberry sauce, preferably whole fruit (if you don't have leftovers, see recipe below)

1½ cups (340 g) raspberries, fresh or frozen

2 tablespoons granulated sugar

½ cup (50 g) sliced almonds

For the filling: Spoon the cranberry sauce across the bottom crust. Smooth with an offset spatula. Scatter the raspberries over the cranberries and sprinkle with the sugar. Remove the chilled dough from the refrigerator and pinch off small pieces, scattering the nubbins across the top of the filling. Top with the almonds.

Bake (on top of the steel, stone, or baking sheet if using) until the almonds appear toasted and the crumble is slightly browned, 50 to 55 minutes. Place on a rack to cool slightly before portioning. Serve with whipped cream or ice cream.

Techniques: Press-In Crusts (page 55), Shortbread Crust (page 59)

Swaps:

• Blind bake (see page 29) a single-crust All-Butter Crust (page 30) and top with Granola Streusel (page 85).

• Make a sauce out of strawberries instead of cranberries.

• Top with diced rhubarb, gooseberries, or fresh currants.

• Meringue the top (see page 76).

MY CRANBERRY SAUCE

Makes 1½ cups

¾ cup (150 g) granulated sugar

¼ cup (60 ml) pomegranate juice or freshly squeezed orange juice

¾ cup (180 ml) water

2-inch-long swath peeled orange or lemon zest

3 cups (330 g) fresh or frozen whole cranberries

I've never thought cranberries needed much coaxing with sugar or other additions, so this recipe keeps those precious berries front and center in a tart sauce. If you prefer a sweeter condiment, add ¼ cup additional sugar.

Combine the sugar, pomegranate juice, and water in a medium saucepan and bring to a boil. Stir in the zest and cranberries. Cook at a quick boil, stirring often and warily to avoid hot sugary splatters, until most of the berries have burst, 16 to 18 minutes. The sauce will firm up as it cools. Once cool to the touch, fill a jar, cover, and refrigerate for no more than a month.

PUMPKIN CHIFFON SLAB PIE

WITH AN AMARETTI CRUST

Serves 12 to 16

I'm going to admit something. I'm not a fan of most pumpkin pies. When faced with a table full of options, it's the last slice I'll put on my plate. However, this chiffon version changed my mind. It's an airy wisp of a fluffy pie, laced with the sultry flavors of fall and a rich almond cookie crust. Gelatin is the key to the cloud-like texture of the filling. There are two critical junctures, so play close attention: First, when beating the egg whites, find the place where they are fluffy and high peaked, but moist, not dry. Dry whites will cause graininess in the finished pie. And next, when cooling the custard, don't let it set up before folding in the egg whites or it will never combine; but don't fold in the egg whites if the filling is still warm or their lift will disappear. It's a tightrope walk. Check the heat of the custard on the inside of your wrist. If it still feels warm, it's too warm.

Make Ahead: Plan for 4 hours or more to chill the pie before serving. The crust may be made a day or two in advance. The entire pie may be made 1 day in advance.

AMARETTI CRUST

29 amaretti cookies (225 g), crushed (about 2 cups)

8 tablespoons (113 g) unsalted butter, melted

¼ teaspoon kosher salt

FILLING

1 tablespoon (7 g) (one ¼-ounce packet) powdered unflavored gelatin

¼ cup (60 ml) cool water

(Continued)

For the crust: Heat the oven to 350°F; if you have one, place a baking stone, Baking Steel, or inverted baking sheet on the center rack to heat (see page 4).

In a large bowl, combine the amaretti crumbs, melted butter, and salt using a firm spatula and pressing the mixture against the side of the bowl until it is cohesive and the crumbs are thoroughly buttered. Dump the wet crumbs into the slab pie pan and press up the sides of the pan before filling in along the bottom. Take your time pressing the crust in, using the side of your hand or a metal measuring cup to form a good edge and a smooth base until the crust feels firm to the touch. Slide the pan into the oven (on top of the steel, stone, or baking sheet if using) and bake until lightly browned, about 20 minutes. Remove from the oven and cool.

(Continued)

1 (15-ounce) can (425 g) pumpkin purée (1½ cups)

½ cup packed (100 g) light brown sugar

5 large eggs, separated

1 teaspoon ground cinnamon

½ teaspoon vanilla extract

¼ teaspoon allspice

Scant ⅛ teaspoon ground cloves

¼ teaspoon kosher salt

¼ teaspoon cream of tartar

TOPPING

1½ cups (360 ml) heavy cream

3 tablespoons powdered sugar

For the filling: In a small bowl, sprinkle the gelatin over the cool water and let it absorb the water for about 5 minutes (this step is called blooming). Set up an ice bath with a large bowl filled with ice water. Place a medium saucepan half filled with water on the stove and heat until simmering. In a large heatproof bowl, whisk the pumpkin, brown sugar, egg yolks, cinnamon, vanilla, allspice, cloves, and salt until well combined and no streaks of yellow remain. Place the bowl over the simmering water. Cook the custard to 170°F, stirring with a rubber spatula as it thickens, dries out a bit, and becomes smooth, 8 to 10 minutes. Remove the bowl from the heat and stir in the bloomed gelatin until it melts. Place the bowl over the ice bath and whisk as it cools to slightly warmer than room temperature, about 85°F. To keep the custard from setting, remove the bowl from the ice bath while whipping the egg whites.

In the work bowl of a stand mixer fitted with the whip attachment or in a large bowl with a hand mixer, whip the egg whites on high until frothy. Add the cream of tartar (which makes the egg whites more stable) and continue whipping until the whites are shiny, the beater leaves a trail, and when lifted, forms medium peaks, another 3 or 4 minutes.

Stir one-third of the egg whites into the pumpkin custard until incorporated and the custard is lightened. Add the remaining egg whites and, using a large, flat rubber spatula, gently fold the custard and egg whites together until thoroughly and carefully combined with no large white streaks, while not deflating the egg whites. Gently pour the mixture into the cooled crust, cover, and refrigerate until firm, about 4 hours.

For the topping: In the work bowl of a stand mixer, whip the cream, increasing the speed as soft peaks form, until it begins to thicken, adding the powdered sugar one spoonful at a time. Beat until the whisk leaves a trail in the stiffened cream and forms high peaks. Spoon the cream on top of the completely cooled chiffon. Make peaks with the back of a tablespoon, smooth the whipped cream from edge to edge with an offset spatula, or add a dollop to each serving. Refrigerate again for at least 2 hours. The pie is even better if it chills overnight and develops an even stronger autumnal flavor.

Note: This pie depends on uncooked egg whites for its lift, so choose the freshest eggs. If serving children, immune-compromised, or elderly guests, use pasteurized eggs instead.

Techniques: Press-In Crusts (page 55), Cookie Crumb Crusts (page 65)

Swaps:

- Trade in an equal amount of strawberry or raspberry purée for the pumpkin and switch white sugar for brown sugar. Cook ³/₄ pound (340 g) berries until softened and jammy, then run the mixture through a blender, food mill, or strainer to remove the seeds.
- Any cookie crust (page 65) is complementary and a Ritz Cracker Crust (page 61) is surprisingly delicious.
- With a Matzo Crust (page 62), this is another Passover-perfect pie.
- To make a dairy-free chiffon pie, use margarine for the crust and trade in the whipped cream for Whipped Coconut Cream (page 75) or another non-dairy topping.

RASPBERRY RUGELACH SLAB PIE

WITH A CREAM CHEESE CRUST

Serves 16 to 24

Cookie-like and slim with a rich cream cheese crust, rugelach pie is reminiscent of the favorite crescent-shaped, jammy, nutty cookie found in my holiday baking lineup. And it's infinitely quicker to make than its fussy cookie cousin, delivering the same fruit and nut goodness pillowed in tender dough. All the joy, none of the fuss. Slice into slim rectangles and serve up for an after-school or teatime treat. Delicate small squares nestled in paper cups are an easy-to-pass-around dessert for a bat mitzvah or a bridal shower. Use the best jam you can find, something made from lots of fruit and not too much sugar, and always use toasted nuts. Have fun creating nutty, fruity combinations.

Make Ahead: Assemble the pie right up to the point of glazing with egg wash and baking. It will keep refrigerated for 2 days or frozen for up to 3 months. Egg wash the pie and sprinkle with sugar right before baking.

CREAM CHEESE CRUST

**2½ cups plus
2 tablespoons (325 g)
all-purpose flour**

**8 tablespoons (113 g)
unsalted butter, cubed and
frozen for 20 minutes**

**8 tablespoons (113 g)
cream cheese, cubed and
refrigerated for 20 minutes**

¼ teaspoon kosher salt

½ cup (120 ml) ice water

(Continued)

For the crust: In the food processor, pulse the flour, butter, cream cheese, and salt until the fat and cheese are in small pieces coated with flour, about 15 times. Add the ice water all at once and process until the mixture almost forms a ball. Form the dough into a 6- by 4-inch rectangle using plastic wrap and a bench scraper to firmly press the dough into a cohesive form. Wrap tightly and refrigerate a minimum of 4 hours.

Remove the dough from the refrigerator and allow it to warm slightly. Divide the dough into two pieces, one slightly larger than the other. Roll out the larger piece to 11 by 15 inches and place in the slab pie pan, pressing it into the corners of the pan and allowing the excess to drape over the sides. Refrigerate. Roll out the second piece of dough to 10 by 14 inches, place it on a lightly floured sheet of parchment, and refrigerate.

Heat the oven to 400°F; if you have one, place a baking stone, Baking Steel, or inverted baking sheet on the center rack to heat (see page 4).

(Continued)

FILLING

10 to 12 ounces (285 g to 340 g) best-quality raspberry jam (1¼ to 1½ cups)

1 cup (115 g) finely chopped toasted pecans

½ cup (21 g) soft bread crumbs

2 tablespoons (28 g) cold, unsalted butter, cubed

1 egg yolk

1 tablespoon cold water

3 tablespoons sparkling sugar

To fill the pie: Remove the top crust from the refrigerator and pierce all over with the tines of a fork or a docking tool. Spoon the jam across the bottom crust and spread evenly from edge to edge. Sprinkle with the pecans and bread crumbs. Dot the surface with the butter. Cap with the top crust and crimp and slash.

Stir together the egg yolk and water. Sprinkle the entire surface generously with sparkling sugar. Slide the pie into the oven (on top of the steel, stone, or baking sheet if using) and bake for 40 to 45 minutes, until shiny golden brown. Cool before serving.

Techniques: Cream Cheese Crust (page 37), Mixing and Rolling Out (page 14), Crimp and Slash (page 24)

Swaps:

- I swoon for the raspberry/pecan combination, but don't let me stop you from trying apricot jam and almonds, or strawberry jam and macadamia nuts, or plum jam and hazelnuts, or blood orange marmalade and pine nuts.

- Omit the bread crumbs and top crust and top the pie with Granola Streusel (page 85) for a chewy treat, making it more like an energy or breakfast bar.

HOW TO TOAST NUTS AND SEEDS

Why toast nuts or seeds if they are going in the oven anyway? To heat the natural oils, making the flavor deeper and richer, and to make sure they will be crisp and never soggy inside the pie. There are two ways to go, in a skillet or in the oven. I use the oven when it is going to be on anyway.

Always chop nuts after toasting, not before. Chopping ahead releases all the fragrant oils too quickly. Toasting the whole nut warms the oils and chopping spreads that scented love throughout. By the same token, do not crush seeds before toasting them. If the nuts or seeds end up overcooked and blackened, do not use them. A burned nut taste is acrid and lasting and permeates the whole pie. You'll need to start again.

IN THE OVEN

Spread the nuts or seeds out on a baking sheet or right in the slab pie pan you will be using. Slide the pan into the center of a 350°F oven and toast seeds for 3 to 5 minutes and nuts for 8 to 12 minutes. The best way to determine they are done is when the nutty aroma wafts through the kitchen, an indication that the oils have warmed up.

IN A SKILLET

When the oven is cold, I lean on my cast iron skillet for this task as the heat is so even and controlled. Use a dry skillet over medium heat and keep moving the seeds or nuts around the bottom of the skillet, flipping and turning them so every edge is exposed to the heat and they do not singe. As with oven toasting, pay attention to the way they smell. That toasty, nutty aroma is unmistakable, usually after 3 to 5 minutes for seeds or 8 to 12 minutes for nuts.

SWEETIE PIES

SUGAR-FREE FIG SLAB PIE

WITH A CREAM CHEESE CRUST

Serves 18 to 24

A rich, satisfying, tender, and delicious pie—and sugar-free to boot. It's actually a big fig cookie that everyone will love. The top crust is intentionally baked without an egg wash so the pie more closely resembles those favorite fig cookies from childhood, but go ahead and cover with Vanilla Glaze (page 79) after baking, if you want.

Make Ahead: The filling may be made a week ahead and kept refrigerated. Bring it to room temperature before spreading it across the bottom crust.

CREAM CHEESE CRUST

2½ cups plus 2 tablespoons (325 g) all-purpose flour

8 tablespoons (113 g) unsalted butter, cubed and frozen for 20 minutes

8 tablespoons (113 g) cream cheese, cubed and refrigerated for 20 minutes

¼ teaspoon kosher salt

½ cup (120 ml) ice water

(Continued)

For the crust: In the food processor, pulse the flour, butter, cream cheese, and salt until the butter and cheese are in small pieces coated with flour, about 15 times. Add the ice water all at once and process until the mixture almost forms a ball. Form the dough into a 6- by 4-inch rectangle using plastic wrap and a bench scraper to firmly press the dough into a cohesive form. Wrap tightly and refrigerate a minimum of 4 hours.

Remove the dough from the refrigerator and allow it to warm slightly. Divide the dough into two pieces, one slightly larger than the other. Roll out the larger piece to 11 by 15 inches and place in the slab pie pan, pressing it into the corners of the pan and allowing the excess to drape over the sides. Refrigerate. Roll out the second piece of dough to 10 by 14 inches, place it on a lightly floured sheet of parchment, and refrigerate.

Heat the oven to 400°F; if you have one, place a baking stone, Baking Steel, or inverted baking sheet on the center rack to heat (see page 4).

(Continued)

FILLING

12 ounces (340 g) dried black mission figs, stemmed (about 3 cups)

6 ounces (170 g) golden raisins (about 1 cup)

½ cup (120 ml) boiling water

Grated zest of 1 orange

½ cup (120 ml) fresh orange juice

4 tablespoons (56 g) unsalted butter, at room temperature

1 tablespoon brandy, cognac, or bourbon, optional

For the filling: Place the figs and raisins in a bowl, pour the boiling water over, and let them steep and plump for 20 minutes. Pour the steeped fruit (including the water), orange zest and juice, and butter into the food processor and blend until smooth. Add the brandy (if using) and stir. Scrape the filling into the chilled bottom crust and smooth the surface.

Drape the top crust over the filling. Crimp and slash. Bake (on top of the steel, stone, or baking sheet if using) until the top crust is lightly browned, 40 to 45 minutes. Cool before slicing.

Techniques: Cream Cheese Crust (page 37), Mixing and Rolling Out (page 14), Crimp and Slash (page 24)

Swaps:

- This pie works especially well with store-bought pie dough (see page 69).

- Or try it with an All-Butter (page 30) or Butter and Shortening Crust (page 33).

- Any dried fruit will swap in for the raisins and figs. Aim for a total of 18 ounces dried fruit (about 500 g).

- Squiggle with Vanilla Glaze (page 79).

MERRY MINCE-ISH SLAB PIE

WITH A BUTTER AND SHORTENING CRUST

Serves 15 to 18

Growing up, holidays always included a mince pie. My grandmother would shop in a fancy food store in Boston and send jars of Crosse and Blackwell filling to my mince pie–loving mother in Ohio. Even as a youngster, I adored the exotic flavors that came from that stout, dark glass jar. When the jars were empty and my mother craved a taste of mince, she made a pie like this and called it *Mince-ish*. I think of this glorious recipe as another way to dress up apples before I wrap them in flaky crust. The glaze is essential, by the way. This is a rich pie; serve in small slices.

Make Ahead: This pie is delicious when freshly made but also holds, covered on the counter, for 3 days. In the refrigerator, it stays fresh for a week.

BUTTER AND SHORTENING CRUST

2½ cups plus 2 tablespoons (325 g) all-purpose flour

8 tablespoons (113 g) unsalted butter, cubed and frozen for 20 minutes

8 tablespoons (113 g) Spectrum or other vegetable shortening, cubed and frozen for 20 minutes

¼ teaspoon kosher salt

½ cup (120 ml) ice water

3 teaspoons vodka, optional

(Continued)

For the crust: In the food processor, pulse the flour, butter, shortening, and salt until the fats are in small pieces coated with flour, about 15 times. Add the water and vodka (if using) all at once and process until the mixture almost forms a ball. Form the dough into a 6- by 4-inch rectangle using plastic wrap and a bench scraper to firmly press the dough into a cohesive form. Wrap tightly and refrigerate a minimum of 4 hours.

Remove the dough from the refrigerator and allow it to warm slightly. Divide the dough into two pieces, one slightly larger than the other. Roll out the larger piece to 11 by 15 inches and place in the slab pie pan, pressing it into the corners of the pan and allowing the excess to drape over the sides. Refrigerate. Roll out the second piece of dough to 10 by 14 inches, place it on a lightly floured sheet of parchment, and refrigerate.

Heat the oven to 425°F; if you have one, place a baking stone, Baking Steel, or inverted baking sheet on the center rack to heat (see page 4).

(Continued)

SWEETIE PIES

FILLING

2 pounds (1 kg) mixed pie apples, peeled, cored, and chopped into ½-inch cubes (about 4 cups)

1 cup (113 g) chopped toasted pecans

1 cup (149 g) golden raisins, plumped in ¼ cup hot water for 30 minutes and drained

¼ cup (30 g) all-purpose flour

1 cup packed (213 g) dark brown sugar

1 cup (240 ml) heavy cream

½ cup (156 g) maple syrup

2 tablespoons brandy or bourbon, optional

1 teaspoon grated orange zest

1½ tablespoons ground cinnamon

½ teaspoon allspice

¼ teaspoon freshly grated nutmeg

¼ teaspoon ground cloves

¼ teaspoon freshly ground black pepper

3 tablespoons (42 g) unsalted butter, cubed

EGG WASH AND GLAZE

1 egg yolk

1 tablespoon water

1 cup (113 g) powdered sugar

¼ cup (60 ml) heavy cream

For the filling: Stir together the apples, pecans, raisins, flour, brown sugar, cream, maple syrup, brandy (if using), orange zest, cinnamon, allspice, nutmeg, cloves, and black pepper in a large bowl, making sure to coat everything in sugar and cream and syrup. Distribute the filling across the bottom crust. Dot with the butter. Drape the top crust over the filling. Crimp and slash. Stir together the egg yolk and water and, with a pastry brush, paint the top generously.

Slide the pie into the oven with a piece of parchment under the pan (and on top of the Baking Steel, stone, or baking sheet if using) to catch any drips. Bake for 20 minutes. Reduce the heat to 350°F and bake for another 40 to 45 minutes, until golden, shiny, and the filling is bubbling through the slashes. Let the pie cool, at least 2 hours.

Mix the powdered sugar with the cream until the glaze is smooth. Squiggle the glaze over the pie using a pastry bag, or opt for a fork held high above the pie for a drizzle rather than a squiggle.

Techniques: Butter and Shortening Crust (page 33), Mixing and Rolling Out (page 14), Selecting Apples for Pie (page 234), How to Toast Nuts (page 253), Crimp and Slash (page 24), Glazes, Squiggles, and Drizzles (page 79)

Swaps:

• All-Butter (page 30) or Leaf Lard Crust (page 45).

• Top with a streusel (see page 85) instead of a top crust.

• Firm pears instead of apples.

• Walnuts instead of pecans.

• Add mini chocolate chips or unsweetened coconut shards to the filling.

• Replace the raisins with dried cherries.

CHOCOLATE PECAN SLAB PIE

WITH A CHOCOLATE CRUST

Serves 12 to 24

It wouldn't be Thanksgiving without a nutty, gooey, sweet pecan pie on the dessert table (along with about five other must-have pies). I like a whisper of bourbon and a healthy slug of maple syrup, anchoring this pie with one foot firmly in the South and the other in New England. Of course, that's my version of pecan pie—after decades spent living below the Mason-Dixon line, there's still a bit of my mother's Boston in me. Big, fat, fresh Texas pecans take it right over the top. Whether you say "PEA-kan" or "puh-CAHN" doesn't matter one bit when serving up this satisfying confection. No need to wait for Thanksgiving, either.

Make Ahead: Make the dough up to 3 days ahead. Toast the nuts up to 1 week ahead and store in an airtight container in the refrigerator.

CHOCOLATE CRUST

1⅓ cups (160 g) all-purpose flour

Scant 3 tablespoons (18 g) natural (not Dutched) cocoa powder

Scant 3 tablespoons (40 g) granulated sugar

8 tablespoons (113 g) unsalted butter, cubed and frozen for 20 minutes

⅛ teaspoon kosher salt

¼ cup (60 ml) coffee, ice cold

Powdered sugar for dusting and rolling the dough

(Continued)

For the crust: In the food processor, pulse the flour, cocoa powder, and granulated sugar. Add the butter and salt and pulse until the butter is in small pieces coated with flour, about 15 times. Add the cold coffee all at once and process until the mixture almost forms a ball. Form the dough into a 3- by 4-inch rectangle using plastic wrap and a bench scraper to firmly press the dough into a cohesive form. Wrap tightly and refrigerate a minimum of 4 hours.

Remove the dough from the refrigerator and allow it to warm slightly. Heavily dust the rolling surface with powdered sugar, roll out the dough to 11 by 15 inches, and place in the slab pie pan, pressing it into the corners of the pan and allowing the excess to drape over the sides. Refrigerate.

Heat the oven to 350°F; if you have one, place a baking stone, Baking Steel, or inverted baking sheet on the center rack to heat (see page 4).

(Continued)

SWEETIE PIES

FILLING

6 tablespoons (85 g) unsalted butter

1¼ cups packed (267 g) dark brown sugar

¼ cup (78 g) dark corn syrup

¼ cup (78 g) maple syrup

2 tablespoons molasses

2 tablespoons bourbon, optional

½ teaspoon grated orange zest

¼ teaspoon salt

3 large eggs

3 cups (340 g) toasted pecans, chopped

2 ounces (56 g) bittersweet chocolate, chopped

For the filling: Melt the butter until foaming in a 2- or 3-quart saucepan over medium heat. Whisk in the brown sugar, corn syrup, maple syrup, and molasses until velvety and smooth. Remove from the heat and cool for 5 to 7 minutes. Add the bourbon (if using), zest, and salt. Beat in the eggs, one at a time, until fully incorporated and no yellow streaks remain.

Scatter the pecans across the bottom crust and pour the sticky filling over the nuts, using a rubber spatula to get every drop. Slide the pie into the oven (on top of the steel, stone, or baking sheet if using) and bake until the top of the pie is browned but the middle is still jiggly, about 55 minutes. Place on a wire rack to cool, about 4 hours.

Melt the chocolate (see box) and pour into a piping bag or a ziptop bag. Snip the end and drizzle chocolate over the cooled pie. Refrigerate to set the drizzle, about 15 minutes. When ready to serve, slice the pie using a knife heated under warm water and wiped clean between cuts. Don't forget the ice cream.

Techniques: Chocolate Crust (page 51), Mixing and Rolling Out (page 14), How to Toast Nuts (page 253), Crimp and Slash (page 24), Glazes, Squiggles, and Drizzles (page 79)

Swaps:

- A store-bought (see page 69) or homemade All-Butter Crust (page 30).

- By weight, substitute toasted walnuts, hazelnuts, pine nuts, almonds, cashews, or a mix of all of them for the pecans.

- Go ahead, drizzle warm caramel across the surface.

HOW TO MELT CHOCOLATE

Chop the chocolate into small pieces, about the size of a pea. The ideal temperature for melted chocolate is 90°F; the butterfats and milk solids will not separate and when it firms up again, it will not have a dusty bloom.

IN THE MICROWAVE

Place the chopped chocolate in a microwave-safe container. Using low power, microwave in short 15-second bursts, stirring between each burst. The stirring is critical or the chocolate will burn. Depending on the quantity of chocolate, this process could take a few minutes. Once the chocolate is smooth, or nearly smooth, stop microwaving and stir until the chocolate is thoroughly melted.

ON THE STOVETOP

Construct a double boiler with a saucepan filled with an inch or two of water and a metal or glass bowl that fits over the saucepan, not touching the water below. Bring the water to a low boil. Place the chopped chocolate in the bowl. With the bowl over the simmering water, stir until the chocolate has melted. Be careful not to cook it, but simply to melt it.

WALNUT "BAKLAVA" SLAB PIE

WITH A CREAM CHEESE CRUST

Serves 16 to 20

Baklava, a phyllo-layered sweet, comes from worlds away and centuries ago. It's crispy and sticky and tender all at once. I set out to make a pie with the intensity of baklava—honeyed dense chewiness—with plump pistachios and plenty of butter. The nutty filling is set on a delicate cream cheese crust for both flakiness and heft. It is the whisper of cardamom and the squeeze of brightening lemon juice that reminds me most of baklava and transforms it from ordinary to exotic. A candy thermometer is useful to keep the filling from turning to taffy.

Make Ahead: Make the dough up to 3 days ahead. Toast the nuts up to 1 week ahead and store in the refrigerator.

CREAM CHEESE CRUST

2½ cups plus
2 tablespoons (325 g)
all-purpose flour

8 tablespoons (113 g)
unsalted butter, cubed and
frozen for 20 minutes

8 tablespoons (113 g)
cream cheese, cubed and
refrigerated for 20 minutes

¼ teaspoon kosher salt

½ cup (120 ml) ice water

FILLING

6 tablespoons (85 g)
unsalted butter

(Continued)

For the crust: In the food processor, pulse the flour, butter, cream cheese, and salt until the butter and cheese are in small pieces coated with flour, about 15 times. Add the ice water all at once and process until the mixture almost forms a ball. Form the dough into a 6- by 4-inch rectangle using plastic wrap and a bench scraper to firmly press the dough into a cohesive form. Wrap tightly and refrigerate a minimum of 4 hours.

Remove the dough from the refrigerator and allow it to warm slightly. Divide the dough into two pieces, one slightly larger than the other. Roll out the larger piece to 11 by 15 inches and place in the slab pie pan, pressing it into the corners of the pan and allowing the excess to drape over the sides. Refrigerate. Roll out the second piece of dough to 10 by 14 inches, place it on a lightly floured sheet of parchment, and refrigerate.

Heat the oven to 350°F; if you have one, place a baking stone, Baking Steel, or inverted baking sheet on the center rack to heat (see page 4).

(Continued)

1¼ cups packed (267 g) light brown sugar

½ cup (156 g) light corn syrup

¼ cup (85 g) mild honey, such as clover or wildflower

3 large eggs, lightly beaten

1 tablespoon fresh lemon juice

2 teaspoons vanilla extract

½ teaspoon cardamom seeds (see box), crushed with the side of a knife

¼ teaspoon kosher salt

1½ cups (170 g) walnuts, toasted and roughly chopped

¼ cup (28 g) roasted salted pistachios

1 egg yolk

1 tablespoon cold water

For the filling: Melt the butter until it foams in a 2- or 3-quart saucepan over medium heat. Whisk in the sugar, corn syrup, and honey until velvety and smooth, then bring to a strong boil. Continue to cook, stirring constantly, until the mixture is thick, the bubbles become lazy, and a candy thermometer registers 240°F. Remove from the heat, cool for 7 to 10 minutes (to 145°F) so the eggs won't scramble. Whisk in eggs, one at a time, until fully incorporated and no yellow streaks remain. Add the lemon juice, vanilla, cardamom, and salt, stir well, and fold in the walnuts and pistachios. Use a flexible spatula to scoop all the filling into the bottom crust. The filling will be sticky and gooey. (Hint: To clean the saucepan, fill with water and bring to a boil.)

Fold the overhanging dough of the bottom crust inward toward the center of the pan to form a wall, using the Three-Finger Crimp (see page 25) to make a double-thick crust that stands up above the rim of the pan. Using cookie cutters or a sharp knife, stamp out cutouts from the top crust. Create an openwork pattern across the surface. We used leaf cutouts. Whisk the yolk and water together and use a pastry brush to paint the cutouts so they will be crispy and glistening.

Slide the pie into the oven (on top of the steel, stone, or baking sheet if using) and bake for 40 to 50 minutes. Check the pie frequently for signs of cratering, when large bubbles form in the center of the pie as a result of the bottom crust rising. Poke the bubbles with a skewer or the sharp tip of a knife and watch them deflate. If you miss the crater and it rises up without a puncture, when it deflates, as the pie cools, the surface may be a little lumpy but the pie is still edible.

Cool for 15 minutes. Use a heated knife, wiping it clean between cuts to portion the pie. Serve slightly warm or at room temperature with crème fraîche or vanilla ice cream.

Techniques: Cream Cheese Crust (page 37), Mixing and Rolling Out (page 14), How to Toast Nuts (page 253), Crimp and Slash (page 24), Lattices, Cutouts, Stamps, and Shapes (page 26)

Swaps:

- Of course, phyllo dough (see page 70) is a natural crust for the filling, but All-Butter (page 30) or Butter and Shortening Crusts (page 33) are suitable, tender alternatives.

- By weight, substitute toasted pecans, hazelnuts, pine nuts, almonds, cashews, or a mix of all of them for the walnuts and pistachios. The pistachios add salt, so add an extra pinch in the filling if you're not using them.

- Go ahead, drizzle warm bittersweet chocolate across the surface.

HOW TO EXTRACT CARDAMOM SEEDS

Cardamom is a sultry spice most often used to scent chai tea or curry powders. As an occasional and classic addition to baklava fillings, it seemed essential in the Walnut "Baklava" Slab Pie. Once it's in the spice drawer, don't stop there. Cardamom is a delightful complement to peach, plum, and apricot pies. Ground cardamom is missing some of the floral tones found in the crushed seeds and grows dull quickly.

For cardamom seeds, look for green cardamom pods in your grocery's spice aisle, at health food stores, and online. Smash a pod with the side of a chef's knife, then pry open the pod and extract the seeds. Crush the seeds with the side of a knife.

PEANUT BUTTER SLAB PIE
WITH A CHOCOLATE WAFER CRUST

Serves 18

A peanut butter cup in pie form—velvety, buttery, and rich. The dark black cookie crust is deeply bitter chocolate with very little sweet; add in a measure of salt for essential balance. Kid-friendly, sure, but I have yet to meet an adult who didn't gasp just a little bit when offered peanut butter pie. Use commercial peanut butter, not "natural" style, for the silkiest filling. When I was a teenager, I spent time in the West Indies. The peanut butter there was highly spiced with roughly ground cinnamon and something spicy. When I first made this pie, it begged for a subtle nudge from the spice cabinet, so I added a pinch of cayenne.

Make Ahead: The crust may be baked and chilled several hours ahead.

CHOCOLATE WAFER CRUST

1 (9-ounce) package Famous Chocolate Wafers (255 g), about 40 cookies, crushed to a fine powder (about 2 cups)

8 tablespoons (113 g) unsalted butter, melted

¼ teaspoon kosher salt

FILLING

1¾ cups (450 g) creamy peanut butter

8 tablespoons (113 g) unsalted butter, softened

4 tablespoons (56 g) cream cheese

1 cup (113 g) powdered sugar

(Continued)

For the crust: Heat the oven to 350°F; if you have one, place a baking stone, Baking Steel, or inverted baking sheet on the center rack to heat (see page 4).

Combine the cookie crumbs and melted butter until cohesive and thoroughly buttered. Press the crust into the bottom of the slab pie pan. I use a metal cup measure or the flat bottom of a glass for this task. Refrigerate for 20 minutes.

Bake the crust (on top of the steel, stone, or baking sheet if using) for 15 minutes, until it feels dry to the touch. Remove from the oven and place on a rack to cool. Sprinkle with the salt.

For the filling: In a stand mixer or with a hand mixer, beat the peanut butter, butter, and cream cheese until smooth and lightened. Beat in the powdered sugar, cinnamon, and cayenne (if using). Continue to lighten the mixture by beating at a high speed for 2 or 3 minutes longer, to make the pie light and fluffy. Scrape the filling into the cooled crust and smooth the top.

Stir the peanuts and chocolate chips together and sprinkle them decoratively along the edges of the pie. Cover and refrigerate for at least 2 hours before portioning.

(Continued)

½ teaspoon ground cinnamon

⅛ teaspoon cayenne pepper, optional

⅓ cup (32 g) chopped salted peanuts

⅓ cup (45 g) mini chocolate chips

Techniques: Press-In Crusts (page 55), Cookie Crumb Crusts (page 65), Birdseed, Crushes, and Rocky Road Garnishes (page 81)

Swaps:

- Any cookie crust (page 65) will do.

- For the filling, other nut butters are rich and delicious, cashew and almond particularly. But not sunflower butter; it is dry and unforgiving.

- Top with a drizzle of chocolate or a splotch of whipped cream.

DOUBLE CHOCOLATE SLAB PIE

WITH A CHOCOLATE CRUST

Serves 12 to 15

This flaky-crusted, chocolate-filled, sprinkle-dotted pie is sensational, but it's also a bit of a project with several steps and chilling times between the steps. Plan it out because it's worth it. Crimped like a chocolate Pop-Tart, it is the answer for a child's party or a Saturday night treat for your best friend, the chocoholic. Use bittersweet chocolate and make it an adult treat: Hold back on the glaze, cut the cooled slab into 2- by 3-inch rectangles, and serve as a snack with warm glogg, *après ski*. If serving it warm, give this pie plenty of time to cool first, then briefly warm the pie before serving (inexplicably, it works best this way).

Make Ahead: The chocolate dough may be made up to 3 days ahead.

CHOCOLATE CRUST

2½ cups plus
2 tablespoons (325 g)
all-purpose flour

⅓ cup (35 g) natural
(not Dutched) cocoa
powder

⅓ cup (67 g)
granulated sugar

16 tablespoons (225 g)
unsalted butter, cubed and
frozen for 20 minutes

¼ teaspoon kosher salt

⅔ cup coffee (160 ml),
ice cold

Powdered sugar for rolling
the dough

(Continued)

For the crust: In the food processor, pulse the flour, cocoa powder, and granulated sugar. Add the butter and salt and pulse until the fats are in small pieces coated with flour, about 15 times. Add the cold coffee all at once and process until the mixture almost forms a ball. Form the dough into a 6- by 4-inch rectangle using plastic wrap and a bench scraper to firmly press the dough into a cohesive form. Wrap tightly and refrigerate a minimum of 4 hours.

Remove the dough from the refrigerator and allow it to warm slightly. Divide the dough into two equal blocks. Roll one of the blocks to about 9 by 13 inches and ¼-inch thickness between two sheets of parchment paper dusted heavily with powdered sugar. Repeat with the second block of dough. Trim the two doughs identically to 8 by 12 inches, leaving each on parchment. Refrigerate for at least 30 minutes before filling.

For the filling: Combine the cocoa powder, brown sugar, milk, salt, and half the chopped chocolate in a medium saucepan. Place the pan over medium heat and whisk until the mixture is smooth. Bring to a gentle boil and continue to whisk until the filling is thick and silky, about 3 minutes more. Remove from the heat and add the

FILLING

¼ cup (21 g) natural (not Dutched) cocoa powder

¼ cup packed (50 g) light brown sugar

¾ cup (180 ml) whole milk

½ teaspoon kosher or sea salt

6 ounces (170 g) semisweet or bittersweet chocolate, chopped

2 tablespoons (28 g) unsalted butter

½ teaspoon vanilla extract

GLAZE

1 cup (115 g) powdered sugar

1 teaspoon vanilla extract

1 tablespoon whole milk

Sprinkles

remaining chocolate, the butter, and vanilla and whisk until smooth. Cool before proceeding, but do not refrigerate. It's easier to put the pie together if the filling has firmed up, about 90 minutes.

Heat the oven to 400°F; if you have one, place a baking stone, Baking Steel, or inverted baking sheet on the center rack to heat (see page 4).

Retrieve the cold rolled-out pie dough from the refrigerator. Without removing the dough from the parchment paper, scoop the filling into the center of one piece. Spread the filling with an offset spatula, leaving a 1-inch border all around. Leaving it on the parchment paper, pierce the second piece of dough all over with a fork. To cover the pie, invert the parchment paper to help drape the second piece of dough over the filling and settle it down corner to corner. Peel away the parchment. Using a fork, firmly crimp the edges all the way around. Slash the top with three vents or otherwise decorate the surface of the pie, keeping in mind the glaze and sprinkles to come. Using the parchment, deftly lift, slide, and settle the pie into the slab pie pan, still on the parchment. Chill for 20 minutes or more.

Slide the pan into the oven (on top of the steel, stone, or baking sheet if using) and bake until slightly darkened at the edges, 30 to 35 minutes. Remove to a rack and cool.

For the glaze: In a medium bowl, whisk the powdered sugar, vanilla, and milk until smooth and thick. With an offset spatula, spread the glaze across the surface of the pie, avoiding the crimped edges. Scatter sprinkles evenly across the glaze. Refrigerate to set, and bring to room temperature before serving.

Techniques: Chocolate Crust (page 51), Mixing and Rolling Out (page 14), Crimp and Slash (page 24), Glazes, Squiggles, and Drizzles (page 79)

Swaps:

- Espresso powder (3 tablespoons) dissolved in boiling water (⅔ cup) and chilled can stand in for the cold coffee.

- Make a Coffee Glaze (page 79) and sprinkle with crushed dark chocolate–covered espresso beans.

NO-CAMPFIRE-NECESSARY S'MORES SLAB PIE

WITH A GRAHAM CRACKER CRUST

Serves 15 to 18

I expect some of you may slap your forehead when you read this recipe and say, "Why didn't I think of that?" Indeed, it's so easy and straightforward, it's almost sinful. There is nothing to beat the smell of wood smoke and the fear your perfectly bronzed and oozy marshmallow will slip from the stick, but this S'Mores Slab stands in when the campfire is miles away. This pie must be baked on top of a hot surface (see Ovens, Steels, and Stones, page 4) to achieve a firm base.

Make Ahead: The crust may be baked and the chocolate layer spread over the crust a day or two in advance. Keep refrigerated until ready to add the marshmallows.

GRAHAM CRACKER CRUST

9 graham crackers (143 g), crushed to a powder (about 1¼ cups)

6 tablespoons (85 g) unsalted butter, melted

⅓ cup (67 g) granulated sugar

1 teaspoon kosher salt

FILLING

2 cups (12 ounces, 300 g) semisweet chocolate chips

5 cups (10 ounces, 285 g) mini marshmallows

For the crust: Heat the oven to 350°F and place a baking stone, Baking Steel, or inverted baking sheet on the center rack to heat (see page 4). Place the graham crackers in a ziptop bag and bash them with a rolling pin until they are in small pieces but not powdered, or use your hands to crush them. Mix the cracker crumbs, butter, sugar, and salt together using your hands or a firm silicone spatula. Knead and press the mixture until it is cohesive and the crumbs are thoroughly buttered. Dump the dough into the slab pie pan and press across the bottom, but not up the sides of the pan. Press down using a metal cup measure, or the flat bottom of a glass, until the crust feels firm to the touch. Slide the pan into the center of the oven, on top of the steel, stone, or baking sheet, and bake until lightly browned, about 10 minutes.

To fill the pie: Remove the crust from the oven; it will still feel damp and soft. Immediately scatter the chocolate chips evenly across the surface of the pie and pop the pie back into the oven for no more than 2 minutes, until the chocolate is softened. With an offset spatula, spread the chocolate evenly across the crust. Refrigerate for at least 2 hours or up to 2 days.

(Continued)

Place a rack at the top of the oven and heat the broiler to high. Scatter the marshmallows thickly across the top of the pie. Slide the pan under the broiler and watch carefully. It takes about 2 minutes to brown beautifully. It takes about 4 minutes to incinerate.

While still hot from the oven, warm a long slicing knife under hot water, make a cut and, wiping and warming the knife between each subsequent cut, portion the pie into serving pieces.

Techniques: Press-In Crusts (page 55), Cookie Crumb Crust (page 65)

Swaps:

- Use any cookie crust (page 65).

- Try bittersweet chocolate instead of semisweet.

- A swipe of caramel atop the crust and below the chocolate is, plain and simple, naughty.

BUTTERMILK CARDAMOM SLAB PIE

WITH AN ALL-BUTTER CRUST

Serves 15 to 18

This recipe is always in my arsenal, the notion tickling my brain when I am searching for a dessert to bring to a party and I don't feel like going to the grocery store. I almost always have buttermilk, but if I don't, a little lemon juice in whole milk creates "sour milk," a suitable stand-in, although with less velvety unctuousness. Considering the limited ingredient list of the pie, its flavor is complex. The filling is dense and a little chewy, with the tang and pleasure of an eggy custard. The pie filling may puff up in a dramatic way while in the oven, but don't worry: It will settle back down as it cools and the crackly browned shell on the filling will do a terrific imitation of crème brûlée, without the shatter but with all the charm.

Make Ahead: This pie may be made and chilled a day ahead. Bring to room temperature before serving.

ALL-BUTTER CRUST

1⅓ cups (160 g)
all-purpose flour

8 tablespoons (113 g)
unsalted butter, cubed and
frozen for 20 minutes

¼ teaspoon kosher salt

¼ cup (60 ml) ice water

FILLING

8 tablespoons (113 g)
unsalted butter, cubed and
slightly softened

1 cup (200 g) granulated
sugar

(Continued)

For the crust: In the food processor, pulse the flour, butter, and salt until the butter is in small pieces coated with flour, about 15 times. Add the water all at once and process until the mixture almost forms a ball. Form the dough into a 3- by 4-inch rectangle using plastic wrap and a bench scraper to firmly press the dough into a cohesive form. Wrap tightly and refrigerate a minimum of 4 hours.

Remove the dough from the refrigerator and allow it to warm slightly. Roll it out to 11 by 15 inches and place in the slab pie pan. Using scissors, trim the overhang. Fold the remaining dough toward the center to make a chubby border. Crimp or pleat the edge all the way around. Place the pan in the refrigerator to stay cold while making the filling.

Heat the oven to 350°F; if you have one, place a baking stone, Baking Steel, or inverted baking sheet on the center rack to heat (see page 4).

(Continued)

3 large eggs

1 egg yolk

3 tablespoons all-purpose flour

1 cup (235 ml) buttermilk

1 tablespoon lemon juice

1 teaspoon vanilla extract

¼ teaspoon cardamom seeds, crushed under a knife blade

For the filling: In a stand mixer fitted with the whisk attachment (or with a wooden spoon, large bowl, and strong arm), beat the butter and sugar until light and fluffy. Add the whole eggs one at a time, whipping after each addition until no streaks of yellow remain and the filling becomes lofty and smooth. Add the egg yolk and whisk in. Sprinkle the flour into the bowl, reduce the speed, and add the buttermilk, lemon juice, vanilla, and cardamom seeds. Beat on low until combined. It will look curdled; that's okay. Pour the filling into the crimped crust. Slide the pie into the oven (on top of the steel, stone, or baking sheet if using) and bake until crackly and bronzed, 45 to 55 minutes.

Cool slightly before cutting. Keep leftovers refrigerated.

Techniques: All-Butter Crust (page 30), Mixing and Rolling Out (page 14), Crimp and Slash (page 24), How to Extract Cardamom Seeds (page 267)

Swaps:

- Try a Shortbread Crust (page 59).
- If you're not a cardamom fan (what?), substitute cinnamon.

LEMON CREAM SLAB PIE

WITH A SPECULOOS CRUST

Serves 16 to 20

Over the years, I've relied on this pie when I didn't have the time to make Lemon Meringue Pie (page 284). It's creamy, velvety, fluffy, and spiked with tart citrus. Using a press-in crust and lightening the eggy, buttery lemon curd with plenty of whipped cream makes all the difference. And, oh, the happy marriage of lemons and Danish Biscoff cookies with their buttery hint of cinnamon! If unable to locate the original Biscoff cookie, a very similar speculoos cookie is available at Trader Joe's.

Make Ahead: The lemon curd may be made (before folding in the whipped cream) and frozen 3 months in advance. The baked crust may be made a day ahead. The cream may be whipped up to 6 hours ahead. Fold the cream and curd together and fill the crust no more than 4 hours before serving or the filling will weep.

SPECULOOS CRUST

29 Biscoff (or other speculoos) cookies (225 g; from an 8.8-ounce package), crushed to a fine powder (about 2 cups), 1 tablespoon crumbs set aside for garnish

8 tablespoons (113 g) unsalted butter, melted

¼ teaspoon kosher salt

(Continued)

For the crust: Heat the oven to 350°F; if you have one, place a baking stone, Baking Steel, or inverted baking sheet on the center rack to heat (see page 4).

In a medium bowl, mix the cookie crumbs, butter, and salt together using your hands or a firm silicone spatula. Knead and press the mixture until it is cohesive and the crumbs are thoroughly buttered. Dump the wet crumbs into the slab pie pan and press across the bottom, but not up the sides, of the pan. Press down using a metal cup measure, or the flat bottom of a glass, until the crust feels firm to the touch. Slide the pan into the oven (on top of the steel, stone, or baking sheet if using) and bake until lightly browned, about 10 minutes. Remove from the oven and place on a rack to cool.

(Continued)

FILLING

3 large eggs plus 3 egg yolks, at room temperature

½ cup (100 g) granulated sugar

¾ cup (180 ml) freshly squeezed lemon juice (about 4 lemons)

8 tablespoons (113 g) cold unsalted butter, cut into cubes

1 teaspoon grated lemon zest

1½ cups (360 ml) heavy cream

For the filling: Heat a medium saucepan filled with 2 inches of water over medium-high heat until the water begins to simmer. In a large stainless steel or glass bowl, whisk the eggs and yolks, sugar, and lemon juice until foamy and a sunny, lemon yellow. Cook until the mixture hits 170°F, when it will be thick like hot fudge sauce and coat the back of a spoon, about 8 to 10 minutes. Remove the curd from the heat and, with a sturdy whisk, beat in the butter, piece by piece, until it has been incorporated into the lemony pudding; this process will take 7 or 8 minutes. The curd will thicken even more and become smooth, silky, and golden yellow as the butter is incorporated. Whisk in the zest. Cover and cool. It will chill to the consistency of firm custard, about 2 hours.

In the bowl of a stand mixer, whip the cream until stiff peaks form and the beater leaves a trail in the whipped cream. Set aside half the whipped cream for the topping. Add a dollop of the remaining whipped cream to the curd and whisk it to lighten the filling. Using bold folding movements, incorporate the remaining whipped cream (that was not set aside for the topping) into the lightened curd using a wide spatula and five or six turns. It's alright if there are some white streaks remaining. Pile the lemon cream filling into the crust and smooth the top with an offset spatula.

Top the pie with remaining whipped cream. Use the back of a tablespoon to make fluffy peaks across the top. Or use a piping bag to decorate. Chill the tart for at least 1 hour and keep chilled until serving.

Techniques: Press-In Crusts (page 55), Cookie Crumb Crusts (page 65), Whipped and Mashed Toppings (page 75)

Swaps:

• Make the cookie crust (page 65) with gingersnaps, vanilla wafers, or amaretti cookies.

• Instead of zest and juice from regular (Eureka) lemons, use Meyer lemons, Ruby grapefruit, Key limes, or Cara Cara oranges.

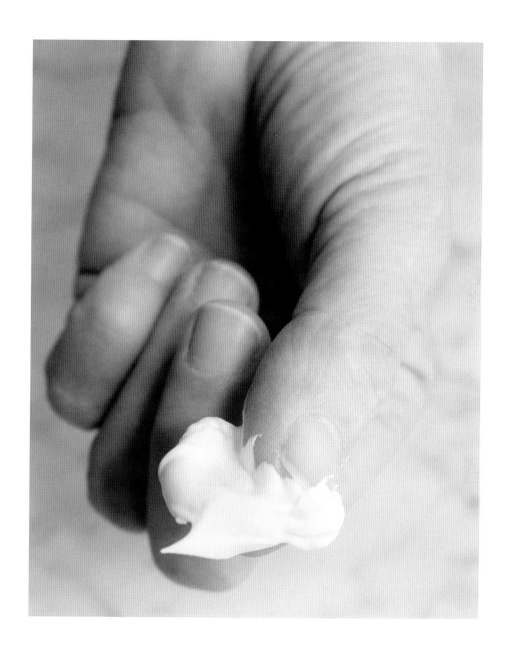

SWEETIE PIES

LEMON MERINGUE SLAB PIE

WITH A GINGERSNAP CRUST

Serves 16 to 20

The combination of a summer day and a slice of lemon meringue pie takes me right back to my childhood because my mother made a stupendous LMP. My classic, lip-puckering slab pie, topped with a cloud of marshmallow meringue toasted to perfection, is a little more effort than the Lemon Cream Pie (page 281), but so worth it. Make sure the meringue touches all the edges of the pie so it has something to hang on to. Meringue has a way of shrinking away to nothing if it isn't anchored.

Make Ahead: The baked crust and the lemon curd base may be made a day ahead and held separately in the refrigerator.

GINGERSNAP CRUST

35 gingersnaps (8 ounces, 225 g), crushed to a fine powder (about 2 cups)

8 tablespoons (113 g) unsalted butter, melted

¼ teaspoon kosher salt

FILLING

3 large eggs plus 3 egg yolks, at room temperature

½ cup (100 g) granulated sugar

¾ cup (180 ml) freshly squeezed lemon juice

8 tablespoons (113 g) unsalted butter, cut into small cubes

1 teaspoon grated lemon zest

(Continued)

For the crust: Heat the oven to 350°F; if you have one, place a baking stone, Baking Steel, or inverted baking sheet on the center rack to heat (see page 4).

In a medium bowl, mix the cookie crumbs, butter, and salt together using your hands or a firm silicone spatula. Knead and press the mixture until it is cohesive and the crumbs are thoroughly buttered. Dump the wet crumbs into the slab pie pan and press across the bottom, but not up the sides, of the pan. Press down using a metal cup measure, or the flat bottom of a glass, until the crust feels firm to the touch. Slide the pan into the oven (on top of the steel, stone, or baking sheet if using) and bake until lightly browned, about 10 minutes. Remove from the oven and place on a rack to cool.

For the filling: Set a medium saucepan filled with 2 inches of water over medium-high heat until the water begins to simmer. In a large stainless steel, ceramic, or glass bowl, whisk the eggs and yolks, sugar, and lemon juice until foamy and a sunny, lemon yellow. Cook until the mixture hits 170°F, when it will be thick like hot fudge sauce and coat the back of a spoon, about 8 to 10 minutes. Remove the curd from the heat and, with a sturdy whisk, beat in the butter, piece by piece. The curd will thicken even more and become smooth, silky, and golden

MERINGUE

**3 egg whites,
at room temperature**

¼ teaspoon cream of tartar

**½ cup (100 g) granulated
sugar**

¼ teaspoon vanilla extract

yellow as the butter is incorporated. Whisk in the zest. Cover and refrigerate. It will chill to the consistency of firm custard, about 2 hours.

For the meringue: Heat the oven to broil with a rack in the upper third of the oven. In a stand mixer, beat the egg whites on medium until foamy. Add the cream of tartar, which helps to stabilize the lift. Continue beating, increasing the speed to high, while adding sugar 1 tablespoon at a time. When half the sugar has been added, add the vanilla. Continue beating and adding sugar 1 tablespoon at a time until the egg whites are shiny and form tall, stiff peaks when the beater is lifted. Check to see if the sugar is entirely dissolved by rubbing a little meringue between two fingers. There should be no grit. If it's still gritty, continue beating and test again after another minute.

Spread the cooled lemon curd across the cooled cookie crust. Plop the meringue here and there over the curd and gently disperse it across the surface with the back side of a large spoon, making fluffy peaks and ensuring the meringue securely touches along the entire edge of the crust, or spoon the meringue into a pastry bag and pipe a pretty design across the surface.

Slide the pie into the oven and broil the meringue until it is browning here and there and smells like toasted marshmallows, 3 or 4 minutes. Cool slightly and serve soon.

Techniques: Press-In Crusts (page 55), Cookie Crumb Crusts (page 65), Whipped and Mashed Toppings (page 75)

Swaps:

- Blind bake (see page 29) a single-crust All-Butter Crust (page 30).

BANANA PUDDING SLAB PIE

WITH A VANILLA WAFER CRUST

Serves 12 to 15

Southern banana pudding was the inspiration for this cookie and banana confection: a Nilla Wafer crust (a beautiful buttery shelf of vanilla) covered with a pillow of pudding and cool, firm banana slices. This is a dangerously delicious pie that hits all my pie-centers. Homey, familiar, velvety, and luscious. I'm partial to a shot of dark, spiced rum for the kick it gives the whole experience, but if the pie is for your kids, hold back the rum for your daiquiri instead. Give the pie plenty of time to chill so the flavors get to know each other.

Make Ahead: This pie benefits from 4 hours of chilling before serving. But do not make this pie a day ahead as the topping will weep.

VANILLA WAFER CRUST

8 tablespoons (113 g) unsalted butter, melted

1 (11-ounce) package standard size Nilla Wafers (311 g), crushed to a fine powder in the blender or food processor (about 2 cups), a few cookie crumbs and shards set aside to decorate the top

¼ teaspoon kosher salt

FILLING

¾ cup (150 g) granulated sugar

¼ cup (28 g) cornstarch

2 large eggs plus 4 egg yolks, at room temperature

(Continued)

For the crust: Heat the oven to 350°F; if you have one, place a baking stone, Baking Steel, or inverted baking sheet on the center rack to heat (see page 4). In a medium bowl, stir the melted butter into the crushed cookie crumbs. Press the crust into the bottom and firmly up the sides of the slab pie pan. I use a metal cup measure or the flat bottom of a glass for this task. Refrigerate for 20 minutes. Bake the crust (on top of the steel, stone, or baking sheet if using) for 12 to 15 minutes, until it feels dry to the touch. Place on a rack to cool, sprinkle with the salt, and then refrigerate until firm, about 2 hours.

For the filling: Whisk the sugar, cornstarch, eggs and yolks, and milk in a heavy 3- or 4-quart saucepan, making sure everything is combined before starting to cook. Cook over medium-low heat, whisking constantly, until it begins to bubble and is thick enough to hold soft peaks when the whisk is lifted, 10 to 12 minutes. Remove from the heat and stir in the vanilla and rum (if using).

Cool slightly before spreading in the cooled crust and smoothing with an offset spatula. Let the pudding set for 1 hour.

(Continued)

SWEETIE PIES

4 cups (960 ml) whole milk

1½ teaspoons vanilla extract

2 tablespoons dark rum, optional

3 ripe bananas, peeled and sliced ¼ inch thick

1 cup (240 ml) heavy cream, whipped to stiff peaks

Line the top of the pudding with the sliced bananas. Top with the whipped cream: Recklessly dollop across the surface or using a pastry bag with a star tip, pipe it prettily, your choice. Place the pie in the refrigerator to chill and firm up, about 4 hours. Garnish with cookie crumbs and shards.

Techniques: Press-In Crusts (page 55), Cookie Crumb Crusts (page 65), Whipped and Mashed Toppings (page 75)

Swaps:

- Chocolate wafers, gingersnaps, or graham crackers also work as a cookie crust (page 65).

- Drizzle a layer of caramel on top of the crust after baking, just before filling.

- Use coconut cream instead of milk.

- Instead of whipping cream, meringue the top (see page 76) and broil until browned like a toasted marshmallow.

COCONUT CREAM SLAB PIE

WITH A SALTINE CRUST

Serves 12 to 15

Coconut cream pie is either loved or loathed. I'm in the love category. Because the balance of crust to filling is crucial, and because the filling can be so sweet, I couldn't stop thinking about a salty undercarriage. And that's when I remembered the iconic Atlantic Beach Pie, a lemony cloud with a salty crust, created by chef Bill Smith at Crook's Corner (Chapel Hill, NC). His pie is an orchestrated balance of a tart-sweet citrus filling and a salty crust. A nod to Smith's originality, my pie offers chewy coconut and shattering saltine crackers. It's textural and smooth, sweet, salty, impossible to resist.

Make Ahead: The crust and filling may be made up to 2 days ahead.

SALTINE CRUST

1½ sleeves (170 g) saltine crackers (about 60 crackers) (about 2 cups crushed)

⅓ cup (67 g) granulated sugar

10 tablespoons (140 g) unsalted butter, cubed, at room temperature

FILLING

¾ cup (150 g) granulated sugar

⅓ cup (60 g) cornstarch

1 cup (235 ml) full-fat coconut milk

2 cups (480 ml) half-and-half

3 egg yolks

(Continued)

For the crust: Heat the oven to 350°F; if you have one, place a baking stone, Baking Steel, or inverted baking sheet on the center rack to heat (see page 4). Place the crackers in a ziptop bag and bash them with a rolling pin until they are in small pieces but not powdered. Alternatively, use your hands to crush them. Pour the crumbs into a medium bowl, add the sugar and butter cubes, and knead and work the crackers until a cohesive dough appears. This will take 8 to 10 minutes of hard work. It's worth it. Press the dough firmly into and across the bottom of the slab pie pan and carefully into the corners and, if you have enough, up the sides of the pan. Bake the crust (on top of the steel, stone, or baking sheet if using) for 20 to 25 minutes, until browned in the corners and on the edges. Cool on a rack.

For the filling: Whisk the sugar and cornstarch in a heavy 3-quart saucepan. Whisk in the coconut milk and half-and-half. Finally, whisk in the egg yolks until no streaks of yellow remain. Place over medium-high heat and slowly bring to a boil, whisking constantly. When it is thick and pudding-like with an occasional bubble forming on the surface of the custard, about 8 to 10 minutes total, remove the pan from the heat. Whisk in the butter and vanilla, which will make

(Continued)

3 tablespoons (42 g)
cold butter

½ teaspoon vanilla extract

2 cups (148 g) sweetened
flaked coconut

2 tablespoons dark rum,
optional

TOPPING

1½ cups (360 ml) heavy
cream

3 tablespoons granulated
sugar

1½ teaspoons vanilla
extract

3 tablespoons toasted
sweetened coconut
(see box), crushed to a
coarse powder

the custard silky and shiny, then add the coconut and rum (if using). Cover with plastic wrap directly in contact with the surface of the custard (so no skin will form) and refrigerate for at least 45 minutes or at most 2 days.

Spoon the coconut filling into the pre-baked crust. Smooth the surface with an offset spatula and put the pie into the refrigerator. Chill for 30 minutes or longer.

For the topping: Beat the cream at high speed with an electric mixer until foamy. Add the sugar, 1 tablespoon at a time, beating until stiff peaks form. Beat in the vanilla. Spread or pipe the whipped cream over the pie and garnish with a shower of toasted coconut.

Chill for at least 1 hour before serving. The leftovers, covered and refrigerated, hold for 3 days.

Techniques: Press-In Crusts (page 55), Cracker Crumb Crusts (page 61), Whipped and Mashed Toppings (page 75)

Swaps:

- Use a Graham Cracker or Vanilla Wafer Crust (page 65).

- Swap in the filling from Lemon Cream Slab Pie (page 281) or Banana Pudding Slab Pie (page 287).

- Omit the garnish of toasted coconut and drizzle with melted chocolate or hot caramel instead.

HOW TO TOAST COCONUT

Toasting sweetened coconut can be tricky. The sugar easily burns, turning tasty to toasty to terrible in no time at all. Patience and vigilance pay off. Do not leave the kitchen. Watch it every moment. And remember—a hot pan will continue to cook the coconut even after removing it from the stove or oven, so immediately pour that perfectly toasted coconut onto a cutting board and lightly chop and crush it with a sharp knife until garnish-worthy. Here are three ways to achieve "coconuttyness" with ½ cup sweetened coconut flakes:

ON THE STOVETOP

Cook the coconut in a small skillet over medium heat, stirring and toasting, until it is lightly browned, dried, and fragrant, 2 to 3 minutes.

IN THE OVEN

I never turn the oven on only to toast nuts or coconut, but if I've made the crust, the oven is already on and it's the easiest way to go. Scatter the coconut over a baking sheet and slide it into a 350°F oven. Bake, stirring every 2 minutes and watching carefully, until the coconut is lightly browned, 5 to 7 minutes.

IN THE MICROWAVE

Spread out the coconut on a microwave-safe plate. Cook in the microwave on High in 2-minute increments, stirring after each time, until it turns toasty brown, anywhere from 6 to 8 minutes.

Store any leftover toasted coconut in a tightly sealed glass jar. It will stay fresh for weeks, but it never lasts that long around here. I add it to everything: granola, scones, roasted salmon, green beans.

DAIRY-FREE AND PASSOVER-PERFECT COCONUT CREAM SLAB PIE

WITH A MATZO CRUST

Serves 12 to 15

"I can't wait for the Passover desserts," said no one ever. Let's be honest: Matzo meal doesn't cut it as a cake flour. Most traditional Seder desserts land like a brick. But here, crushed matzo become the base for a sweet, textured, crunchy, chewy pie with a crust worth *kvelling* over. It's kosher and dairy-free and delicious all year round, but especially at Passover when it's a welcome change from Aunt Rose's sponge cake. Make this pie once and be prepared to bring the Seder dessert forevermore. There are three types of coconut called for here: milk, cream, and sweetened, flaked. Look for coconut milk in the international foods aisle at the grocery store. The best-quality coconut milk has a thick layer of coconut cream at the top of the can. Shake well before using. Cans of coconut cream are usually in the aisle devoted to drink mixers and sodas. If unavailable, scoop the thick cream from the surface of two additional cans of coconut milk for the topping, discarding the watery liquid below. Sweetened, flaked coconut is in the baking aisle.

Make Ahead: The crust and filling may be made up to 2 days ahead.

MATZO CRUST

8 to 9 sheets (225 g) matzo (about 2 cups crushed)

¼ cup granulated sugar

1 teaspoon kosher salt

10 tablespoons (140 g) unsalted margarine, cubed, at room temperature

(Continued)

For the crust: Heat the oven to 350°F; if you have one, place a baking stone, Baking Steel, or inverted baking sheet on the center rack to heat (see page 4). Place the matzo in a ziptop bag and bash with a rolling pin until they are in crumbs and small shards but not powdered. You should have 2 cups. Alternatively, use your hands to crush them. Pour the crumbs into a medium bowl and add the sugar, salt, and margarine cubes. Knead the matzo until a cohesive dough appears. Press the dough across the bottom of the slab pie pan and carefully into the corners and, if you have enough, up the sides. Bake the crust (on top of the steel, stone, or baking sheet if using) for 20 to 25 minutes, until browned in the corners and on the edges. Cool on a rack.

FILLING

¾ cup (150 g) granulated sugar

⅓ cup (60 g) potato starch

2½ cups (588 ml) full fat coconut milk, stirred or shaken well before measuring

3 egg yolks

3 tablespoons (42 g) cold margarine, cubed

½ teaspoon vanilla extract

2 cups (148 g) sweetened flaked coconut

2 tablespoons dark rum, optional

TOPPING

1 can (350 ml) coconut cream, chilled in the can in the refrigerator for several hours

¼ cup (59 g) powdered sugar

½ teaspoon vanilla extract

3 tablespoons toasted sweetened coconut, crushed to a coarse powder

For the filling: Whisk the sugar and potato starch in a heavy 3-quart saucepan. Whisk in the coconut milk. Finally, whisk in the egg yolks until no streaks of yellow remain. Place over medium-high heat and slowly bring to a boil, whisking constantly. When it is thick and pudding-like with an occasional bubble forming on the surface of the custard, about 8 to 10 minutes, remove the pan from the heat. Whisk in the margarine and vanilla, which will make the custard silky and shiny. Add the coconut and rum (if using). Cover with plastic wrap directly in contact with the surface of the custard (so no skin will form) and refrigerate for at least 45 minutes.

For the topping: Beat the icy cold coconut cream at high speed with an electric mixer until foamy. Add the sugar, 1 tablespoon at a time, beating until peaks form. Beat in the vanilla. Chill for 1 hour. Spread or pipe the whipped topping over the pie and garnish with a shower of toasted coconut.

Chill for at least 2 hours before serving. The leftovers, covered and refrigerated, hold for 3 days.

Techniques: Press-In Crusts (page 55), Cracker Crumb Crusts (page 61), Whipped and Mashed Toppings (page 75), How to Toast Coconut (page 293)

Swaps:

• Any week but Passover, the dairy-free filling sidles up to any cookie crust (page 65), but try it with a Saltine Crust (page 61) first.

GRANDE MOCHA CAPPUCCINO SLAB PIE

WITH A SHORTBREAD CRUST

Serves 12 to 16

Combine a crumbly buttery crust and a silky coffee-chocolate filling and it's my favorite barista beverage in a pie. It's a cup of coffee and a cookie with a glorious whipped cream topping. This is a slab pie to take to new neighbors, serve at brunch, or bring to the office to feed your fellow cubicle dwellers.

Make Ahead: The crust may be baked 1 day ahead. The pudding may be made several hours in advance.

SHORTBREAD CRUST

6 tablespoons (85 g) unsalted butter, at room temperature

⅓ cup (67 g) granulated sugar

1 egg yolk

1½ cups (180 g) all-purpose flour

¼ teaspoon kosher salt

FILLING

2 cups (480 ml) whole milk

¼ cup (15 g) coffee beans, lightly crushed

2 tablespoons cornstarch

¼ cup (50 g) granulated sugar

¼ cup (22 g) unsweetened cocoa powder

(Continued)

For the crust: Heat the oven to 350°F; if you have one, place a baking stone, Baking Steel, or inverted baking sheet on the center rack to heat (see page 4). Using a stand mixer, hand mixer, or strong wooden spoon, beat the butter and sugar until lightened and fluffy. Add the egg yolk and beat until fully incorporated. Add the flour and salt and stir until a crumbly dough is formed. Dump the dough into the slab pie pan and, taking walnut-sized pieces, press the dough up the sides and well into the corners before worrying about the bottom. Use a metal cup measure or a flat-bottomed glass to press the remaining crust as uniform as possible with about a ¼-inch thickness. Chill the crust for at least 20 minutes.

Bake the crust (on top of the steel, stone, or baking sheet if using) for 15 to 20 minutes, until pale golden brown on the edges. Cool the crust before filling.

For the filling: Warm the milk in a small saucepan or the microwave until it is steaming but not boiling. Remove from the heat and add the crushed coffee beans. Set the saucepan aside and let the flavors marry while the milk cools, about 30 minutes. Strain the milk through a fine strainer and discard the beans.

Whisk the cornstarch, granulated sugar, cocoa, espresso powder, and salt in a heavy medium saucepan. Gradually whisk in the coffee-flavored milk. Place the pan over medium-high heat. Whisking all the time, bring to a quietly bubbling boil and cook for 3 minutes or so, until

1 tablespoon espresso
powder

¼ teaspoon kosher salt

3 ounces (85 g) bittersweet
or semisweet chocolate,
chopped (about ½ cup)

1 tablespoon unsalted
butter

2½ cups (600 ml) chilled
heavy cream

3 tablespoons powdered
sugar

¼ teaspoon vanilla extract

Chocolate-covered
espresso beans to garnish,
optional

thick like pudding. Remove from the heat and whisk in the chopped
chocolate and butter until they are melted and the filling is shiny.

Transfer the pudding to a glass or metal bowl set over another
bowl filled with ice (an ice bath) and stir continually until cool, about
8 minutes. Cover with plastic wrap pressed against the surface of the
pudding so a skin will not form.

In the bowl of a stand mixer fitted with the whisk attachment
(or with a hand mixer), whip the cream, increasing the speed as soft
peaks form, until it begins to thicken, adding the powdered sugar one
spoonful at a time with the mixer running. Beat in the vanilla and continue beating until the whisk leaves a trail through the cream. Spoon
half the whipped cream into the bowl with the pudding and fold in
until no streaks remain. Scoop this lightened pudding into the cooled
pie crust and level the surface.

Spread or pipe the remaining whipped cream across the surface
of the pie. Refrigerate for 4 hours, until well chilled. Decorate with
chocolate-covered espresso beans if you like.

Techniques: Press-In Crusts (page 55), Shortbread Crust
(page 59), Whipped and Mashed Toppings (page 75)

Swaps:

- Omit the coffee beans and the espresso powder and it's a silky
  chocolate cream pie.
- Press in a Chocolate Wafer or Speculoos Crust (page 66) instead.
- Swipe caramel over the crust before adding the coffee filling.

GOOD MORNING CHEESE DANISH SLAB PIE

WITH A PUFF PASTRY CRUST

Serves 8 or 12

This pie blends two of my favorite breakfast treats: the cheese Danish and the blintz and satisfies my desire for savory (cheesy) and sweet (fruit). Here, a buttery puff pastry foundation pillows a bright, creamy filling and a whisper of tart, sweet jam. As pretty as it is tasty, this pie deserves a place at your next brunch table. Farmer cheese is pressed cottage cheese, like a firmer version of ricotta, divinely creamy and melty. You can usually find it in the dairy section near the cream cheese, cottage cheese, and sour cream. The filling makes more than is needed for the pie, so do as my grandmother did and stir the cheesy blintz filling into eggs before scrambling in plenty of butter for a creamy, child-friendly breakfast.

Make Ahead: Make the filling up to 2 hours ahead. Roll out the crust, cover, and refrigerate up to 2 hours before baking. Assemble the pie up to 1 hour before baking. Keep covered and refrigerated until ready to bake.

1 sheet puff pastry
(7 to 10 ounces, 200 g to
285 g), defrosted if frozen,
but still cold

¾ cup (6 ounces, 170 g)
farmer cheese, at room
temperature

¼ cup (2 ounces, 56 g)
cream cheese, at room
temperature

2 tablespoons granulated
sugar

2 tablespoons whole milk

1 teaspoon vanilla extract

½ teaspoon grated orange
or lemon zest

(Continued)

Heat the oven to 400°F; if you have one, place a baking stone, Baking Steel, or inverted baking sheet on the center rack to heat (see page 4).

Cut a piece of parchment to fit the slab pie pan. Dust lightly with flour and use it as a guide to roll out the puff pastry to size. With a sharp knife, score the surface of the pastry nearly all the way through the dough in a tic-tac-toe pattern, to mark off either 8 or 12 portions. Slide the parchment with the pastry into the pan and refrigerate.

In a stand mixer, or by hand, whisk the farmer cheese, cream cheese, granulated sugar, milk, vanilla, zest, and juice until lightened. Whisk in the egg yolk and salt and beat until no yellow streaks remain. Use a small scoop or two spoons to plop cheese filling on top of each portion, no more than 1 or 1½ tablespoons each. Less is more: Too much cheese will overwhelm the pastry and tamp down the layers, so hold back.

(Continued)

1 teaspoon fresh orange or lemon juice

1 egg yolk

Pinch kosher salt

2 to 3 tablespoons cherry or raspberry jam

About 2 tablespoons powdered sugar, for dusting

Use the back of a spoon to make a well in each dot of cheese and spoon in a scant ½ teaspoon of jam. Bake the pie (on top of the steel, stone, or baking sheet if using) until the cheese is beginning to brown here and there and the pastry is toasty brown, 21 to 23 minutes.

Cool the pie for no more than a moment. Dust with the powdered sugar. Ideally, slice and serve this pie barely warm. I use sharp scissors or a pizza wheel to cut the portions along the score lines.

Technique: Puff Pastry (page 72)

Swaps:

- Ricotta or cottage cheese, well drained, can stand in for the farmer cheese. But substitute 3 tablespoons of powdered sugar for the granulated sugar called for in the recipe and cut out the milk altogether.
- Crème fraîche is an alternative to the cream cheese.
- Any jam is delicious but know if using apricot or peach, the pie will closely resemble sunny-side-up eggs.
- Chopped or crushed fresh berries, sprinkled with a whisper of sugar and left to sit for 20 minutes, can swap in for the jam.

SLAB PIE STRATEGIES
SLICE, STORE, AND FREEZE

OU'VE MADE A BEAUTIFUL PIE BUT YOUR JOB IS not over. Here's how to slice, store, and freeze that beauty.

Smart slicing strategies can allocate a slab pie to portion out to serve a few or many. When your kid brings home three friends for dinner, slab pie accommodates.

Slicing a slab does not have to be daunting. First, choose your weapon. I like to use a metal bench scraper to make swift up and down cuts into and through the crust. It makes clean cuts and is easy to use. A sharp chef's knife or a pizza wheel work to cut the pie, too,

a SLAB PIE

but there's something very solid about the bench scraper (but it can scratch the bottom of the pan). Once portioned, lift each pie piece with an offset spatula or another flexible flat lifting tool.

18

15

20

1

PERSONAL
SLaB Pie

STORING LEFTOVER SLAB PIE

Most of the pies in this book have great staying power, which makes them serve double duty: Eat now and eat later. I'm always happy for leftovers, especially when faced with the daily lunch quandary. Slab pie leftovers belong in a lunchbox.

Pies made with eggs, poultry, meat, or dairy must be stored covered in the refrigerator. Fruit pies without custard may be held, covered, on the counter for a day and then will need to be refrigerated. By day three, the bottom crust will be soggy and unappealing, so invite a neighbor for a cup of coffee and a slice of pie on day two and eat up.

Conveniently, as far as leftovers are concerned, pie is frequently served at room temperature. Remove any leftovers from the refrigerator in plenty of time, usually 2 hours or so.

If you prefer a warm pie, cover loosely with foil and reheat at 350°F for 15 to 20 minutes. For the lunchbox, wrap individual pieces in foil; then, if you can, heat in a (toaster) oven at 350°F for 10 to 15 minutes.

FREEZING WHOLE SLAB PIE

And now that you've got your pie skills honed, I promise you whole frozen slab pies are like buried treasure. The next time you're making one pie, if you've got the time and inclination, make a second one. Freeze that second pie hard inside the pan, tip the fully frozen pie out of the pan, and wrap it first in plastic wrap and then in foil. It'll keep in the freezer for a month or two. When you're ready for pie, unwrap the frozen slab and pop it back in a slab pie pan, then bake it straight from the freezer according to the instructions in the recipe.

Do not freeze pies with dairy, eggs, or gelatin in the filling.

RESOURCES

EQUIPMENT

Slab Pie Pans, also known as quarter sheet pans, are baking sheets that are 9 by 13 inches and only about 1 inch deep. They are widely available at places like Sur La Table, Bed Bath & Beyond, World Market, and any restaurant supply store, as well as online. I am partial to the ones that come with a snap-on plastic cover. I have a few with a pebbled or ridged surface which seems to make lifting the slices out of the pan even easier.

Using a **scale** will help you make pies that are consistently delicious. I'm fond of the OXO scale because it offers a flat base on which to place the food processor bowl, the numbers are large enough to read easily, and backlit. You'll find this and other scales available at Bed Bath & Beyond, Sur La Table, and Williams-Sonoma. I promise you will see results in your baking as well as fewer dishes to wash!

I don't use my **food processor** all the time, but I do use it every time for pastry. Nothing cuts in butter faster and more consistently than the food processor. I've used an 11-cup model from Cuisinart for years. It's a dependable kitchen workhorse and worth the investment. Food processors can be found at all department store kitchen departments, Sur La Table, Williams-Sonoma, Bed Bath & Beyond, Target, Walmart, and Costco. A big motor and a big workbowl are nice to have. Replacement workbowls, lids, and blades are available from the manufacturer or from websites like kitchenworksinc.com.

I resisted the call of the **Vitamix heavy-duty blender** for a while, but I'm very glad I gave in. It's a useful machine, sturdy and strong. Available at Sur La Table, Target, Walmart, Costco, and every so often, Whole Foods, where the manufacturer does a demonstration and offers the machine at a discount. I use the Vitamix to pulverize bread crumbs and Parmigiano, to make the silkiest squash and apple soup, to make sauces, juices, and so much more.

Pastry brushes, bench scrapers, cookie cutters, and fluted pastry wheels are available at kitchenware shops like Sur La Table, Bed Bath & Beyond, Williams-Sonoma, and Target. I like to find vintage tools when I'm out poking around yard sales.

Finding your **rolling pin,** the one that fits your hand, may take some time. Be deliberate. Borrow your friend's. Use your mom's. Figure out what shape and weight works best. The helpful staff at Williams-Sonoma or Sur La Table can help sort the wood from the silicone, the handled from the cylindrical from the tapered.

Cherry pitters are very nice to have. When faced with two big flats of cherries, I appreciated the type with a hopper, but for a few quarts at a time, I am partial to the handheld version from OXO.

INGREDIENTS

King Arthur flours are available in many grocery stores, at Target, some Costcos, and online directly from the Vermont headquarters, KingArthurFlour.com.

White Lily flour is a soft wheat flour that makes exquisite biscuits (but is not appropriate for pie crust). It's found throughout the South on grocery store shelves. If you live elsewhere, it's available online.

For decorating, **sparkling and pearl sugars, white and multicolored and chocolate sprinkles** can be found in most grocery store baking aisles. Larger containers (which are more affordable, ounce for ounce) are available at Sur La Table, Michael's, Bed Bath & Beyond, and online. Fancy decorating baubles from Sweetapolita (sweetapolita.com) are special occasion worthy, but spendy.

Instant ClearJel is found online at KingArthur Flour.com and other places. It keeps for years.

The recipes in this book use Diamond Crystal **kosher salt.** I find it at my grocery store, restaurant supply stores, and Costco. If using Morton's kosher salt, cut back just a little as it's heavier by weight.

Nuts and dried fruit from Nuts.com are so delicious and fresh, I'm converted to ordering online. When I don't have the time to order, I think the fruits and nuts at Trader Joe's are superior to most of the other stores. They're fresher and available in reasonably sized packages.

Jarred spices purchased at the grocery store can be old and dusty. I order **spices, chile peppers, salts, and vanilla** from Penzeys (penzeys.com).

Fresh apricots delivered from Frog Hollow Farm (froghollow.com) are indulgent, yes, but so delicious. Frog Hollow also grows beautiful peaches and plums.

Meyer lemons are a weakness of mine. Lemon Ladies Orchard (lemonladies.com) will ship Meyer lemons in season. The lemons are big and juicy and wonderful and so pretty, I always fill a bowl with them and just look at their cheery yellow. Make and freeze lemon curd (page 282) for emergency lemon meringue pies.

ACKNOWLEDGMENTS

I always believed that pie was just another word for happy, and the joyous way in which this book came together makes me even more certain. Bonnie Benwick asked me to write about slab pie for the *Washington Post*. Marilyn Pollack Naron (see her work on pages 304 and 305), mentioned the story to her agent, Lori Galvin, who thought the world needed a book about slab pie. Lori became my agent and, over a few weeks while I moved from one home to another, we conjured up a book proposal with dozens of telephone calls, a messy, shared Google document, and text messages at all hours. And then she helped *Pie Squared* find a home at Grand Central Life & Style.

I thank my lucky stars this book was in the capable hands of a pie-loving editor, Karen Murgolo. I am grateful for her sharp pen, insightful take on organization, and encouraging words at just the right moment. I knew we would bond when she declared sour cherry pie to be her favorite. Me, too! Morgan Hedden was the unflappable in-house shepherd for the manuscript. I am encouraged that she's come around to Pop-Tart-style pies. It can't be easy to keep all these square pies in order, and for that I am in awe of the crack production team that oversaw the move from manuscript to book. Tareth Mitch was unflappable, her suggestions made the book better. Deri Reed copyedited with a keen eye for consistency and clarity. Designer Shubani Sarkar brought both whimsy and order to the pages.

Spending time with the ace photography team of Christopher Hirsheimer and Melissa Hamilton is a sublime experience and it comes through in the photographs in this book. I spent a couple of summertime weeks driving through Buck's County on tree-shaded roads, finding orange-yolked eggs, thick cream, bicolor corn, and tomatoes as big as my head. I ate the most glorious white peaches from Manoff's and drank coffees from the Early Bird, as pie after pie emerged from the oven. I am grateful for Melissa's clever pie toppers, her calligraphy letters, and her precise crimping. I admire Christopher's pairing of background and subject. The way she plucked the flower from a sprig of mint and snuggled it onto a plate. The way she chases the light. This book is infused with those summer days and the happy times we had putting pies on the long table.

My official recipe tester, Christine Rudalevige, she of the fish pie, provided great insight and an eye for streamlining steps. She's the only person I know who has made more pies than I have. Her insights are peppered throughout this book. Jennifer Steinhauer and Jonathan Weisman and their try-any-pie household tasted dozens of pies, helped focus and analyze flavors, and buoyed me along the way with bourbon and conversation.

Ingredients are everything. Sandra Kay Miller at Painted Hand Farm provided sensational lard, eggs, chicken, and lamb. Fruits and vegetables came from Bending Bridge Farm and Norman's Farm Market. Pork and beef were sourced from Whitmore Farm and Springfield Farm. Dairy products from South Mountain Creamery.

Pie makers Abbie Argersinger, Sabina Behague, Sue Bogan, Julia Devine, Alanna Dickson, Gail Dosik, Alex Gehring, Marie Benbow Genrich, Emily Hanhan, Janice Lavigne, Mary Ann Livegood, Ashley Lusk, Rick Pearson, Jen Reichenbach, Mary Reilly, Carol Sacks, Anna Saint John, Misty Sasai, Gigi Schumm, Stephane Simon, Claire Stotts, Ann Stratte, Amy Stromberg, Alexandra Mudry Till provided recipe testing and input. And I have to shout out to my neighbors at the National Park Seminary condominiums who helped eat all the pies.

And to my darling Dennis, thank you for your patience. I am so grateful for our happy life together (and your appetite for pie).

INDEX

ABOUT THE AUTHOR

CATHY BARROW, an award-winning author, knitter, traveler, cook, teacher, and gardener, is published in the *New York Times,* the *Washington Post, Serious Eats,* the *Local Palate, Garden & Gun, Southern Living, National Geographic,* and NPR's *The Salt.* Cathy believes in the power of home cooking and the stories that connect us to food, culture, home, friends, and family.